It's About
Excellence

Building
Ethically Healthy
Organizations

David W. Gill

WIPF & STOCK · Eugene, Oregon

Wipf and Stock Publishers
199 W 8th Ave, Suite 3
Eugene, OR 97401

It's About Excellence
Building Ethically Healthy Organizations
By Gill, David W.
Copyright©2008 by Gill, David W.
ISBN 13: 978-1-61097-609-1
Publication date 7/1/2011
Previously published by Executive Excellence Publishing, 2008

Advance Praise

David Gill's *It's About Excellence* explains a tough topic in a very concise and even captivating manner. It doesn't just "talk" about the topic, as so many books do, but actually provides great guidance on how to integrate ethics "into" business strategies. As an executive I was drawn into key ethical decisions I've made for my business. *It's About Excellence* is a perfect guide for any executive or entrepreneur planning their business and should be required reading for business school students.
— Rand Morimoto, President/CEO, Convergent Computing (www.cco.com), White House advisor on cyber-security and cyber-terrorism; co-author of *Network Security for Government and Corporate Executives.*

Our company incorporated the ideas and concepts put forth in David Gill's *It's About Excellence* with resounding success as measured by the acceptance and enthusiasm of our employees. Now we have a moral and ethical guide for our company going forward that really describes our "heart and soul" to our employees and clients. It makes good business sense to me.
— Carl Harris, Chairman of the Board, Harris & Associates, Concord, CA (www.harris-assoc.com)

Practical, comprehensive, and concise, David Gill's *It's About Excellence* is the perfect introduction to business ethics. CEOs looking to create ethical organizations should give copies to all their managers.
— James O'Toole, Professor, Marshall School of Business, USC, author *Leading Change: The Argument for Values-Based Leadership, The Executive's Compass, Creating the Good Life* (www.jamesotoole.com)

It's About Excellence is thorough, compelling, and urgently needed to bring us back—and then keep us on the right track—to excellence in our business life.
— David M. Gilmour, Founder and President, Paradise Foods, Corte Madera, CA (www.foodsofparadise.com)

David Gill's book title is right on target. *It's About Excellence* is a fantastic, highly motivating book that every business owner, CEO and entrepreneur should read and implement. It is the first book I've seen that successfully shows how ethics, vision, and mission must be integrated from the start as key elements in building a company beyond average to excellent and exceptional.
— Rich Ferrari, Managing Director, De Novo Ventures (www.denovovc.com)

What a treat to find an ethics text that is readable, practical, and still based on solid ethical theory! David Gill's book will be of value to anyone who has to run an organization, for profit or otherwise.

—Lisa Newton, Professor and Director, Program in Applied Ethics, Fairfield University (www.fairfield.edu); co-author of *Taking Sides: Clashing Views on Controversial Issues in Business Ethics and Society*; author of *Permission to Steal: Revealing the Roots of Corporate Scandal*.

At a time when consumers, investors and employees are demanding transparency from the companies they purchase from, invest in, or work for, David Gill's *It's About Excellence* is a timely and practical manifesto for not only doing well but doing the right thing. Anyone who invests time in recruiting talented people and developing high-performance organizations should also invest time with this book. A great resource for a management retreat.

—Doug Sterne, Senior Vice President, Clear Channel Radio

Business leaders need a new method, a new generation of tools and guidelines, to compete today both ethically and excellently. What ISO 9000, Malcolm Baldrige, and *In Search of Excellence* did for business quality twenty years ago, David Gill captures for today in *It's About Excellence*.

—Peter Jackson, President & CEO, Intraware Inc. (www.intraware.com)

David Gill's book is a must-read for any leader who wants to create a culture in an organization in which people are ethical because it's the right thing to do, not just because it works.

—Dennis Bakke, Co-Founder & CEO emeritus, AES Corporation, president, Imagine Schools, and author of *Joy at Work* (www.dennisbakke.com)

This is an accessible, compelling and useful architecture for "ethically healthy organizations." Based upon his long-time engagement with the private and non-profit sectors, David Gill's "blueprint" is a major contribution toward the construction of excellent and caring organizations.

—Roy Allen, Dean, School of Economics and Business, St. Mary's College, Moraga, CA (www.stmarys-ca.edu)

David Gill has provided a compelling manifesto for a creative, proactive approach to ethics. Whether as an aid in making the case for ethics training, as a guide for designing and evaluating training proposals, or as the foundation for an integrated, systemic ethics program, *It's About Excellence* is a rich and versatile manual, an essential resource.

—Maria I. Marques, Senior HR Analyst, Employee Development, East Bay Municipal Utility District (www.ebmud.com)

Successful businesses understand the fundamental and paramount importance of relationships with customers and employees. David Gill provides a useful blueprint for ethical stewardship of these essential relationships in any company. The key is a clear vision for the long term. In our post-Enron world, where greed and cutting corners are a daily reality on a global scale, this book sounds a much needed drum beat for what's truly important.

—Clark Sept, Co-Founder/Principal, Business Place Strategies, Inc. (www.businessplacestrategies.com)

It's About Excellence is a must-read for any company leader who wants to establish a culture of ethics and excellence—and it is an excellent tool and guide for on-going training in any company that already has such a culture. Absolutely enjoyable reading!

—Guy Erickson, President, Harris & Associates, Concord, CA (www.harris-assoc.com)

David Gill's *It's About Excellence* poses probing questions every manager should seriously contemplate. His mission-control "blueprint" is a powerful synopsis of how to improve the ethical health of organizations—with a set of tools for aligning corporate cultures with ethical decisions and behavior.

—Jana Kemp, author of *NO! How One Simple Word Can Transform Your Life* and *Building Community in Buildings* (www.janakemp.com)

It's About Excellence is a densely packed, realistic, flexible, and proactive guide for developing ethical leadership and businesses. Owners of the very smallest businesses—not just big corporations—can mine a wealth of practical information to help them become and remain excellent in this challenging business climate. As the sole proprietor of a small bookstore for over thirty years, I highly recommend David Gill's book for other "Main Street" businesses.

—Carol Spencer, Proprietor, Russian Hill Bookstore, San Francisco, CA

David Gill's *It's About Excellence* is a well written, theoretically rich, insightful and practical book. The concepts and tools contained within its pages can assist business leaders in the critical tasks of developing healthy organizational cultures and restoring overall trust in business. The book is a wonderful resource for students and practicing managers alike.

—Kenman Wong, Professor of Business Ethics, Seattle Pacific University (www.spu.edu); co-author, *Beyond Integrity: A Judeo-Christian Approach to Business Ethics.*

It's About Excellence demonstrates convincingly that ethics is hardwired into the fabric of successful organizations. Much more than regulatory compliance, sound ethics is fleshed-out-excellence manifested in daily work life—from CEO to mid-level manager to entry-level staff. Anyone seeking to build sustained organizational excellence should keep this resource close at hand.

—Greg Zegarowski, President, Financial Leadership Corporation (www.financialleadership.com)

David Gill provides a compelling and insightful manifesto linking ethics to healthy, excellent organizations. He doesn't just preach at us about what to do but also provides why and how to implement an ethics program—a program that weaves throughout an organization and guides people to achieve more than what they may have thought possible, in ways consistent with innate desires for fairness. *It's About Excellence* helps us see the power of authenticity and integrity.

—Randall L. Englund, Englund Project Management Consultancy; author, *Creating an Environment for Successful Projects* (www.englundpmc.com)

For any business student or working professional, *It's About Excellence* is a must-read book. Drawing on more than three decades of ethics teaching and practice, David Gill explains in detail the theory of ethics as well as how to apply it in the workplace, with several practical questionnaires, diagnostic tests, and matrixes to put into your ethics toolbox.

—Kendall Mau, International microfinance consultant & banker (www.microfinancetravels.typepad.com)

David Gill powerfully shows why good ethics is in the best interests of business and masterfully brings together ethical theory and practical application tools. *It's About Excellence* gets to the heart of the matter for anyone from a budding entrepreneur to a seasoned business leader. More than theory, more than bright ideas, this book provides a working roadmap to a sound ethics that is woven into the fabric of an organization.

—Trish Fisher, Assoc. Chair, School for Professional Studies Business Program, Vanguard University (www.vanguard.edu)

It's About Excellence is a fascinating read. Starting with the basics for ethics "neophytes," David Gill builds a sound framework for analyzing the issues managers face, from crisis management to longer term strategy and planning. Discussions of mission/vision, culture, practices, and leadership have been augmented with real-world cases, pragmatic guidelines, and checklists; this is a workbook which executives can immediately apply to their own situations.

—Juan P. Montermoso, President, Montermoso Associates (www.montermoso.com)

For Jonathan

Founder and proprietor of Gill's Fitness (San Diego, CA).
Consistent exemplar of both ethics and excellence.
Beloved and admired son.

Contents

Blueprint, Toolbox & Manifesto

Executive Summary

For all super-busy, on-the-fly business leaders and managers, I have provided a one-paragraph executive summary at the head of each of the seven chapters, the Prelude, Interlude, and Postlude of It's About Excellence. *If you don't have time to read the whole book right now, then browse through it and read these summaries to get the basic message. Then keep the book close at hand so you can come back and get the substance beneath the surface. The devil really is in the details when it comes to building ethically healthy organizations. So keep it close by for future reference—or give it to a colleague who can take on the detailed study, planning, and execution for your organization.*

The Prelude that follows describes briefly the purpose, orientation, structure, and flow of It's About Excellence.

It's About Excellence provides a practical, concise, and well-tested *blueprint* for building companies[1] that are both ethical and excellent, that *do right* as well as *do well*. It is also a veritable *toolbox*—full of action plans, analytical charts, ethics audits, and how-to ideas. Finally, though, it is a *manifesto*—not a dispassionate, soulless, philosophical treatise but a call to action. Good business is good for everyone. More good business means more good jobs, reduced unemployment, more opportunities for creativity, meaning, achievement, and personal pride. The ripple effects of good business are a wonderful thing. Lack of good work has a terrible fall-out in terms of crime, family breakdown, personal discouragement, and even despair. So consider this book *a call to entrepreneurship and business development.*

Calling for more business development, of course, has its risks in our era of daily business scandals and outrages. Frankly, there is a deep corruption in

11

parts of our business world today. I don't think that the majority of businesses and their leaders are unethical—but neither is it a matter of a just few isolated instances, a few "bad apples." No doubt that every day countless businesses open their doors to employees who will find good and satisfying work, customers who will appreciate the products and services they buy, and investors pleased with their returns. But also every day the business news reports another story of drugs rushed to market with questionable safety test results, a major default on long standing pension benefit commitments to workers, a refusal of a corporate board to listen to shareholder protests, a boatload of cash and stock for some CEO whose performance ranges from average to negative, or something equally troubling. Every day there's some story like this. The ethics problem in business is not just a matter of theft, sexual harassment, and irresponsibility on the part of employees. From the very top on down, greed and moral blindness can sometimes look like an epidemic out of control.

This cannot continue. History is replete with lessons about aristocracies and oligarchies which pushed the envelope too far, too long. Locally and globally, the chickens will of necessity come home to roost. Investors, employees, customers, and citizens will eventually rebel. We must reform now or face a rebellion later, take the initiative now or experience the initiative of a radical opposition later. Never has the business landscape been so in need of more good leadership. So consider this book *a call to ethical leadership in the business domain*.

Despite this opening mini-rant, however, *It's About Excellence* is not a fundamentally negative, pessimistic, or reactive treatise. The answer to unethical business is not to become an expert in malfeasance or in techniques of blame and denunciation. Rather, it is to get creative, positive, and proactive. A major theme is that business and organizational ethics has far too often been practiced as a kind of "damage control." Headline, brand-reputation-threatening crises have too often been allowed to set the business ethics agenda both in companies and in business schools. But if ethics is little more than an "emergency service" to contain damage and assign blame after the fact, we will never make real progress in addressing the causes and conditions of such crises.

This book is about a better, more proactive, way. Ethics is first and foremost about *excellence*. I am not alone in arguing that doing right and doing well, ethics and excellence, are intimately related. No doubt, there are exceptions where good ethics is accompanied by business failure—and where bad ethics is accompanied by apparent business success. There can be no guarantees in these matters but *most of the time*, especially *in the long term*, sound ethics is a key factor in achieving and maintaining successful for-profit and non-profit organizations. This book explains how it works—and what you can do as a manager/leader to strengthen your company.

Here is the basic plan of attack:

Chapter One cuts to the chase with a clear working definition of "ethics"—"right and wrong"—for the business context. We certainly want to learn, on this topic, from the great moral philosophers and ethics teachers through history, but our interest is not in ivory tower debates or abstract, technical jargon. Let's get our definitions and starting points right, and then let's hit the ground. Since we carry out our business in diverse, even global contexts these days, it is essential to find a share-able, common way we can follow together, to figure out what is right. I propose six basic common grounds to guide us toward what's ethically right.

Chapter Two is about *motivation*. Why should we care about and pursue the right thing in business? If we, with our workforce, our board, and our colleagues, are not adequately motivated, nothing—NOTHING—is going to change. We will explore "Twelve Good Reasons to Run a Business in an Ethical Manner." Most of these reasons provide a common sense business case for being ethical. At the end of this chapter, we will also ask what has motivated some business leaders to be *unethical*—to cut ethical corners and get themselves and their companies into serious trouble. Why would they risk it? Part of it is "greed," one of the most popular of the classic "Seven Deadly Sins," but it is more complex than that, as we will see.

Chapter Three is about *decision-making, trouble-shooting, and crisis management*—"ethical ER," I call it. While I often criticize business ethics approaches that are *nothing more than* damage control, the fact is that our organizations must know how to recognize and resolve ethical dilemmas and crises when they arise. I'd prefer to make this chapter an Appendix at the end, included just in case some unexpected problems arise. But the reality is that our organizational "boats" are often already leaking as we take over the captain's post. So right away we must put in place, and into action, a patch and repair process so that we don't sink before our larger, more positive, remodeling project can be carried out.

After Chapter Three I have a brief "interlude" (hence a "prelude" here and a "postlude" at the end). The Interlude is an explanation of the transition from the problem orientation of the first chapters to the proactive building orientation in the remaining chapters.

Chapter Four is about *phase one* of a three-phase blueprint for building ethi-cally healthy, excellent companies. How can we build or rebuild the business "boat" so it is seaworthy and less prone to spring leaks or run aground? Answer: If we want to build ethical, excellent organizations, our mantra must be: "First, get the *mission* straight." What is our *purpose* (or "End," as the classi-cal thinkers would say)? What is our "envisioned future"? Where do we want to go? What do we want to accomplish? It is this fundamental choice that, more than any other single factor, leverages (and specifies) the quality of the ethics and the level of the excellence in an organization. We are going to call this "mission-control ethics" (replacing the usual "damage-control" approach).

Chapter Five is about figuring out the *core values* that are essential to guid-ing and enabling the achievement of the organizational mission and fulfilling the vision. And after we figure out these core values, how do we practically, effectively embed them in every part of the *corporate culture,* from our architec-ture and physical equipment to our policies and systems to the personnel we hire to our company rituals and atmosphere? It's all about what kind of organi-zation we *are*—our corporate character and culture. It's about building our *capa-bility* of carrying out and fulfilling our mission and vision. I call this "building ethical muscle" in our organization. We won't be able to "lift the weight" with-out it, no matter how good our intentions.

Chapter Six is about our organizational *practices*—the things we *do*, the ways we spend our time and effort in pursuit of our vision and mission. Here is the distinction I am making: our *culture* is about who and what we *are*, about our capabilities; our *practices*, then, are about what we *do*, about our activities. After mapping out these practices, the essential activities of our company, we then figure out, articulate, and disseminate our basic *guidelines* ("principles," we will often call them) for "how we do the things we do." This is where we call on our people to join together to write (and regularly update) our organiza-tional code of ethics (or conduct). *Principle-guided practices* are built out of our *value-embedded culture* in our *mission-controlled organization.* That is the grand plan.

Chapter Seven is about *leadership* and governance. If we don't have good leadership and a solid approach to corporate governance, none of the preceding is going to happen. The blueprint will only be haphazardly followed: Employees will become cynical, directors will be asleep on the job, and the company will flounder. So *who* is going to lead? Everyone has a leadership role to play in the company—but not the same one. *How* will effective ethical leadership take place? How will we measure our success—or lack of it? (partial answer: regu-lar, no-holds-barred ethics and values assessments in employee performance reviews—*and*—employee assessments of company and management ethics).

At the end of each chapter are (1) a brief "Afterword" reflection on a topic related to the concerns of that chapter, (2) some questions for personal reflection or group discussion, (3) a couple suggested "exercises" to help you take the ideas of the chapter to the next level, and (4) a paragraph describing further resources (books, articles, web sites, etc.) for study of the topic of that chapter. With these addenda and the occasional footnotes, readers can take their study of organizational ethics several levels deeper. At the end of the book I have included three appendixes, including two "thought pieces" about (1) core values of healthy corporate cultures and (2) key principles guiding ethical leaders and organizational practices along with (3) some commentary on ethical problem cases described in Chapter Three.

I mentioned at the beginning of this preface that reading the Executive Summary paragraphs heading each chapter will be a quick way to get the basic message if speed is your priority right now. If you can beef up your diet just a tad, you can get the "reader's digest" version by reading just the boxed statements that occur every page or two. Reading all the fine print of the audits and other examples takes some time, but the payoff for including these items will come when you can get started inventing and implementing the ethics building project in your company.

Despite the presence of these detailed tools, and despite my professorial temptation (to which I have yielded many times in the past) to try to answer every possible objection, meander down every byway, and document every assertion—I have tried to resist, stay strong, and *stay lean* in this book. Most of my argument is common sense. Most of it is really just summarizing and applying to our workplace the best ideas and best practices of the past and the present.

Readers will note the frequent reference to Harris & Associates, a construction and project management firm based in Concord, California, and operating throughout the western United States. The ideas and strategies in *It's About Excellence* have been put into practice at Harris in a truly exemplary way, and they serve as a great illustration of how to make it all real. This book is not just about some vague theory. I am grateful to founder Carl Harris, Guy Erickson, Jeff Cooper, Vern Phillips, Marie Shockley and the entire Harris team for permission to share their example with a broader public.

My last name brands a lot of the tools in this book that I have designed over the years (interview and research questions, values and principles lists and questionnaires, audit and case analysis forms, etc.). It's not my ego but my experience that made me do this. I am, of course, happy to share my stuff with a broader audience here. I would just ask that you properly credit the source both for the sake of justice and so that those who wish to make their way to this book will know where to go. Also, I am eager to hear your response to this book and its approach to ethics—and about your own innovations and applications. Please shoot me an e-mail and let me know.

David W. Gill
www.ethixbiz.com
dgill@ethixbiz.com

NOTES

[1] My primary concern is with for-profit businesses—small, medium, or large—anywhere in today's global marketplace. But when reference is made to "businesses," "organizations," and "companies," the lessons almost always apply equally well to non-profit organizations (including schools and churches) and government agencies. In fact, even neighborhoods, families, and other social groups can be helped by the "mission-control" blueprint.

Chapter 1

Ethics Isn't Pretty
(but the alternatives are *really* ugly)

Executive Summary

Ethics and morality are terms (with Greek and Latin roots respectively) that refer to our efforts to figure out and then carry out the right thing in business and in other areas of life. In a world of great and growing diversity, six criteria can help us work toward a shared conclusion about what is ethically, morally right. (1) Our laws are not perfect, but they represent politically based judgments about right and wrong behavior; if it's not legal, it's probably not ethical. (2) Company and professional codes of ethics must also be taken seriously as guidelines to right and wrong. (3) All human beings have some kind of conscience, moral intuition, or "moral compass"; we need to listen to it in ourselves and others. (4) Golden Rule: Treat others the way you would want to be treated. (5) Publicity and transparency: Don't do things that you wouldn't want on the front page of tomorrow's newspapers.
(6) Bottom line: Never do anything that irresponsibly exposes others to serious harm (physical, financial, reputational, etc)."

I was always amused when comedian Steve Martin would put on his most serious face and tone of voice and remind us that "comedy isn't pretty." Well it's no joke to say that "ethics isn't pretty." Much of the time business ethics is mucking around in this scandal or that. I confess that there are times when I look down the road a few years and fantasize about getting up in the morning and not having to read some more aggravating news stories in the business section (or on the front page) of the *Wall Street Journal, New York Times,* or *San Francisco Chronicle*. It is depressing to read of another modern-day Robber Baron looting his or her corporation (or public utility or state university) while simultaneously stripping basic benefits from his or her workforce. Frustrating to read about corporate lobbying and political contributions defeating legislation that would have helped the people and protected our environment. You know what I'm talking about. Ethics isn't pretty.

But there is another side to the story, and that is the main theme of this book. To borrow the well-phrased challenge: "It is better to light a candle than to curse the darkness." My parents constantly drilled into me that I was either going to be "part of the solution or part of the problem." Ethics is not just (or primarily) about cataloging (and ranting about) the evil, unjust, and ugly. Its historic focus is on the good, the just, and the excellent. Ethics is about excellence. The ancient Greek philosophers actually used one word, *arête*, for both "moral virtue" and "excellence." (How and why did we ever separate them?). It doesn't always get on page one, but there are lots of great examples of ethical, excellent, successful businesses.

So, with this more classical, holistic, positive understanding, ethics can start looking good, actually. Ethics is not just a "patch and repair," or still less an "identify and blame" enterprise. Nor, let us be clear, is it about a head-in-the-clouds, idealistic "who cares about profits and bottom lines?" attitude. Ethics is about excellence. Ethics is about a robust, big-view, building program for companies that seek to be financially profitable as well as morally praiseworthy, doing well as well as doing right. It is not either/or: either financial success or corporate social responsibility and ethics. No, it is both/and.

Ethics is looking prettier every minute.

> *Ethics is not just (or primarily) about cataloging and ranting about the evil, unjust, and ugly. Its historic focus is on the good, the just, and the excellent. Ethics is about excellence.*

So let's get clear about our definitional starting points: What is ethics? What is an "ethical business"? What does it mean to "run an organization in an ethical manner"?

"Ethics," in the most general sense, is about matters of right and wrong, good and bad.[1] It is about what we "ought" to do (our duties, obligations, and responsibilities to do the right thing). Our ethical *values* and *principles* are our *guidelines* for addressing these matters. An ethical individual or organization is one that *does* the right thing (and avoids doing the wrong thing)—or at least it is one that *cares about* what's right and makes a good faith effort to do it.

This description still does not go far enough, however. Such a broad use of terms like "right," "wrong," and "ought" could still apply to baking a cake or solving mathematical problems ("here is how you ought to solve this equation," "that's right!" etc.). We need to get more precise about *ethical* right and wrong. This is not always a simple task.

In a simpler time and place we might have all agreed that (let's say) the Bible decides what's right. Others could agree that the Koran decides it. Or perhaps tradition, common sense, or utilitarian moral philosophy could provide our guide to what is right. But a real problem arises when we are faced with ethical questions and the players are not all from the same tradition or background. Certainly, there is a place for us to express our personal convictions in business ethics, as we shall see below. But we need a shared foundation and one religion alone—or one philosophy, or one political perspective—cannot provide it in our era of diversity.[2]

Welcome to today's marketplace and workplace: swirling change, driven by technology and globalization, and amazing diversity in ethics and values as in other matters.

> *"Ethics," in the most general sense, is about matters of right and wrong, good and bad—figuring it out and carrying it out in the various domains of human experience.*

But diversity is no reason to bail out on right and wrong. The stakes are too high. And diversity is not just a challenge—it is also an opportunity and an asset when it means that we can now benefit from multiple ethical perspectives, experiences, and insights. Ethical imperialism will never work; ethical cynicism and apathy, on the other hand, are disastrous. It's not always pretty and it's not always easy—but the common pursuit of doing the right thing today is an adventure that is both essential and rewarding.

Nor, we must add, are ambiguity, paradox, or uncertainty reasons to bail out on ethics. Life is complex. Our challenges are thorny. Perfect clarity is elusive. But it is far better to think carefully through our ethical challenges and work hard to come up with the wisest possible resolution than to just shoot from the hip. Sometimes we will feel like we are just "muddling through." But the pursuit of ethics and excellence lessens our risk of personal and corporate harm and increases our chances of long term, sustainable success.

Six Criteria for Recognizing and Deciding Right & Wrong

So how can we determine ethical right and wrong? How can we find common ground in this world of diversity? In today's context, six basic test questions can help us begin to recognize, sort out, and resolve the ethical problems we face. Perhaps none of these six litmus tests is sufficient by itself (although the last of the six comes real close); taken together, however, they provide a pretty reliable set of filters (or "foundation stones," if you prefer that metaphor). Our task is simply stated: When should we regard something in business as unethical? Or to phrase it positively: On what grounds could we argue that something is the ethically right thing to do?

The first two of the six test questions are "compliance" questions (i.e., they test whether our actions are in accord with acknowledged, written standards).

First: Does it violate—or comply with—the law? We hope (and often have good reason to think) that our governmental laws are *grounded* in, and reinforce, what is ethically right. Thus, we have laws that prohibit murder, theft, and libel—and most ethical value systems (like the Ten Commandments or Kantian deontology) also designate these behaviors as wrong. So if we see something going on that breaks the law, it is usually ethically as well as legally wrong. Normally, our ethical antennae (along with our legal ones) should perk up if a law is broken. Our laws and regulations are our "social contract" defining the right way to behave in our political community. If we think a law is wrong or unethical, we should use the appropriate legislative channels to change it.

The caveat is as follows: Throughout history there have been times when something was legal, but was nevertheless unethical (slavery, environmental destruction, taking advantage of a buyer's feeblemindedness or lack of command of a language, etc.). There are also things that might be unethical and wrong—but that we, nevertheless, decide we can't or shouldn't make illegal (e.g., racist attitudes, smoking in private, gambling). So there is not an exact, precise equivalence between law and ethics, but compliance with governmental laws and regulations is the opening test. *An ethical organization does its best to know and obey the laws and regulations of its host societies.*³

Second: Does it violate—or comply with—company (or professional) ethics? Not only do governments promulgate standards of behavior (in the form of laws), companies and professions do so as well (in the form of codes of conduct or ethics). The Hippocratic Oath (from about 600-400 B.C.) served for centuries as the statement of professional ethical standards to which physicians were expected to subscribe, no matter whether these ethical standards (e.g., concerning confidentiality, protection of life, etc.) were reinforced by surrounding laws or not. Attorneys, clergy, civil engineers, HR directors, therapists, and CPAs are examples of other professional groups which have attempted, with greater or lesser success, to hold fellow professionals to a clear, high standard of ethics. If you go online, it is easy to find the codes of ethics for these and many other professional specializations.

In recent years, many businesses have also developed codes of ethics for their employees.[4] Levi Strauss, Bechtel, Arthur Andersen, Enron, and Ben and Jerry's are examples (also illustrating the point that merely having such a company code is no guarantee of its observance at all levels). Many company codes of ethics are posted on-line and it is worthwhile to visit a few web sites and take a look. Ethical codes and principles spell out "law-like" boundary conditions, but these are based not on the judgments of political authorities but on what members of the profession (or the company) think is ethically right. Such professional or company ethical boundary conditions are usually drawn well back from those legal edges we might otherwise trespass.

Obviously, professional and company codes of ethics vary in scope and quality, and may affirm or prohibit activities which, on other grounds, we find unethical or ethical. At their best, however, organizational and professional ethics statements summarize right and wrong in a way that would pass the other five test questions on this list. In any case, non-compliance with (or "violation of") company or professional codes of ethics is another red flag indicating that we should take a close look at what's going on. *An ethical business complies with corporate and professional ethical standards.*

Two Compliance Criteria
- *An ethical organization does its best to obey the <u>laws and regulations</u> of its host societies.*
- *An ethical business complies with <u>corporate and professional ethical standards</u>.*

But these two sorts of compliance tests, while the appropriate starting point, are not sufficient. Three other questions will help us catch ethics problems that might slip through the compliance cracks.

Third: Does it violate—or agree with—your (and others') conscience and personal values? Of course people sometimes disagree about moral and ethical values.[5] "Don't impose your moral values on me!" is not an uncommon (or unjustified) sentiment in many cases. People's consciences and values can be twisted, dulled, inconsistent, conflicted, and unhelpful. Nevertheless, as just one of our six test questions, it is worthwhile to pay attention if you or others are seriously troubled by what is going on. Our internal "moral compass" may be blinking a warning light for good reason as we observe or engage in some action or business practice. If so, pay attention. And if you find that others around you are also very troubled—some would call it a "gut feeling"—by what seems to them unfair, dangerous, or wrong—take it seriously and follow through.

Think of it this way: The first test (the law) is about taking seriously the ethical standards espoused by the larger society or political entity; the second test is about taking seriously the ethical standards espoused by our profession or company; now the third test is about taking seriously the ethical standards espoused by individuals.

This, by the way, is a place where faith, religion, or personal philosophy of life can play positively into the process. If something is going on that violates the clear ethical teaching of your religion or philosophy, it may be important for you to share that concern with others. Your religion or philosophy might be helping you to be sensitive to some injustice the rest of us are missing. Speak up! We don't have to (and indeed can't) always agree on these things, but we could help each other by honestly sharing our values and concerns. *An ethical company respects the consciences and deeply held values of its stakeholders.*[6]

Fourth: Would you like it done to you and yours? This fourth ethics test moves from attitude to behavior. This adds some crucial realism to our questioning. It's not just "does this bother my conscience" but "would I tolerate this actually being done to me (or my loved ones)?" For example, I might somehow justify selling some dangerous or defective product to others, even though it violated my values and troubled my conscience to some extent. I might still give the "go ahead" sign because I'm uncertain and others are pressing me not to be so uptight. But when you ask me if I would be willing for my daughter or grandson to buy or use that product, some moral clarity emerges: No way! It is not right! This is, of course, the ancient Christian "Golden Rule": "Do unto others as you would have them do unto you." Confucius had taught a few centuries earlier the negative version of this: "Do not do to others what you would not want done to you."

Note well, however, that while your preferences are one valid test, they may not be the only one. It is not always reliable—or right—for us to project our desires and standards onto others. Just because I like to be treated in a certain way does not automatically mean that everyone else wishes for the same. Part of the solution to this possible problem lies in the fact that Jesus taught his Golden Rule to a community, not to some sort of rugged American individualist. By asking our colleagues "how would we like to be treated" rather than just asking myself "how would I like to be treated" we will be on safer ground.[7] *An ethical company treats others as it would like to be treated.*

Fifth: Would it cause a scandal or uproar if it was publicized? The fifth test question is sometimes called the *New York Times* test (in our wildly partisan era, we probably need to add a "Fox News" test or a *Wall Street Journal* test to be inclusive enough). The basic question is "would this be tolerated if it was on the front page of the newspaper" (or the lead story on the evening television news—or the dominating story in the "blogosphere"). This ethics test is not about me and my conscience or desires but about the *community* conscience and standards. This is actually a classic observation. The Book of Genesis gives the famous story of Adam and Eve fleeing and hiding after they have done something wrong—a pattern repeated ever since. In their recent book, *The Naked Corporation*, Don Tapscott and David Ticoll argue that transparency requires (and produces) more ethical business behavior.[8]

Of course, some things are actually right and good which we would, nevertheless, not want publicized on the evening news (making love to my spouse, having a heart-to-heart talk with my colleague, etc.). So the publicity test is not sufficient by itself. But it remains one of six great questions to raise.

Three Basic Business Ethics Standards (beyond compliance)
- *An ethical company does its best to respect the consciences and deeply held values of its stakeholders.*
- *An ethical company treats others as it would like to be treated.*
- *An ethical company is transparent and defends its actions in public.*

Sixth: Could someone be seriously harmed—or will they be helped? In my opinion, the only test question that can stand by itself is this sixth one, regarding potential harm (or help). In the end, even this test question works better if it is linked to the preceding five (which can be seen as five ways of distinguishing harmful and nonharmful behavior). But we really are at the fundamental, bottom line in ethics with this test question. Think about it: What is the difference between breeches of *ethics* and breeches of *etiquette* (customs, manners)? Answer: breeches of etiquette *offend*, but breeches of ethics *harm* (or risk harm). It's the difference between belching and beating someone. Since the ancient Hippocratic Oath, "do no harm" has commonly been called the "first duty of professional ethics."

Of course, saying that ethical wrong is about "harm" is just the beginning of a debate, not the end. We will have to debate what constitute acceptable risks of harm (knowing that there is no such thing as a completely harm-free, risk-free life) and how this varies for adults and children. We will not all agree on where to draw the line or in our calculations and predictions of harm. But that is ok. The point is to get this serious, core issue on the table. To be ethical is not necessarily to be perfect but to care, to be responsible, in protecting others from harm in its various forms. *An ethical company acts responsibly to prevent serious harm to any of its stakeholders.*

So we have six basic questions. The first five expose us to the summaries and standards of right and wrong that governments, companies and professions, we and our families and friends, and the larger community have articulated or internalized and embraced in some way. Ethics is partly personal and individual—paying attention to your own conscience and internal moral compass is an important part of it. But ethics is always a social phenomenon as well—standards embraced by communities to guide and govern our relationships. Anthropologists, sociologists, and historians argue that every culture, every social group in history requires some kind of morality to guide its behavior. But it is not quite deep enough to say that ethics is about "generally accepted principles and standards of behavior" (or words to that effect). At rock bottom it is about harm.

The Bottom Line Issue in Ethics: Harm

• *An ethical company acts responsibly to prevent serious harm to any of its stakeholders.*

• *It is wrong to knowingly, irresponsibly risk harm (physical, psychological, financial, reputational, relational, etc.) to others ("stakeholders"—those affected by our actions) without their participation in the decision to accept such risk.*

• *If no risk of harm or hurt can be established, we are talking about differences of taste and personal preference, not about ethics.*

• *Our ethical values, principles, and rules (concerning integrity, honesty, privacy, safety, fidelity, confidentiality, service, and the like) are summaries of important ways we protect each other from harm and act for each other's good and well-being.*

Our ethical values, principles, and rules (concerning integrity, honesty, privacy, safety, fidelity, confidentiality, service, and the like) are summaries of important ways we protect each other from harm and act for each other's good and well-being.

An ethical business or organization, then, holds itself accountable and is willing to run its operations past the six checkpoints or test questions. One way to describe an ethical organization is to say that it is concerned about, and committed to, doing the *right* thing—rather than just the *profitable* thing, the *legal* thing ("compliance"), the technologically *possible* thing, or the *everybody-else-is-doing-it* thing. An ethical company wants to do the thing that *helps* rather than *harms* people and the environment. In the language of *good* and *bad*, an ethical company wants to be *good* for *shareholders*—but also good for *customers*, good for *employees*, good for *business partners*, good for *community/neighbors*, and good for the *environment*—good for all its *stakeholders*. An ethical company cares about right and wrong, is willing to discuss it, and will actually do something about it. Companies are not perfect in either discernment or performance. What we are looking for is responsible effort—not perfection.

It is difficult to imagine many people disagreeing with the basic idea that avoiding harm and being ethical are desirable goals. The theory is great. But moving from theory to practice is another thing. Many are too busy or too focused on other things to believe ethics deserves their time and attention. Others are cynical and don't believe that anything can actually be done to improve ethical performance in our "dog-eat-dog" business world.

Defining the "Ethical" Organization
"Running a company in an ethical manner" means caring about right and wrong, not just about profits. It means putting (and keeping) ethical values and concerns on the table. It means acting with due diligence and responsibility. It doesn't mean perfection, but it does mean a good faith effort.

Business Ethics, Social Responsibility, Governance, and Sustainability

As we begin this study, some readers may ask how "business ethics" relates to "corporate social responsibility," "corporate governance," and "sustainability." None of these terms have clear and consistent definitions and usages. In the perspective of this book, "corporate social responsibility" (CSR) (along with corporate environmental responsibility) is a subset of business ethics. It is focused on how companies do (or not) the right thing vis-à-vis their social (and natural) environments. Any "business ethics" that fails to care about business's social (and environmental) responsibilities is a wimpy, pathetic, lame, unworthy fraud. But any authentic business ethics is *also* concerned about doing the right thing toward investors, suppliers, governmental agencies, employees, customers and all other stakeholders. The CSR rubric is a worthy focus for organizations, but business ethics is (or should be) a broader, more inclusive concern. A company that has a CSR program and emphasis, but no business ethics program, is missing something very important.

"Corporate governance" refers to the structures, authorities, and procedures by which major strategic decisions are made and directions set in businesses. Corporate governance is about how businesses are to be controlled, guided, influenced, or led so that they behave properly and fulfill their fiduciary and ethical responsibilities. The organization and behavior of corporate boards of directors, as well as executive leadership and internal management of companies, are all part of corporate governance. Government regulations, industry and professional standards and oversight, global business covenants and institutions are sometimes also part of this picture. Any "business ethics" worthy of the name is certainly concerned with these corporate governance matters. But an authentic business ethics is equally (or more) concerned with voluntary, organizational "self-governance" in service of a mission and vision, through ethical values and guidelines, training programs, and the like. Depending primarily or exclusively on legal compulsion or improved board oversight to assure good business behavior can be, by itself, narrow and short-sighted—not a strategy likely to bring out the best up and down the line in a company culture. A company that works hard to improve its corporate governance but has no business ethics program is missing something important.

Finally, how does business ethics relate to "sustainability"? The "triple bottom line" (financial, environmental, and social) and sustainability literature over the past decade has become more and more impressive, insightful, and helpful. I like the "triple bottom line" rubric although the terminology of "stakeholder" is even better because it is more holistic, fluid, and inclusive (i.e., why just three bottom lines?). And "sustainability" is *almost* always the right thing to pursue. But sometimes organizations are appropriately "built to flip" rather than "built to last." Our lives and societies and environments, and most of our business *processes*, need to be sustainable—but not every *organization* should be sustained. Furthermore, mediocrity and, worse, disease sometimes have interminable sustainability. So when it comes to our organizations there is a higher notion than "enduring" (built to last, persisting, sustainable), and that is the notion of "right"—ethics and excellence—doing the right thing and doing things right.[9] Much of today's "business ethics" has gotten narrow, individualistic, reactive and off track. But the answer is to go back to the grand, classical approach and rearticulate it for our era.

Afterthought: How Do Religion & Philosophy Relate to Business Ethics?

A large majority of people say that they got their basic ethics and values from their religion. Most religious believers say that their ethical values and standards come from God (through inspired, sacred texts like the Bible or Koran and through religious authorities like priests, rabbis, and mullahs). In the six-fold foundation for ethics I have described, religion can play into our expressions of personal values (test three) in a direct way, but it is undoubtedly the case that religion has also affected the formation of laws, ethical codes, and social mores and values in profound ways.

We can hope that people in different religious communities will engage in some serious reflection about business and its ethics. There is a lot of potential insight from Judaism, Buddhism, Christianity, Islam and other traditions, and it is regrettable that many religious people have not seriously explored what their traditions teach about good work and business. But today's workplaces and marketplaces are diverse, multi-faith, pluralistic environments. While it is sometimes appropriate for people to share their ethical values and sensitivities with their colleagues, there is never a place for any sort of religious (or ideological) "imperialism" which tries to force everyone into line. Christians, to take one important example, need to remember always that Jesus called his followers to be the "salt of the earth"—not the bulldozers of the earth—the "light of the world," not the lords of the world.

What about philosophy? Certainly, at the very least, moral philosophy challenges business leaders to think clearly and reason logically. One distinction sometimes made in ethical theory, worth mentioning here at the outset, is between "act" and "rule" theories. "Act" theories say that in every given moment we must decide afresh what is right or wrong (helpful or harmful); by contrast, "rule" theories say that people develop rules that provide general guidance so that we don't need to review every situation afresh. For example, an "act" ethicist would repeatedly ask, in every given situation, whether it is right to tell the truth or not. A "rule" ethicist would say something like "We should always tell the truth unless doing so clearly leads to harm of another person" (e.g., identifying a hidden runaway slave to a brutal master). As we review the six test questions for ethics, we can see that the two compliance questions are rule-oriented and the four others tend to be more act-oriented.

Not unlike the various religions, philosophical schools (from Chinese philosophy to Plato to Kant to postmodernism) have some valuable insights to share in the business context. But there is no room for philosophical imperialism by any one approach. We can hear and learn from many different perspectives and then work our way forward in the best, most practical way we can to figure out and do the right in the business context.

It should also be said that it is not just traditional, formal religious and philosophical schools and movements that can provide our marketplace with some helpful moral/ethical sensitivity and insight. Feminism, ethnic and social identity and liberation movements, therapeutic and psychological traditions, environmentalism, self-help movements, and other affinity groups and movements have something to offer as well in the ethics domain. We are potential losers if we banish their adherents and practitioners from contributing their ethical insights.

In all cases, we must express our ethical concerns and values in ways that are respectful of others and that contribute to a positive, collective result. If an individual cannot in conscience participate in a consensus resolution, it may be time for them to find another job where their personal values will be more comfortable.

For Reflection or Discussion

1. How would you define "ethics" and "an ethical company"?

2. How would you rank the helpfulness and importance of each of the six test questions for ethics given in this chapter? Can you suggest any other questions or guidelines for deciding on right and wrong?

3. How would you describe your own personal moral compass as it relates to the business environment? Do you have a clear and articulate sense of your core values and principles? Can you defend your position and give reasons why you adhere to it?

Exercises

1. Ask a couple business colleagues or friends how their personal ethics and business ethics are the same—and/or different?

2. Over the coming week, pay special attention to the ethical aspects of the business news as you read (or watch or listen to) it. What seem to be the important issues of business right and wrong this week?

Resources for Further Study

The easiest and quickest way to broaden one's introductory knowledge of business ethics is to do an Internet search and visit some of the good web sites devoted to this topic. The Ethics Resource Center (www.ethics.org), the Institute for Business Ethics (www.ibe.org.uk) and the Markkula Center at Santa Clara University (www.scu.edu/ethics/practicing/focusareas/business) are three great web sites with abundant resources on business ethics.

One of the best business ethics textbooks is *Managing Business Ethics: Straight Talk About How to Do It Right* by Linda K. Trevino and Katherine A. Nelson (John Wiley & Sons, 4th edition, 2007). Their approach is broad, holistic, deep, and practical (rarely can one use all four of those adjectives about one business ethics textbook). Their textbook includes lots of cases and discussions.

Two of the better collections of articles on topics in business ethics are the *Harvard Business Review's Corporate Ethics* (Harvard Business School Press, 2003) and *The Blackwell Guide to Business Ethics* edited by Norman E. Bowie (Blackwell Publishers, 2002). In later chapters, other books on particular aspects of business ethics will be mentioned.

For those interested, Edward D. Zinbarg's *Faith, Morals, and Money: What the World's Religions Tell Us About Ethics in the Marketplace* (Continuum, 2001) gives a fair and even-handed introduction and overview of what Judaism, Christianity, Islam, Hinduism, Buddhism, and Confucianism teach about sales, product safety, financial ethics, corporate governance and other topics.

NOTES

[1] "Morality" terminology, by the way, refers to the same subject matter as "ethics" terminology. Morality terms have Latin roots, ethics terms have Greek roots; some authors stipulate differences (e.g., "Ethics is the study of morality.") but there is no etymological basis for such a distinction, nor is there anything like a consistent distinction in usage. We will use the terms interchangeably.

[2] Any religion or philosophy can potentially *contribute* to our shared company ethics; but none is *sufficient* by itself as a guide in our diverse era.

[3] "Does its best" may sound too weak, but I am trying to allow for cases where compliance with the law can be a bit ambiguous; a good faith effort is what counts. No excuses.

[4] In Chapter Six we will look in detail at how best to create and implement company codes of ethics.

[5] For what it's worth, I include two ethical values and principles statements as appendixes. These can serve as reference or starting points for clarifying your own personal moral compass. It's good to be clear and articulate about these personal convictions.

[6] A "stakeholder" is anyone affected by ("with a stake in," "with something at stake") something. It is a common principle of justice that I ought to have some voice in things that will significantly affect me.

[7] Pop business writer John Maxwell's misbegotten book *There's No Such Thing as 'Business Ethics'* (Warner Books, 2003) misleads its readers into an individualistic reading of the Golden Rule (among its other failings).

[8] Don Tapscott & David Ticoll, *The Naked Corporation: How the Age of Transparency Will Revolutionize Business* (Free Press, 2003).

[9] My quibble is largely a terminological one. I have a similar issue with Steven R. Covey's justly famous book on *Seven Habits of Highly Effective People*: "effective" for what? Some cruel tyrants could claim to be effective in their own terms. So too, "sustainable" what? I'm interested in effective, sustainable *ethical/excellence* (the Greek term *arête* captures this combination precisely).

Chapter 2

Ethics Carrots & Sticks:
The Motivational Challenge

Executive Summary

We can't assume or take for granted that everyone wants to do the right thing or run an ethical organization, so we must address the motivational angle. Running through this discussion are two basic motivators: fear (of negative consequences) and love (passion and desire for positive consequences). Ethical leaders will need to use a dose of fear once in a while but should accentuate the positive (i.e., "We can achieve our vision if we will treat others fairly," etc.). There is an eight-reason business case for ethics. The first four reasons have to do with the context or environment in which business operates. Ethical businesses (1) minimize or avoid litigation, (2) enjoy greater regulatory freedom, (3) have public acceptance and a good reputation, and (4) are environmentally sustainable. The second four reasons concern the core components of the business. Ethical businesses (5) build investor confidence, (6) enjoy business partner trust, (7) have loyal customers, and (8) recruit and retain high performance employees. Finally, some managers and leaders will find it possible to motivate their people by appealing to one of four deeper reasons, i.e., (9) personal pride and honor, (10) corporate mission and identity ("This is just who we are as a company"), (11) corporate citizenship (our duty to our host government and community), and (12) "just because it's right" (the intrinsic rightness of it all). A motivation audit form is included.

What motivates the behavior and ethics of individuals and organizations? Some people and companies are exemplary in both business excellence and business ethics. What can we learn from them about motivating this kind of positive performance and achievement? Other people and companies are doing unethical things and we'd like them to stop, to change their ways, even though old habits are hard to change. We've got to address this motivational issue, figure out how to motivate more ethical business, then train and educate everyone involved. We just can't skip over this issue.

When I was a full-time professor teaching ethics to university students, I didn't pay enough attention to the motivational side of ethics. My students were already motivated to learn the material by the grade hanging over their head. As I moved from the academy to the marketplace, academic grades and degrees no longer mattered to my audiences, and I had to begin building a different sort of case.

Getting Employees Interested

An initial question is how to get company personnel interested in ethics training and performance. The answers are fairly obvious at this level. Be sure the ethics training is interesting and practical; make the training a pleasant experience; give away coffee cups, certificates, and other items to those who complete training programs; recognize and praise individuals and teams for displaying good ethics; make ethics part of employee performance and self-reviews, and so on. Ask other companies and training leaders what their most successful motivators have been.

> *Obvious steps: Make ethics and values performance part of annual reviews (individual, departmental, company-wide). Make ethics training interesting and practical. Give recognition to exemplary ethics. Reward and recognize completion of ethics training.*

All of this is important, but it is still not very deep. Why is good ethics important to me in my career and to the company and its success? It's not just because I'll get some trinket or certificate, or even a raise in pay for completing ethics training exercises. As I reflected on this question, I came up with a list of "seven good reasons to run a business in an ethical manner." As I discussed and debated it with colleagues and friends in both business and academia, the list grew . . . to eight . . . then nine . . . and finally *twelve* good reasons.[1] All of these twelve will not be equally *convincing* to everyone. All of them are not equally *appropriate* to every business context. Think of this list as a sort of menu from which to order what you need. Take a careful look at the twelve reasons and then construct the most convincing and appropriate case possible for your company and context.

Love and Fear, Carrots and Sticks

Running through all twelve reasons are two very basic motivational forces: *love* and *fear*. "Carrots and sticks." Fear of the stick and love of the carrot. Ethical behavior and change is more complicated than simple fear or love by individual agents, of course. Context matters a lot. People behave better, sometimes, because the temptation or the opportunity to misbehave have disappeared. Because of this reality, we must pay attention to the environments and structures we create—not just to the will and choice of individuals and groups. Removing temptations and possible incentives to act unethically is very important. Nevertheless, all temptation and opportunity cannot be eliminated. Freedom (basic to a "free" enterprise system) presents an opportunity for ill as well as for good.

So we return to fear and love. Think about how fear can affect us. People sometimes act a certain way (or change) because of:
  • Fear of death, sickness or injury (so we might quit smoking or other risky behavior—although sometimes people give up and go off the deep end, despite their fears);
  • Fear of failure, disgrace, and shame (sometimes we shape up and change our ways, sometimes we cheat and lie to try to stave off the inevitable);
  • Fear of financial loss, penalties, or disaster.

We could extend the list considerably. Many of the "Twelve Good Reasons to Run a Business in an Ethical Manner" contain a "fear factor." And that's not all bad. Sometimes we should be afraid and change our ways. Sometimes leaders must instill a bit of fear and reality in their employees and colleagues. Sometimes we are living in a dream world and need to wake up and change our ways.

> *Fear is a strong motivator, and good leaders need sometimes to "put the fear of God" into the troops; but as soon as the threat subsides, the old ways can reappear. And will business creativity and excellence really flourish long-term in a repressive, fearful atmosphere?*

Machiavelli argued that, if they had to choose, it was better for princes to rule by fear than by love. In my view it is the opposite: better to rule by love than by fear (though a dose of the latter is sometimes appropriate). For one thing, love can operate in a more long-distance fashion. Fear is a great motivator—as long as it is a felt threat. When it is removed it is easy to slip back into our old ways. Think of how some long-time smokers or overeaters suddenly shape up when given a bad report of serious threats to their health—but then relapse immediately when they get a better report. Think of how some individuals will be unfaithful as long as the fear of discovery is low or nonexistent; but think of how rigorously faithful someone is who is deeply in love, even with a distant lover.

What I mean by *love* is a "passionate desire" for something. Why does someone known as a kind of "slob" undergo an amazing change and start dressing and acting in "sharper" ways? Often it is because he or she has fallen in love with someone and is now all about impressing and winning the object of affection. Love (passionate desire) for a particular job one has applied for might (alone) get someone to clean up their act. Love of money and material things, love of praise, fame, power, or God, also get a lot of people going. Later in our discussion of business mission and vision (Chapter Four) we will reflect more carefully on what sorts of goals and purposes move individuals in positive and ethical directions. The wrong love can wreak havoc. But the basic point remains: People change because of passion (love) for things. There is a "love factor" along with a fear factor embedded in most of the twelve reasons which follow.

Love (passion and desire) is a powerful motivator, even at a distance.
But what we love has a lot to do with how we behave. We need an
inspiring, worthy object to love and pursue.

Twelve Good Reasons to Run a Company in an Ethical Manner

There are at least Twelve Good Reasons: twelve reasons to recruit, hire, and continuously train an ethical workforce; twelve reasons for leaders to focus some serious attention on building ethically healthy organizations. We can simplify things a bit into *three categories*: four external reasons, four internal reasons, and four deep reasons. The basic motivations of fear and love run through all twelve reasons in the sense that there is trouble to be feared and success or satisfaction to be pursued. A business can work it either way motivationally. My recommendation is: a little fear and realism, a lot of passion and love.

Four External Reasons to Build an Ethical Business

The first set of reasons for businesses to care about ethics relates to the political-social-natural environment in which a business must operate. It has to do with keeping good relations with the communities, political authorities, neighborhoods, and ecosystems—the external stakeholders, we could say—in which a company is based. This context around a business can gradually become hostile or negative or apathetic toward a business—or it can suddenly slam down and crush a company. We ignore these external factors and forces at our peril.

Reason #1: Litigation & Penal System Avoidance.

The first reason (though not the highest or most admirable!) to be ethical in business is to reduce the likelihood of getting arrested, indicted, convicted, fined, or imprisoned. A long list of business leaders is suffering the consequences of illegal behavior. Boeing, one of the world's great corporations, with a large ethics office and mandatory training programs for employees, saw Michael Sears, once in line to become CEO, indicted, tried, convicted, and sentenced to four months in prison, $250,000 in fines, two years' probation, and 200 hours of community service. He was abruptly fired after a promising 34-year career, losing an estimated $10 million in salary, stock benefits and future compensation. A management book Sears was about to publish, "Soaring Through Turbulence," was withdrawn after his arrest. Boeing CEO Phil Condit resigned under a cloud shortly after Sears was fired. Condit's successor, Harry Stonecipher, announced that he had "the highest confidence in the integrity and systems of the Boeing Company" and would "exert all energy to address any inadequacies that need to be corrected." (*New York Times* 10/2/04), but was fired a few weeks later for his own personal ethical lapses. John Rigas, Jeffrey Skilling, Bernie Ebbers, Sam Waksal, Martha Stewart: the list goes on for pages.

The Enron and Arthur Andersen stories show that it is not just individuals who get caught and punished; whole companies can go out of business. These stories of high profile misbehavior landing people and companies in court (and often prison) go on and on, day after day, in our business news. Small businesses, and employees at all levels, also get caught, sued, convicted, and fired, for behavior that starts by not caring about basic ethics. It's a career-wrecker and a company-wrecker.

> *Unethical behavior easily descends into illegal behavior. But even if you manage to get off legally unscathed, think of how much money must be diverted to legal defense rather than into research, product development, marketing, and other activities which add value.*

Running a business in an ethical manner helps a business avoid trouble with the law in four ways.

First: while ethics is more than compliance, *legal compliance often stands as a sort of "minimum ethics."* Respect for the law is the first step in being ethical, most of the time.

Second: simply having an ethics and compliance program *can significantly reduce any fines and penalties* if you do get caught doing something wrong. Not a very high-minded reason to care about ethics, but it still counts: the United States Federal Sentencing Guidelines for White Collar Crime (1991) specify that companies which create Compliance and Ethics programs can have their penalties reduced by up to 40 percent.

Third: ethical guidelines *establish a company's behavioral boundaries a safe distance within the law.* Thus, the law may permit a greater exploitation of customer data (or a larger dose of impurities in a food product) than a company believes is ethically right. But a company that works the extreme edges of the law is more likely to step over the line and get into trouble.

Fourth: laws are best at telling us *what not to do*—while ethical principles often give us not just negative boundaries but *positive standards and ideals to aim at*. (In Chapter Six, we will take a close look at ethical boundary and mandate guidelines). An ethical guideline like "treat all customers with respect, consideration, and friendliness" creates a different business from one which tries only to avoid getting indicted or sued for questionable handling of customer transactions. Think about it: If your customer service or sales people are only guided by the limits of the law, that creates a much different (and riskier) environment than one in which their conscious thought is focused on providing excellent service with integrity.

Reason #2: Regulatory Freedom.

The second good reason to be ethical is "regulatory freedom" or "red tape avoidance." Red tape (bureaucracy, regulations, forms, etc.) can eat up a great deal of time and money. All regulation is not bad of course. Some is always necessary to help level the playing field and establish fair "rules of the game." It is not true that healthy capitalism needs only the "invisible hand" of the market. Just ask those doing business in Russia after the fall of the USSR or take a look back at the unregulated vices of the Robber Barons who led American business in the late 19th Century. Anarchy is not the context in which markets thrive.

But excessive or poorly drawn regulation harms business and then society as well. Provided there is a basic, adequate legal and social infrastructure, business thrives on maximized freedom. Red tape, bureaucracy, and excessive regulatory demands inhibit free enterprise, promote conformity, restrain innovation, and mishandle novel situations. Government will always, inevitably, be somewhat ham-fisted in its regulations. Given the complexity of each field, insiders and practitioners are usually the best positioned to know how to operate ethically in their own domains. But if they fail to self-regulate, government will step in. If businesses abuse their freedom by doing things that, while legal, are unethical, legislative agencies will create new regulations to prevent such abuses. If we want freedom, *we must regulate ourselves* by sound ethical values. "Govern yourself, or be governed" is another way to put it.

Two recent examples are the legislation prohibiting telemarketing calls and the Sarbanes-Oxley legislation which followed the Enron and Andersen scandals. The sins of the few brought regulatory compliance costs to the many—some estimate an annual Sarbanes-Oxley cost of 30 billion dollars to American business. For their part, if telemarketers had used some self-imposed restraint they might still be in business.

If excessive compensation and stock options are given to CEOs without shareholder approval and strong performance, if computer users suffer from excessive spam (over 50 percent of all e-mail now is unsolicited junk), if medical experts (nine out of ten, they say) write treatment guidelines while having undisclosed financial ties to the pharmaceutical industry, if ranchers fight efforts to ban the use of sick animals in our meat supply, if big oil drilling companies evade American taxes by taking addresses in Bermuda and Barbados and then turn around and qualify for business contracts open only to American companies, if companies abuse the privacy and confidentiality of customer financial information, if restaurants don't voluntarily follow safe and sanitary food handling procedures, if workers are exploited and harmed, if video game players go nuts, if investment brokers rip off the vulnerable, if boards of directors of publicly held corporations are hopelessly compromised and ineffective . . . tighter regulations will follow. Of course, thankfully, all businesses do *not* push (or cross) the ethical limits described in this paragraph, but these things do happen; and if they become more frequent and unchecked are likely to prod greater regulation.

> *__Aggravate__ people by irresponsible business behavior . . . __activate__ the regulators. Regulatory responses may be slow but they will come . . . and bring a significant cost. Smart business leaders get their companies to __self-regulate__ with sound ethics.*

Business is always better off voluntarily creating and submitting to ethical values and principles rather than grudgingly, involuntarily submitting to government laws and regulations. The long-standing, traditional, self-governing practices of nurses, lawyers, clergy, and other professionals are a better way to go. The growing practice of self-reporting on corporate social and environmental responsibility (now being done by more than 500 corporations, including 3M, General Motors, McDonald's, and Siemens) is another positive example.

Reason #3: Public Acceptance, Social & Reputational Capital.

Wendy's lost (permanently) millions of dollars and (temporarily) some 30 percent of its business after a severed finger was found in its chili in early 2005. It turned out not to be Wendy's fault but rather a scam by a customer trying to collect. But it illustrates the sudden and swift power of public opinion on a business. The obvious impacts of a reputational disaster are customer and investor flight. But it's not just about investors and customers: the whole community perks up.

Think of how Procter & Gamble has been hurt over the years by false rumors of a Satanic logo. Think of how Arthur Andersen's great reputation vanished overnight with the Enron debacle that some of its people had helped facilitate and cover up. Wal-Mart's expansion plans often face stern public resistance by local people, based on Wal-mart's perceived bad reputation. The point is that if you act (or are believed to act) in an unethical fashion, public sentiment may turn against you in ways that constrict your business freedom and possibilities.

On the other hand, a reputation for being ethical creates a kind of public approval and acceptance that is a business plus. For every community or neighborhood that organizes to fight off Wal-Mart there is one that organizes to try to get Trader Joe's to come. Such a reputation helped Johnson & Johnson to rebound very strongly and quickly from its costly Tylenol scare. Southwest Airlines has built widespread public acceptance because of its values, ethics, and trustworthiness. They have business opportunities almost anywhere they want to go. Competitors fight against letting Southwest into this or that airport—but the people are on their side.

> *A bad reputation is like tilting the playing field and forcing your team to try to move uphill all the time. Everything gets harder. Doors close and companies are forced to engage in damage control and in aggressive public relations that may not be enough to counter the criticism.*
>
> *A good reputation is like having the wind at your back. Build a reputation for being ethical and you will likely win public praise, a favorable press, and the conditions and environment conducive to experimentation, expansion, and business success.*

Reputational capital and public acceptance are built up by operating in an ethical manner toward your various stakeholders. If you pay attention to this reality you may be lauded in the press. If you don't, investigative journalists (*60 Minutes, Frontline, Mother Jones, Business Week, Fortune*) might feature you in a negative lead story! Old and new activist groups might create a huge ruckus, demonstration, or boycott. The new era of Internet-driven transparency makes it increasingly difficult to hide—and increasingly easy to organize. Even a small group with limited resources can affect your company. Better to proactively embrace transparency, integrity, and the social bottom line, than to try to resist or hide. It's not just about avoiding harm and ethical scandal but about the fair treatment of business's societal stakeholders.

Of course, the public square is fickle and not always fair. Rumors and accusations can be unfounded. The Internet circulates lies as well as truths. The road to rebuilding a reputation can be long, winding, and unfair. The public can remain suspicious and cynical. But all of this is an argument for companies to be proactive in developing a strong and visible ethics and values identity and to take the initiative toward transparency and open communications with the public.

Reason #4: Environmental Sustainability.

My barbecue won't be fired up nearly as often this year. The price of wild salmon (my favorite thing to grill) is double or triple what it usually is. Why has the price jumped like this? Because the wild salmon population has been so badly overfished since 2002 that there is now a serious shortage. Consumers are hurt. The fishing business is hurt. Local seafood merchants are hurt. Restaurants are hurt. If salmon fishermen don't respect and care for the health of the salmon population, they not only disrespect and harm the salmon population, they undermine their own business. So too the timber industry. Over-log and disrespect the health of the forest, and the timber business will not last long. This isn't just about sympathy for nature (though that is a valid point in its own right); it is about the "bite back" consequences of harming the very basis of our business. We must replenish (or allow nature to replenish) what we use.

It is unethical to harm Mother Nature. Maybe we can get away with a lack of environmental ethics in the short term, but there can be no sustainable, long-term success without careful stewardship of the environment and the earth's resources.

Depletion is one major harm to the environment. Another is the pollution of our water, land, and air which makes for contaminated food and water, sick workers, and severe harm to the ecosystem. Again, the bite back effects may be slow, but they can be catastrophic. In more and more cases, human defenders of nature and of human health will also come after you if you pollute or harm nature. The wreck of the Exxon oil tanker *Valdez*, the Union Carbide chemical plant explosion in Bhopal, India, and the toxic waste at Love Canal illustrate how very costly it is, at many different levels, to ignore or violate environmental ethical standards.

The Ford Motor company, ranked last among the six automakers in fleetwide fuel efficiency, experienced protests at more than 100 dealerships across the USA in recent years. Greenpeace activists temporarily shut down a Land Rover factory owned by Ford in the UK by chaining themselves to plant equipment. After two years of protests, Dell was forced to change its policy and recycle any computer at no charge from customers who buy a new Dell. Chevron has been challenged by Ecuadoran Amazon and Alaskan Arctic National Wildlife Refuge environmentalists over its business practices.

There is good news though: General Electric polluted the Hudson River with its industrial waste discharges, ruining the fishing industry and related businesses, became a national scapegoat, and was forced to fund a very expensive dredging and clean up process. But now GE's CEO, Jeff Immelt, is leading a campaign, called Ecomagination, to invent green technology at GE. The world seems to be "going green," and GE wants to be the one to service that transition. It's about business, not altruism, Immelt said. (*SF Chronicle* 5/29/05). The inventive Rocky Mountain Institute has shown how ecological practices can lead to greater business efficiency and profits. Bay Area restaurants have discovered that they can make money by going green and sustainable—using locally grown organic ingredients, antibiotic-free meats, fish species that are not endangered, recycling cans and bottles, composting food scraps, and using environmentally friendly cleaning products.

Just in the past few years, concerns about global warming and climate change and about the political complexities of energy needs and usage have made the environmental ethics and sustainability discussion front and center for many businesses. It is not going away.

Four External Reasons to Build Ethically Healthy Organizations
- *Litigation, indictment, and penal system avoidance*
- *Regulatory freedom*
- *Brand reputation, social responsibility, and public acceptance*
- *Environmental stewardship and sustainability*

Four Internal Reasons to Build an Ethical Business

The second set of reasons for businesses to care about ethics relates to four key components in almost every business. Every business needs investors—or owners or donors (for non-profits). Every business needs business partners. Every business needs customers (or clients, patients, etc.). Every business needs employees (workers, etc.). We could refer to these four groups as the internal stakeholders in the company. My argument is that each of these four components will function better in an ethical company than an unethical one. The argument is common sense—but is easily overlooked. I'll give some examples, but they are almost unnecessary.

Reason #5: Investor Confidence.

Tom Friedman's best-selling book on globalization, *The Lexus and the Olive Tree*, describes an "electronic herd" of investors swarming around world markets by means of the Internet, looking for investment opportunities.[2] Obviously, the prospect of a good return on investment is on the minds of this electronic herd. But these investors want to be sure that the companies to which they give their money will count it properly and manage it securely. Friedman creates the image of putting on a "golden straightjacket" for businesses which agree to submit to basic rules of accounting and ethics. If companies put on this "straightjacket," they receive the investors' "gold." This is not just an issue of third world economies; investors in the USA also punish companies that abuse their trust. Here is the lesson: Make investors jittery about your ethics and watch them withhold or withdraw their investments. Without capital there can be no capitalist success.

After Enron and other scandals came to light in 2001, *Business Week* editori-alized: "There's an unusual kind of mass protest going on in America. A new investor class feels betrayed by the financial manipulation, managerial arro-gance and political connivance now revealed to be widespread in the aftermath of Enron Corp.'s collapse. These investors are educated, suburban, well-off, white- and blue-collar workers who placed their trust and their future in the stock market in the 1990s. They eagerly embraced the high-risk, high-growth economy of deregulated markets and individual choice and now feel deceived by insiders who hid the truth and rigged the odds against them . . . The investor class is taking its revenge by crushing certain stocks and pummeling companies." (*Business Week*, 25 Feb 2002, p. 150).

There is a second level to this argument. Some investors care not only about their own ethical treatment as investors, they also want the company to treat others right. They do not want to profit from or support unethical behav-ior toward employees, customers, the environment, or anything else. "Socially Responsible Investing" (SRI) has a growing, if still small, percentage of the overall market.[3]

• If investors cannot trust a company to have honest, ethical account-ing and financial management practices, and if they can't really count on a fair, just return on their investment, they will move their money elsewhere.

• Some investors will also move their money if they find out you are unethical toward your other stakeholders—even if you are straight with them as investors.

The argument about investor confidence applies to non-profit corporations as well. With the fraud conviction of their CEO William Aramony, United Way's donations went from $26 million in 1992 down to $15 million by 2002. The 2003 Pipevine scandal (misspending millions in donations they had helped collect for United Way) had a further negative impact. Excessive execu-tive compensation, wasteful spending, and needlessly high overhead are good ways for schools, charitable groups, religious organizations and other nonprof-its to discourage their donor bases. I don't give much to my beloved alma mater, UC Berkeley, because of the compensation practices of its leadership, squeezing the bottom while feathering nests at the top.

Reason #6: Partner Trust.
The old vertically integrated business "silo" organization is pretty much

dead. Instead, companies form partnerships with other companies, often out-sourcing various functions to companies that are expert in those particular business areas, rather than trying to be expert on everything. Agility and speed matter in a fluid, shifting business landscape. It's about the capacity to form and maintain business partnerships, for example, with "upstream" suppliers and "downstream" distributors.

Ford Motors and the Firestone Tire Company had a long and fruitful business partnership. But it all came unglued when Ford's Explorer SUVs experienced a series of deadly turnovers as their Firestone tires blew out. Ford blamed faulty tires manufactured at a Firestone plant allegedly manned by scab workers during an extended strike. Firestone's Japanese parent company, Bridgestone, clammed up and stonewalled. In the end it was clear that Ford's executives had chosen high SUV profit margins over their own engineers' recommended safety upgrades to stabilize the high-center-of-gravity vehicles. But Firestone also was guilty of stonewalling inquiries and evading responsibility for tire quality. Ethics broke down, then trust, then business.

Imagine a partnership where you understand each other, trust each other, shake hands and get to work. Imagine a second relationship where you've been burned before so you get your lawyers to draft voluminous protective agreements and disclosure documents, all of which have to be reviewed, negotiated, and signed by all sides. Who wins here? Agility, speed, flexibility—built on a foundation of trust and trustworthiness—win over stacks of legal protections for partners who don't trust each other. In the era of virtual corporations and extended enterprises, prospective partners will avoid unreliable, unethical companies and seek out reliable, ethical partners.

The great contemporary theorist and analyst of this phenomenon is Francis Fukuyama, author of *Trust: The Social Virtues & the Creation of Prosperity* (Free Press, 1995), an exhaustive historical study of economic and business history in several national and cultural contexts. Fukuyama discovered that business flourished and prosperity came where people had traditions of "spontaneous sociability"—the capacity to form relationships not based on blood and family ties but spontaneously, based on a shared purpose and values. He found that, in different ways, the USA, Germany, and Japan had been "high trust societies" and that this helped explain their economic success. Some other countries, by contrast, had wonderful extended family, kinship traditions—but these often precluded trusting (and working with) people outside the family or tribe. Businesses in low trust societies could only grow to a size manageable by a single family.

Getting the lawyers involved to cover all possible exposures and vulnerabilities with detailed contractual agreements may work in some fashion. But these measures increase "transaction costs," in Fukuyama's terms. They slow down and undermine business.

Erich Schlosser's book *Fast Food Nation*, describes costly breakdowns in fast food business relationships when meat packers, truckers, executive leaders, and franchise workers are not on the same page. By contrast, Getty Images, has become an extremely successful business (collecting, archiving, marketing photographic and art images for use by advertisers, illustrators, journalists, and others) on a basis of trust. There is simply no way for field photographers around the world and business workers in Seattle to check up on each other. It is all based on trust, and on shared values.

> *If we don't want to be slowed down (and financially drained) by armies of lawyers and stacks of fine-print, legal agreements—our business-to-business relationships will need to be based on trust. Trust is itself based on a reliable foundation of shared values and ethics.*

Reason #7: Customer Loyalty.

Companies can lose their customers in two ways: (1) treat them badly (cheat, hurt, or disrespect them), or (2) let them know you treat others badly. It's the same basic argument that related to investors. Customers will definitely go elsewhere for better treatment; they may also go elsewhere just for a better feeling about the business. Customers are attracted by price, quality, convenience, and such factors. But they are also attracted by *how they are treated* (including fairness, honesty, ethics) and by *brand image and reputation* (ethics included).

Business is about customers. Everybody knows that it is cheaper to retain an old customer than to find a new one (by a factor of five, according to one report). Ethical practices and a good reputation will help attract new customers and retain existing ones.

Consider these examples of customer loss: Denny's Restaurant lost customers big time because of its mistreatment of some of its black customers. It wasn't just blacks who stopped going; it was many of their non-black sympathizers as well. The old Texaco oil company (now merged into Chevron) also lost customers—in its case because of its racist treatment of black employees. In my home town, the professional football Oakland Raiders rarely sold out their home football games after they returned to Oakland in 1995. Why? Partly, of course, it has to do with a poor, losing product and high priced tickets. But the deeper reason has to do with how their local fans have been treated. From the late 1960s when the Oakland Coliseum was built for them (and for the Oakland Athletics) until they suddenly moved to Los Angeles in 1984, the Raiders sold out every game they ever played in the Coliseum. Their fans were fanatically loyal, even when they didn't win championships. But after Al Davis jilted and abandoned this loyal fan base, and then came back to town without an apology ten years later, those fans are staying home or supporting the cross-bay 49ers. Be fair to your customers.

Of course, many customers go into Wal-Mart or other stores and buy whatever they want, simply because it's cheap. Some customers don't really care if workers were whipped and beaten as they made their items—or if harbormasters were bribed to move the merchandise—or if their own next door neighbors were thrown out of a job three weeks before retirement by a company that, pressured by Wal-Mart, offshored its manufacturing jobs, cut its costs, lowered its prices, and rewarded its top brass with obscene bonuses. They don't care about things like that (until its hits home to their family). We can't say that such customers are all evil people, either. Sometimes it is "care exhaustion"—just impossible to muster the passion to find out about these things and look for a more ethical (and probably more expensive) alternative. What is certain is that if you shaft the customers themselves, they will go to another company if there is an alternative. That much is clear.

That's the fear side, the "stick" side. What about the love, "carrot" side of the argument? Many customers become fanatically loyal to companies that treat them—and their other stakeholders—well. The Odwalla juice company survived and even prospered after a contamination scare because their customers believed in their values and ethics. In'n'Out Burgers customers are also loyal, not just because of the taste (real dairy in their milk shakes!—not artificial, chemical concoctions; actual potatoes cut up into french fries!—not just processed, industrial potato meal shaped into fry-like sticks seered in boiling lard) and price—but because of the ways In'n'Out treats and compensates its employees from front-line workers to managers.

Starbucks coffee may not always measure up to Peet's or other local coffee houses we love, but it is the sort of place many of us feel good about patronizing because of the way they have provided health care benefits even to their part-time employees and because of their efforts to increase their use of fair trade coffee and be ecologically responsible. Costco may be too much of a big box warehouse experience for some people, but it turns many others into loyal fans by its policies toward its customers (never marking merchandise up more than 14 percent) and toward its employees (insisting on paying them industry-leading wages). No surprise that Costco has both a talented, stable, happy workforce and a loyal customer base.

- *Treat your customers with honesty and respect and see them again . . . and again.*
- *Cheat, disrespect, or lie to them and watch them migrate to your competitors.*
- *Exploit employees or trash the environment and watch some customers leave.*
- *Run a company admired for its ethics and watch customer pride and loyalty reinforced.*

Reason#8: Employee Performance.

Surveys show that prospective employees (recent MBA grads, workers in transition) are attracted to companies with good reputations for ethics and fairness. Given a choice, employees will choose to work for companies with good reputations. Honest, hardworking people tend to prefer honest hard-working organizational cultures. "Best Places to Work" survey award winners often highlight the ethical dimensions of their employers. No doubt that compensation factors play a key role in recruiting good employees. But company ethics can also be an important recruiting help. As with the customers, this is first of all about whether employees themselves are treated fairly. But it is secondarily about how the company treats others (customers, business partners, government agencies, etc.). If the company is cheating and deceiving others, it loses respect and loyalty with its own people.

It's not just about recruitment but *retention*. As with customers, it is much better and more cost-effective to retain your people than to have high turnover. New employee training costs are even more significant than new customer orientation costs. Ethics helps retain good workers.

Beyond recruitment and retention is employee *performance*. A company that exploits or mistreats—or even *appears* to exploit and mistreat—its workers, will likely get a second-rate performance out of them. If we think our boss or colleagues will rip off our best, most creative ideas, or tell lies about us . . . will we freely and openly share those ideas? I don't think so. In our *knowledge* economy, our best assets are people and their knowledge and creativity. But knowledge sharing must be based on and facilitated by trust and trustworthiness. If we think that we're here for the long haul and that we are a team that will share in the upside as well as the down, we will deliver a better performance.

Impacts of Bad Company Ethics on Employees
- *Employee recruitment (more difficult). Employee retention (down; turnover increases)*
- *Job satisfaction (down). Job performance levels (down)*

Lincoln Electric Motors, outside of Cleveland, is a longtime industry leader, whose employees routinely, consistently, out-produce, by wide margins, all their competitors. Why? Lincoln has a culture of strong job security, an egalitarian management/labor culture (with lots of symbolic equality in office furnishings, the company cafeteria, etc.), and opportunity to work hard and be paid (bonuses) for what you have done. It is a culture that manages simultaneously to stimulate individual effort and team sacrifice. Treat workers well and watch them perform.

There are many other examples of ethical companies benefiting in employee recruitment and performance: office furniture manufacturer Herman Miller, Southwest Airlines, Men's Wearhouse, Costco, the SAS software firm. Stanford business professors Charles O'Reilly and Jeffrey Pfeffer's *Hidden Value: How Great Companies Achieve Extraordinary Results with Ordinary People* argues that "Great people want to work at places where they can actually use their talents, where they are treated with dignity, trust, and respect, and where they are engaged by the values and culture of the organization."[4]

Four Internal Reasons to Build Ethically-Healthy Organizations
- *Investor confidence*
- *Business partner trust*
- *Customer loyalty*
- *Employee recruitment, retention, & performance*

Two Levels to the Business Case for Ethics

What we have then is an eight-part business case for running a company in an ethical manner. It's about treating eight stakeholders fairly and wisely. You've heard of the "triple bottom line"; this is the "octoval bottom line." Generally speaking, it will cost you if you don't pay attention, and it will benefit your business if you do, to these eight factors. On the most obvious, common sense level these eight arguments have the following logical structure: Treat nature in the right way, and nature will not bite back; treat your customers honestly and respectfully and they will be loyal; treat your investors ethically and honestly and they will give you more of their money; treat your employees right and they will perform better; or, conversely, mistreat any of these groups and they will take their business elsewhere.

On a second level, the business case is less clear. Here is what I mean. Will your investors care if you abuse your workers as long as you are honest and fair with the investors themselves? Some care, for sure. This is the "socially responsible investing" community. SRI is a growing but still relatively small fraction of the investment community. And will your customers care if you abuse your workers, so long as you are honest with the customers and they get a good deal? Not at all clear. Will your employees be affected if you disrespect and cheat your customers and business partners, so long as you treat them (the employees) generously and honestly? Some employees wouldn't care; some would. So the business case on this second level is not as compelling and certain as on the first level. The first level argument is a slam dunk, common sense case; the second level argument becomes increasingly compelling as a long term, "built-to-last" orientation is taken.

Four Deep Reasons to Build an Ethical Business

Finally, we come to four "deep" reasons to operate a business in an ethical manner. I say "deep" because for many people, these reasons are convincing enough to be ethical, even if the preceding eight-part "business case" does not seem to be playing out as we would wish.

Reason #9: Pride, Honor, & Conscience.

The first deep reason has to do with *pride*, *honor*, and a *clear conscience*. Pride means that we can look in the mirror—or at others—without shame. We can walk anywhere with our head held high. It is about *honor*, a sense of personal value that will not let me stoop to treat people in bad ways. Even if nobody else knows, I know what I did. I want to be proud of my work. When you achieve success (or survive difficulty) without cheating or compromising your ethics, you sleep well at night and take pride in what you have accomplished. As Peter Drucker has written, "The test is a simple one: What kind of person do I want to see when I shave myself in the morning?" It's about *who we are* and what kind of a team or company we are. Can we feel great about not just *what* we accomplished but *how* we did it?

> *Pride, honor, and a clear conscience are at the foundation of a mean-ingful career, life, and legacy. It's about who we are and what kind of a team or company we are. Can we feel great about not just what we accomplished but how we did it? Can we hold our head high, knowing we didn't cut corners, step on others, and deceive people? It is about getting into alignment with our deepest, best self. Many of us would absolutely loathe ourselves if we were hypocritical, sniveling, decep-tive, wormy, phony, abusive, cheaters.*

The classic idea of "conscience" says that everyone has some kind of moral "antenna," or "moral compass," an innate as well as learned sense of right or wrong. Even if we don't agree on all the details, we all have a con-science that tells us when something is wrong. The ninth reason to operate an ethical business is to keep this conscience clear, untroubled, and not pointing an accusing finger at us. Conscience, pride, and honor are about who we are as human beings. Doing the right, ethical thing is about getting into alignment with our deepest, best self.

The human capacity for rationalization and denial is truly awesome, of course, and some high profile business malefactors may go to their graves protesting their innocence and victimization by others. But how would you feel if you were caught in a lie? How did George O'Leary feel when he was abruptly fired as Notre Dame football coach—just days after getting the job—when it came out that his academic background was not what he had claimed? Just a little embarrassing. How do the formerly high rolling corporate crooks feel now at their family gatherings or high school reunions or when they are alone thinking about their lives?

There is a lot of cheating going on in the world. People justify it by saying that others are cheating and they are really just evening up the playing field. Certainly there are lots of pressures to cut corners and not enough pressures, and not enough praise for doing the right thing and living with pride, honor, integrity, and a clear conscience. But what is truly most important often comes out at the end of our lives and careers—e.g., in retirement speeches, and even more, funeral eulogies. Most of the time it is our kindness, generosity, integri-ty, toughness under challenge, that sort of thing, that gets lauded and praised. No one seems to want to mention or take pride in the scandalous behavior or duplicity of their lives and careers. It is a powerful argument, an inspiring call—when someone challenges us to live with pride and honor, with integrity, "no matter what."

Reason #10: Business Excellence & Success.

The second "deep" reason to be ethical is about being in alignment with the essential character and purpose of our business organization. In some ways, this argument is a kind of summary of all the preceding ones—it is about the total business and its overall ethical health. It's a *broad*, comprehensive perspective. But it is also a *deep* reason. It is an argument about the "corporate DNA," the "genetic" structure, the essential nature of the organization, about being in alignment with the mission and vision at the core of the whole enterprise.

This tenth reason is really the launching pad into a new way of thinking about business ethics that is proactive instead of reactive, holistic instead of fragmented, positive instead of negative, practical instead of theoretical, contextual instead of abstract. This kind of ethics is not "damage-control" but "mission-control." Instead of letting crisis cases and troubling dilemmas set our business ethics agenda, instead of relying just on our personal values and consciences, we are building on our shared, fundamental, business purpose.

So the first question here is not, "What is right and wrong"—but "Why do we exist?" "Where are we going?" "What is our core *purpose* and *mission*? Our *vision*?" Right and wrong cannot really, fully be spelled out until we figure out where we are going. It is the mission that *leverages* and *motivates* our ethics. And the mission *specifies* our ethical guidelines and values. Without a positive, inspiring, worthwhile corporate mission, all of our other efforts at ethical business will be piecemeal and of uncertain impact. Fear of jail or shame or failure or customer loss may motivate some ethical behavior. Passion for a worthy, inspiring mission works like love: It will overcome a lot of obstacles to find its satisfaction.

Ethical guidelines spell out the *means* to the *end* (our purpose or mission), but they are also the *"realized presence"* of that end. That is, they are not separable but integral to the character of the End. This approach to business values and ethics, by the way, has ancient roots (in Aristotle and the Bible, for example)—and contemporary support from authors such as Jim Collins and Max DePree. The second half of this book develops this sort of mission-control approach.

What does it mean to say that *"ethics is about excellence"*? The terms "success" and "excellence" are ways of saying "we made it." To succeed or excel is to fulfill our purpose or goal in a praiseworthy, admirable manner. I mentioned earlier that in classical Greek the word *arête* means *both* "ethical virtue" and "excellence." In this way of thinking, ethics and excellence are inseparable, almost identical. "Doing the right thing" and "doing things right" are tightly intertwined. There just is no success and excellence that mean anything that can be separated from being good and doing right.

> *Paying attention to our ethics and values is fundamentally about paying attention to the characteristics and guidelines that will make us and keep us great. It's all about excellence, about our corporate DNA, about making clear who we are as a company. Ethics is all about getting into alignment with who we are and where we are going as a company.*

Like Hewlett-Packard in the old days, Harris & Associates, a highly-regarded construction and project management firm based in Concord, California, is a great example of this tenth motivation for paying attention to ethics. Carl Harris founded his company with two other people back in 1973. Thirty years later Harris & Associates was approaching five hundred employees. Rather than everyone operating out of one headquarters location, there were now some twelve satellite branch offices around the western United States. Carl Harris and his generation of the founding leadership were at or nearing retirement age.

When Harris & Associates was small and centered in one place, when the leadership was looking forward to decades of hands-on presence, it sufficed to have its values and ethics embodied personally in its leaders and articulated person-to-person. Thirty years later the growing numbers, the geographical dispersion, and the generational leadership transition all led Harris & Associates to take action to articulate and implement an aggressive mission, values, and ethics program. For them it was not about damage control but about taking steps to guard and perpetuate into the next generation, the things that have made their company great. And Harris is a great company—growing and hiring new people all the time. If someone comes on board, perhaps in a remote branch office, bringing the values and style of their previous employer (like Haliburton or Bechtel), Harris & Associates wants its own culture, values, and ethics to be clearly identified and distinctively present.

The ninth reason (pride, honor, conscience) was about acting in harmony and alignment with our best selves. The tenth reason is about ethics and action that are in harmony and alignment with what our company represents and aspires to, our best corporate self, we could say.

Reason #11: Corporate Citizenship.
A third "deep" reason for being ethical that doesn't really depend on a

pragmatic, business case has to do with "corporate citizenship." Much has been written, pro and con, about the American legal definition of corporations as "persons." The corporate citizenship view actually brings the best out of the concept by calling for a fuller understanding of the obligations as well as privileges that go with such citizenship. Citizens have responsibilities as well as privileges by *definition*. It just goes with the territory. Non-citizens don't share the same rights and responsibilities. Citizens pay taxes, obey the laws, defend the commonwealth, and do their part for the common good.

Corporate citizenship sees the ethical responsibility of business based not on business benefits, personal values, or grand philosophical or theological theories but on the necessary relationships among citizen-participants in civil society. Corporations are seen as complex communities and institutions existing in relationships within civil societies. Ethics for corporate "persons" is about being aligned with the requirements of a healthy, well-functioning civil society.

Some companies understand and willingly embrace this responsibility as citizens. David Packard writes, "Among the Hewlett-Packard objectives Bill Hewlett and I set down was one recognizing the company's responsibility to be a good corporate citizen. . . This means being sensitive to the needs and interests of the community; it means applying the highest standards of honesty and integrity to all our relationships with individuals and groups; it means enhancing and protecting the physical environment and building attractive plants and offices of which the community can be proud; it means contributing talent, energy, time, and financial support to community projects."[5]

Harris & Associates articulated its long-standing mission to explicitly include the following: *"We protect and improve our community and environment through responsible stewardship of our shared resources"*. . . and its vision to include *"We want to be valued as model corporate citizens by all the communities in which we operate, with a reputation for generosity, responsiveness, and wise stewardship."*

Of course, this kind of corporate stance can pay off in greater public acceptance, higher brand reputation, increased customer loyalty, and employee pride. But the fundamental argument is that, *even if there is no other direct business pay-off*, operating ethically and responsibly is part and parcel of being a citizen in this society. It just goes with the territory. It is about being in harmony and alignment with our host society and community.

> *If corporations are to be granted the* privileges *of legally defined "persons," it is appropriate to expect them to accept the* responsibilities *that normally attach to such citizenship. It is a two-way street. Ethical responsibility goes with the territory. It is about being in alignment with our civil society in its most constructive sense.*

Reason #12. "Just Because It's Right."

Shouldn't we do the right thing "just because it's right," i.e., even if there is no benefit to us or our business? The short answer is "Of course!" We shouldn't need a business or personal payoff to get us to do the right thing. In fact, we shouldn't even need the reward of feeling pride or honor or having a clear conscience. We should do the right thing "just because it's right." It certainly simplifies things if this answer is convincing. For one thing, it could be a real distraction to stop and calculate probable benefits each time before deciding whether to do the right thing. Such a calculating approach to the moral life would soon be very tedious personally and impossible for organizations in our high speed society.

Another concern behind this "reason" is that motivation by the benefits of being ethical can appear hypocritical. The famous Machiavelli, quoted earlier about the virtues of ruling by fear, also said that rulers only needed to "appear to be virtuous"—not actually be virtuous. But the people are not as naïve as Machiavelli thought. Wayne Alderson, leader of the "Value of the Person" business seminars, often said that if a leader treats employees with love, dignity, and respect, productivity will virtually always go up; but, he insisted, if a leader treats employees with love, dignity, and respect *so that* they will be more productive, they will see right through him or her and it will fail.[6] Dennis Bakke's recent account of his CEO experience at AES, *Joy at Work*, makes the same kind of argument: Do the right thing because it's right. That's enough.[7]

A famous tradition in European philosophy is one source of this thinking about ethics. Immanuel Kant (1724-1804) argued that ethical imperatives are never "hypothetical" but always "categorical"—independent of all conditions and results. Kant thought that this was the only rational way to live and think. Another source of "just because it's right" thinking is religion. "Divine Command" ethics say that something is right just because God decrees it to be so. (Though the Bible itself, by the way, never urges ethical behavior with a "just because" or a divine "pulling of rank." For example, for those who follow the Ten Commandments, "It will go well with you and you will live long in the land" (Deut. 5:33).

> *The "just because it's right" argument is really about something like "getting into alignment with God and the universe"—seeking harmony with the moral universe.*

In any case, there is an important problem that this argument is trying to address. If one is only ethical when one can see a concrete business benefit, some bad things are going to be done. Calculation, hypocrisy, and manipulation will poison any atmosphere, any organization. Nobody can make the case that every ethical act will result in a personal (or business) benefit in the short term. Another way of explaining this argument is to say that it is really more about "*when*" to do the right thing than about "*why*" to do it. In other words, do the right thing even when the benefit of being ethical is unclear or deferred. Sometimes being ethical will cost us one way or another; sometimes it will pay-off in *many* different ways; but sometimes we just can't tell. The best we can say is that being ethical will *often* bring benefits to you and your organization, especially in the long-term. So the best "working" rule of thumb is always "do it just because it's right."

A good analogy here is physical health. If you will stop your excesses and control your bad habits, if you will exercise regularly and eat wisely, you will likely live longer and feel better. But this is not guaranteed; you might get hit by a truck or die of a heart attack anyway. Nevertheless, good habits will increase your odds of a good and long life. So with business: Good ethics increases your odds of success and excellence. No guarantees—but better odds.

But even that bit of long-term pragmatic thinking troubles some of the devotees of this twelfth reason. Maybe the best way to put it is to say that we ought to do the right thing in business because it keeps us in harmony and alignment with the moral universe and its Creator.

<u>**Four Deep Reasons to Build Ethically Healthy Organizations**</u>
- *Honor, pride, & conscience: alignment with my best self*
- *Success & excellence: alignment with our corporate mission and vision*
- *Corporate citizenship: alignment with our public responsibility and privilege*
- *Just because it's right: alignment with a moral universe and Creator*

Getting Real About Ethical Motivation in Our Organizations

There are four basic processes in "making ethics real" in an organization. We will return to this four part process again and again in coming chapters. The first process is *identification*. We must identify or "figure out" and describe the best, strongest case for being ethical in our company. This chapter has discussed twelve good reasons. But every organization needs to engage in a serious conversation about *why* it should be ethical. You can't just piggy-back on someone else's convictions (though we can and must learn from others). Get a committee together and hash out the strongest case possible.

The second process is *education*. This process is about making sure everyone in our organization (perhaps also our customers and business partners) *knows* our reasons for being ethical. It does no good to have a great argument if the people don't know it. How do we educate and train our people? It starts with leaders from the top on down communicating our "good reasons" to be ethical, defining and explaining them, and constantly telling stories (that instill fear and love as appropriate) in support of each of our good reasons. The company newsletter can circulate these communications. A letter from the CEO at the front of the code of ethics can give the reasons. Speeches, presentations, and staff meeting agendas can be teaching opportunities and motivational opportunities. My caution is to be sure to give at least as many positive examples as negative ones. Carrots, not just sticks.

The third process is *implementation*: living out what we have identified and taught, practicing what we preach. In the case of ethical motivation it is a relatively straightforward matter of *arguing* for good ethics and then *acting* ethically. Giving reasons, persuading others . . . that is how we implement the concerns for motivation. But we can't just give a strong argument and then ignore it or violate it; we must also act on our arguments.

The fourth process is *evaluation*. We must be aggressive in finding out if our people *know* the argument and actually *believe* it. I will say more about the general process of evaluation later, but one component I strongly recommend is an annual or perhaps biennial ethics audit of all employees (and directors, executive management, et al). We must find out whether and how the people are motivated to be ethical—and what they think of the company and its leadership. Below, I have given a *generic* version of an ethical motivational audit; I believe each organization needs to *customize* its own audit. In addition to an audit like the one below, there is no substitute for focus groups, staff discussions, and the insight one gets from "management by wandering around."

Gill's Company Ethics Motivation Audit

Does our company take ethics & values seriously?	Strongly Disagree 1	2	3	Strongly Agree 4	5
1. Our company leaders communicate frequently about the importance of ethics and social responsibility. They really care and see these things as a priority.	❏	❏	❏	❏	❏
2. Avoiding trouble with the law is an important reason why ethics matters at our company.	❏	❏	❏	❏	❏
3. Earning and maintaining a good public reputation for ethics and social responsibility really matters at our company.	❏	❏	❏	❏	❏
4. Being good stewards and caretakers of the environment is important at our company.	❏	❏	❏	❏	❏
5. Maintaining strong financial health and committed investors/owners is an important reason why ethics matters to our company.	❏	❏	❏	❏	❏
6. Maintaining good working relationships with business partners is an important reason why ethics matters at our company.	❏	❏	❏	❏	❏
7. Customer acquisition and loyalty depends in an important way on our treating clients ethically—and on our overall reputation for ethics.	❏	❏	❏	❏	❏
8. Recruiting and retaining good, enthusiastic employees depends, to an important extent, on our maintaining an ethical organization.	❏	❏	❏	❏	❏
9. Our people take pride in the high ethics they practice, so that any success they have was not achieved by cutting ethical corners.	❏	❏	❏	❏	❏
10. Ethics and values at our company are not just an external standard but are part of our core identity. Living by our company values and ethics is essential to fulfilling our corporate mission.	❏	❏	❏	❏	❏
11. Our company stresses the importance of being a responsible, ethical corporate citizen in the communities in which we operate.	❏	❏	❏	❏	❏
12. Our company would do the ethically right thing even if it cost something, even if didn't have a financial benefit, even if its competitors didn't follow suit. It would do it just because it is right.	❏	❏	❏	❏	❏

Make a list of the top four reasons you think our company should operate in an ethical manner, from the #1 reason down to #4:

1. _____

2. _____

3. _____

4. _____

Comments on our company's motivation and commitment to being ethical:

Afterthought: What Motivates Unethical Business?

It is worth asking the opposite motivational question: Why are people and organizations unethical? Are we up against a separate "twelve good reasons to be unethical"? What motivates bad things in business?

If we focus on the vices of attitude that lead to unethical action, greed would certainly be one of the top answers in any survey. Inordinate, obsessive desire for more and more and more—this can blind people to all other considerations and cause them to lie, cheat, and steal. Pride may be a cause in some cases; people are so afraid of appearing (or being) unsuccessful that they cheat. Arrogance can play a role—some individuals are so drunk with power they believe they are above the law and conventional morality.

This could lead into a focus on the character of the individual players. One common explanation is to blame the "bad apples" in our midst—bad individuals who do unethical things. The message seems to be that a few "bad apples can spoil the barrel." Some people are so corrupted by greed and pride that they will stop at nothing to get what they want. The bad apples justify themselves by thinking they are above the law, unique in their situation. Or they argue that others in their position would do the same (unethical) thing. Sometimes they argue that their private moral standards are one thing but the business world is a dog-eat-dog, kill-or-be-killed environment with no place for a soft ethics of altruistic values.

The implication of the "bad apple" argument is that companies need to be careful to hire "good" people. HR recruiting processes must look for character, values, and ethics, not just for technical skills, experience, or academic pedigree. That is unquestionably important, but things are rarely so simple. None of us completely lives up to our ideals. And people of high ideals sometimes fail or fall under the extreme pressure of business situations. The character of the individual (apple) is very important, but it doesn't fully explain unethical business.

Another explanation focuses our attention on the environment, either the organization or the broader economy and society. Some point the finger at defective systems and policies in companies. This is the "bad barrel" argument. The barrel causes (or enables) the rotting of the individual apples. For example: The compensation system might reward quantitative achievement so heavily that corners are cut to "make the numbers." Perhaps the system encourages cronyism rather than accountability on boards of directors. Perhaps the company does nothing to promote or implement its formal values statements so that cynicism reigns in daily practice. Perhaps there are just too many "opportunities" left open for individuals to be corrupted and make bad, unethical decisions.

The systems explanation certainly is important and urges business leaders to be clear and articulate about values and then implement those values in organizational systems, policies, and daily business activities. The "bad barrel" argument is no excuse for letting the guilty off the hook, but it is an explanation of why people and organizations sometimes yield to temptation. The implication of this argument is that we need to build organizations that reduce the pressures and opportunities for unethical behavior and that, conversely, reward and encourage ethical behavior.

We can go even broader and blame the larger global marketplace, economy, and society. Today's intense economic and cultural pressures, the competitive environment in which companies operate, cause ethical lapses. This is just a larger version of the preceding systems argument. Now it is not the individual company but something larger: "the market made me do it!" We "had to do it to stay competitive," to survive (employment practices, pricing, pollution, etc.) in the global economy. What can possibly be done about this third factor? Changing an individual is very tough; changing a company is so much tougher; changing the national or world economy seems impossible.

The legislative and regulatory environment might be improved, of course. Perhaps national governments and international bodies (World Bank, United Nations, etc.) can have an ethical influence on business. Perhaps the media, religious organizations, and other popular movements can have an impact. Perhaps businesses can work together to improve things. Some companies may choose to back off from the competitive, global environment and operate on a smaller scale in some area. The point is that it will not be easy to modify the intense, competitive forces of global capitalism. We will have to look elsewhere for solutions to the epidemic of unethical business behavior.

For Reflection or Discussion

1. As you think about your own business experiences, what fears (worries, anxieties, things to avoid) and what loves (positive passions and desires) have influenced you?

2. Which of the twelve reasons do you find most convincing for your career and your business arena? Which will be easiest to use in motivating your company?

3. Which of the twelve reasons do you find unconvincing or unhelpful in motivating your company to be ethical? Why? Can these weaker arguments be strengthened at all?

4. On a more general level, are there other reasons or arguments to be ethical in business? What are they?

Exercises

1. Go out on the web and visit a few web sites of both competitors and companies in other industries that you admire. Some of them post their mission/vision, values, and ethical guidelines with an introductory statement (usually signed by the President or CEO) saying *why ethics is important.* What are their reasons? Could you write a more compelling statement about the "why"?

2. Do some brief interviews of a superior, a peer, and a subordinate in your company. Ask each of them to define "ethical business" and say why it is (or should be) important to our company.

Resources for Further Study

One place to go for the "why care about ethics?" discussion is Milton Friedman's famous little essay "The Social Responsibility of Business Is to Increase Its Profits" (originally published 13 September 1970, *New York Times Magazine;* widely available on the web). Friedman argues for a "minimalist" perspective, that executives serve only the profit-maximizing interests of the business owners, limited only by the "rules of the game," i.e., free and open competition and avoidance of deception and fraud. Friedman is not really attacking business ethics, but for him, obligations to other stakeholders (beyond investor/owners) are distinctly secondary. It is a great thought and discussion piece.

Of the many fine books arguing (with lots of examples) that good ethics, social responsibility, and the triple bottom line approach are (or at least can be) good for business here are a handful of the best: Andrew W. Savitz (with Karl Weber), *The Triple Bottom Line* (Jossey-Bass, 2006); Raj Sisodia, David B. Wolfe, and Jag Sheth, *Firms of Endearment: How World-Class Companies Profit from Passion and Purpose* (Wharton School Publishing, 2007); Steve Hilton and Giles Gibbons, *Good Business: Your World Needs You* (Texere, 2002); Philip Kotler and Nancy Lee, *Corporate Social Responsibility: Doing the Most Good for Your Company and Your Cause* (John Wiley & Sons, 2005), and John Dalla Costa, *The Ethical Imperative: Why Moral Leadership Is Good Business* (Addison-Wesley, 1998).

Charles A. O'Reilly and Jeffrey Pfeffer's *Hidden Value: How Great Companies Achieve Extraordinary Results with Ordinary People* (Harvard Business School Press, 2000) and Francis Fukuyama, *Trust: The Social Virtues and the Creation of Prosperity*

(Free Press, 1995) are fascinating, well-documented studies of how valuing people and building trust (respectively) bring business value. David Vogel, *The Market for Virtue: The Potential and Limits of Corporate Social Responsibility* (Brookings Institution Press, 2005) is a thorough study of what we can know today about the contribution of CSR and ethics to financially successful companies. The verdict is mixed, but Vogel is mainly discussing what I called the "second level"—i.e., how stakeholders respond to the company's treatment of other stakeholder groups. (The first level has to do with how stakeholders respond to their own treatment).

Many books chronicle the successes of ethical leaders and companies (and the books listed above give many such examples). Another way to come at things is to read about the disintegration of Enron and others companies that bent and broke the law and ethics. One of the best of these studies is Barbara Ley Toffler with Jennifer Reingold, *Final Accounting: Ambition, Greed, and the Fall of Arthur Andersen* (Broadway Books, 2003).

NOTES

[1] "Nine Good Reasons to Run a Business in an Ethical Manner" was published by Al Erisman and me in our *Ethix Magazine,* Issue 22 (March-April 2002), p. 11. I would not have included the "Just because it's right" argument (number 12 on my list here) without Al's strong insistence. We don't all have to feel the force of these various arguments in the same way. What we want is to find meaningful, effective ways of persuading businesses to do the right thing. We can leave the metaphysics to someone else.

[2] Tom Friedman, *The Lexus and the Olive Tree* (Anchor Books, 2000), Chapters 6 and 7.

[3] See David Vogel, *The Market for Virtue* (Brookings Institution, 2005) for a careful report on the potential and limits of SRI funds.

[4] Charles O'Reilly and Jeffrey Pfeffer, *Hidden Value: How Great Companies Achieve Extraordinary Results with Ordinary People* (Harvard Business School Press, 2000), p. 3.

[5] David Packard, *The HP Way: How Bill Hewlett and I Built Our Company* (HarperCollins, 1995), pp. 165-66.

[6] Wayne T. Alderson & Nancy Alderson McDonnell, *Theory R Management* (Nelson, 1994), p. 47.

[7] Dennis W. Bakke, *Joy at Work* (PVG, 2005), pp. 27, 31.

Chapter 3

Ethical ER:
Trouble-Shooting & Crisis Management

Executive Summary

Some kind of ethics trouble-shooting, decision-making, and crisis management system needs to be put in place in every organization—to be able to respond quickly, wisely, and effectively when ethics problems arise and to act before things spin out of control. A five-phase process is proposed here: (1) Recognize (when serious ethical issues arise), (2) Strategize (what to do when we recognize a problem), (3) Analyze (understand the problem in depth—facts, values, options), (4) Resolve (the immediate problem), and (5) Reform (the organization so that this sort of problem is less likely to recur in the future). Sample cases, a case analysis form, and a trouble-shooting audit form are included.

It would be great if we could just get motivated to build ethical organizations, take out the blueprint, and get to work on our ideal organization. Unfortunately, our experience is less like going to a vacant lot and starting to build—and more like getting dropped into a leaky boat already out at sea. Bailing water and patching some leaky holes are urgent necessities. "Damage control" is essential. An ethical "emergency room" team needs to treat some serious cases ASAP. Later we can move the patient from the hospital to the gym, from reactive intensive care to proactive muscle building.

So we start where we are. How can an organization manage its ethical questions, dilemmas, and crises? This chapter is about decision-making, trouble-shooting, and crisis management.

Ethics Trouble-Shooting & Crisis Management: Why?

Why not just improvise and "shoot from the hip" when we see an ethical problem? Better to develop a method, a strategy for coping with ethical crises so that we can respond with wisdom and courage rather than panic. We want to minimize and contain the damage—as well as learn the appropriate lessons from each case. Putting a thoughtful, effective trouble-shooting method in place will also mean we can address ethics problems before they get *too* hot, before positions get hardened and options become limited. We want to stop unethical practices before things spin out of control and destroy careers and companies.

One of my favorite statements about decision-making was in Woody Allen's "My Speech to the Graduates" (1980): "More than at any other time in history, mankind faces a crossroads. One path leads to despair and utter hope-lessness. The other, to total extinction. Let us pray we have the wisdom to choose correctly."[1] Often enough our options in business ethical decision-making seem to range from the unpleasant to the tragic. But, as in the case of Woody Allen's speech, we may not be seeing all the possibilities. In this chapter we want to design the best possible strategy.

Certainly one obvious argument for renewed attention to our subject is the long and depressing list of bad decisions made by business leaders in the scandals of the past decade. Kenneth Lay, Andrew Fastow, Dennis Kozlowski, Martha Stewart and so many others made bad decisions with terrible consequences not just for themselves but for many others, most of them innocent. It is rare to open the daily newspaper and not find multiple reports of unethical and illegal business behavior—despite the growth of business ethics education and training in recent decades. So it is a very practical concern that drives our quest for improvement in our approach to ethical decision-making.

It is worth asking, of course, whether Ken Lay and the other corporate malefactors failed because they lacked a good decision-making and trouble-shooting method. I'm not at all sure that the standard decision-making schemes would have saved them (or us). The critical decisions they mishandled were at a deeper level (What are my values? Am I above the law? What is my mission? What will be my legacy? Do I really want to serve my self-interest alone?). The typical approach to decision-making may fail by being too narrow; that is, so focused on immediate dilemmas and quandaries that it overlooks more basic and fundamental decisions.

> *We need to set up a business ethics "Emergency Room" so that we can recognize and wisely manage ethical problems and dilemmas before they get out of control and ruin careers and companies.*

Today's pop business writers have not helped us on this topic. I will only call attention to one example, and only because I'm afraid a lot of people buy books like this: *There's No Such Thing As "Business Ethics"—There's Only ONE RULE for Making Decisions* by best-selling "leadership" writer John Maxwell.[2]

Maxwell writes: "An ethical dilemma can be defined as an undesirable or unpleasant choice relating to a moral principle or practice. . . Do we do the easy thing or the right thing?" (p. 5). Here is the first problem with Maxwell's approach: A dilemma is indeed a problematic, difficult situation, but for him to describe it in terms of being "undesirable" and "unpleasant" puts far too much emphasis on psychological factors (desire, pleasure) and fails to high-light the issue of *harm* that is at the core of ethics. Second, for Maxwell to sug-gest that the core dilemma is choosing between "easy" and "right" is also naïve and misleading.

Ethical dilemmas are such because of the difficulty in figuring out what is the right thing to do; what is right is not self-evident. For example, do we lay off these loyal workers and offshore their jobs? Maybe that will be good for our customers and shareholders, and good for the offshore economy. But it will likely be bad for our loyal workers, and may be bad for our long-term rep-utation and brand. It is very superficial to say this is about a choice of "easy" versus "right."

Maxwell goes on to say "There are really only two important points when it comes to ethics. The first is a standard to follow. The second is the will to follow it." (p. 23). But he then glosses over the difficulties in figuring out the relevant "standard" in a given situation. Nor is the "will" to do the right thing so easily attained. This is why we spent a whole chapter on ethical motivation. Motivation and will cannot be taken for granted or treated simplistically.

Assuming we can figure out the relevant "standard" (value, principle), how should we apply it to this or that situation and dilemma? What is our method? Who needs to be part of the decision-process? Who are the stake-holders and how do we respect their various interests and claims, especially when they conflict? These are tough questions that demand careful considera-tion and best practices.

Maxwell argues that, in practice, the one and only ethical guideline needed is the Golden Rule: "Do unto others as you would have them do unto you." No doubt this is a powerful, often helpful principle aiding our decision-making. What I want done to me may (unless I am a masochist) prevent me from doing some injustice. It may lead me to do some good things. But it would not, for example, prevent a tough guy-type from misapplying his tough guy tactics to all others. That is why Jesus (author of the Golden Rule) and other wise ethical teachers always fought against hard-core individualism of the Maxwell type, and emphasized community discernment and action. Maxwell is also wrong to say that the Golden Rule is the one and only rule we need. It has wide *generality*, but not does not have exclusivity or sufficiency, as Maxwell claims. It is not the only ethical principle. Unlike Maxwell, Jesus didn't limit his ethical teaching to the Golden Rule. I won't weary my readers any further by critiquing Maxwell's decision-making model, but it is very clear that it fails by being simplistic and naïve. I don't mean to suggest that Maxwell's other books or ideas are without value—or that other pop writers are necessarily better—but we need to find and promote a better way when it comes to business ethics. Contra Maxwell, "There is such a thing as business ethics," but his book is not the place to find out about it.

The Nature of Ethical Dilemmas and Crises

"Dilemmas" are cases, crises, quandaries, and challenges where there is a conflict of ethical values and principles and the right thing to do is unclear. In the offshoring example above, what are our moral obligations to the various stakeholders? How do we balance the competing values of loyalty, profit, low cost to customers, etc.? In other situations, how do we balance employee privacy and management need-to-know? How do we balance a downside risk of harm with an upside potential for help? How do we pay competitive executive salaries while providing fair, living wages and benefits to our workforce?

> *Today's list of ethical challenges and dilemmas is long and complex. Diversity and globalization mean that we don't all share the same values, language, and decision-making styles. In addition, we move at high speed, with decreasing time for study, discussion, and reflection on the complex, important matters of ethics.*

Some of these ethical dilemmas have been perennial problems throughout history (fair wages, just prices, safe working conditions, etc.). Today's list of problems and dilemmas has been amplified by rapid change and growing complexity in the workplace. We never had to figure out property issues for information flying around the web. Until recently the concept of patenting a genetic modification was not on our radar screen. Some of our problems have increased difficulty because of an unprecedented and growing diversity among the players and stakeholders. It is harder to address problems when we all come with different values, traditions, and even languages. The overall speed of life also means it is difficult to plan ahead and difficult to slow down and seek wisdom in these matters. All of this is why I said in chapter one, "Ethics isn't pretty."

Mapping the Ethical Dilemma Terrain

Let's do a quick and dirty overview of the business ethics problem areas: First, in business relations with government and its agencies the dilemmas and challenges concern things like (a) compliance with laws and regulations, perhaps especially in doing business in other countries than our own, (b) providing adequate, truthful reports to government authorities about finances, hazardous wastes, pollutant emissions, and so on, (c) paying a fair share of taxes (smart business vs. tax evasion), (d) influencing government fairly and ethically through lobbying, campaign contributions, and the like.

Second, there are many significant ethical issues relating to business relations with, and impacts on, the surrounding social and natural environments (the social and environmental bottom lines in the "Triple Bottom Line"). Some of the issues here include (a) externalizing business costs on to the surrounding community (e.g., traffic congestion, waste disposal, etc), (b) disclosure of risks to the health or lifestyles of business neighbors, (c) cleaning up pollution and replenishing depletion of natural resources, (d) appropriate citizenship and corporate social responsibility vis-à-vis the host community.

Third, we can list issues related to owners (investors, shareholders, donors) (the traditional financial bottom line, now part of the "Triple Bottom Line") such as (a) fair return on investment, (b) accurate and adequate information and communication, and (c) fair and competent stewardship of invested (or donated) funds.

Fourth, issues related to business-to-business partnerships upstream and downstream would include (a) fulfillment of contracts and agreements, maintaining trust, (b) financial fairness, (c) tampering with the workforce or work processes of a business partner, and (d) supply or distribution chain ethical practices.

Fifth, customer ethics issues include (a) product/service information: truth in advertising, disclosure of risks, understandable and accurate product information, (b) product/service safety, reliability, and quality, (c) treatment of customers themselves (responsive, competent service, prompt and respectful interaction, complaint handling), and (d) maintaining the confidentiality/privacy of customer information.

Sixth, and finally, we have a wide range of issues concerning the personnel employed at the company. This includes (a) recruiting, screening, hiring, promoting, disciplining, and firing employees (is it done fairly?), (b) downsizing and outsourcing issues (job loss, workforce loyalty, work standards in distant places, etc.), (c) compensation (salary and benefits at employee and executive levels: what is fair?), (d) workplace safety, relationships, and communications (including issues regarding dating, harassment, growth opportunities, privacy, etc.), (e) conflicts of interest (personal vs company benefit, competing secondary jobs) or improper influence (e.g., hiring relatives or friends), (f) improper, compromising relationships with those outside the company (bribes and kickbacks, gifts and entertainment, divulging company secrets and plans), (g) improper use of corporate resources (company name and reputation, equipment, finances, intellectual or physical property, etc.).

Ethical dilemmas and crises can arise in many different business relationships and arenas: with government and its agencies, with the surrounding communities and neighbors, with investors and owners, with business partners, with customers, and with employees.

So the range of ethical dilemmas and problems is huge. Managers need to have their eyes open to this whole range of possible challenges. Our ethical concern should extend beyond shareholders to all stakeholders, i.e., everyone having a significant "stake" in—or significantly affected by—a company's presence and activities. This is because it is a basic principle of justice that I should have a significant say about any of your actions that may affect me. It is unfair for you to violate my freedom or space without asking me. If you break or harm something that is mine (or ours in common), justice says you should fix it or pay me damages. This includes the air I breathe, the water I drink, the noise I hear, and so on. The era when it took money, property, race, class, or gender to confer moral and legal rights is long gone. All stakeholders have a right to be protected from harm and loss. Furthermore, enabled by communication technology and encouraged by a democratized culture, today's stakeholders *will* raise their voices and claim the rights they believe are their prerogative. Businesses ignore their stakeholders at great peril.

One way to map out an organization's stakeholders is to differentiate between *primary* stakeholders (those with contractual relationships: partners, customers/clients, employees, investors/owners, government)—and *secondary* stakeholders (those with informal relationships: the surrounding community the natural environment, perhaps even competitors in the industry). Another kind of map identifies *internal* stakeholders (employees, owners, managers, et al), *value chain* stakeholders (customers, partners), and *external* stakeholders (environment, press, society, etc.). Whatever map works for your organization, it is essential to keep it accurate and up-to-date and to carefully identify and review potential ethical trouble spots on the map.

A Community of Ethical Discernment and Action

Especially in light of the scope and complexity of the business ethics challenge, it is essential to stress that ethics is a community affair, not an individual one; a "team sport," not a solo one. This is one of my major criticisms of John Maxwell's approach—but frankly it is a problem far beyond his little book. Much of today's business ethics literature and training is highly, if not exclusively individualistic. The standard compliance and ethics training programs the big consulting firms want to sell you will sit your employees as Lone Ranger individualists in front of their computer screens to interact with some artificial, multiple choice scenarios. Companies are fooling themselves if they think this approach can do the necessary job (to say nothing of the vast amounts of money being squandered).

Anthropologists and sociologists who seriously study real people in real groups making life decisions have shown that morality is always a social construction. The great classical philosophers like Plato and Aristotle always saw ethics as embedded in politics, the individual good interdependent with the community good. Religious ethics over the centuries and around the world has consistently emphasized the importance of community discernment and action. Our modern individualism runs against the ethical thinking and practice of most people throughout history.

> *Especially in light of the scope and complexity of the business ethics challenge, it is essential to stress that ethics is a community affair, not an individual one; a team sport, not a solo one.*

Ethical decision-making is not just an individual exercise in abstract reason and logic. Determining the relevant rules, predicting the likely consequences, and arriving at the wisest decision—these challenges are always more effectively addressed if we are working with input from others. This sort of community helps us *figure out* what is right and then helps us *carry out* what is right. One clear implication for business is to always try to recruit *team* players and then both teach and reward teamwork rather than just individual accomplishments.

Building an Ethics Trouble-Shooting Strategy and Method

As we saw in the discussion of ethical motivation, there are four basic processes in building the components of an ethically healthy organization.

First comes the *identify* process. This task is to figure out the best strategy and method for handling ethical questions, dilemmas, and crises. What kind of structures, policies, methods, and procedures do we need? Who will be responsible and oversee this part of our ethical practice? Again: Ethics cannot be taken for granted. Don't wait until a big crisis comes. Put a good plan in place before trouble arrives.

The second process is to *educate* and *train* the company in this method and strategy—from the board of directors to the newest, lowest person on the totem pole. Everybody needs to know the strategy we have chosen. Teaching and training are a critical process. Many companies fail to make sure their recommended process is well-known to everyone in the company. I often ask my Executive MBA students, "What does your company say you should do if you have an ethics question or want to report a possible violation?" It is amazing how often I get a blank stare or an "I'm not really sure."

Third, the trouble-shooting strategy and method needs to be *implemented*, practiced. It can't just be known intellectually, it must be used. Here the trick is to get people used to deploying the method and system before a big problem arises. It's a little like the old fire drills in school. Practice the process regularly so that it will be used when the fire actually happens.

Fourth, the trouble-shooting process must be *evaluated* regularly and rigorously. There is no room for wishful thinking here. We need to find out if our trouble-shooting method is well-conceived, if it has any weaknesses, if it is well-known and respected and practiced. We must ask all of our people to tell us the truth and help us do it better.

Figuring Out Our Trouble-Shooting, Decision-Making Method

So how do we figure out our best decision-making and trouble-shooting method? The business ethics textbooks contain models of varying quality and appropriateness. *Unfortunately, they are often more helpful in determining what the different philosophical schools would think about a problem than in helping managers and people in the business trenches.* Many business ethics teachers and writers are still captive to the theoretical philosophers they once studied. Certainly there is something to be learned from the moral philosophers, but frankly, the ivory tower context is not the same as Wall Street or Main Street. A better approach, in my view, is to look at what highly regarded or ethically admirable companies (and leaders) do. What kind of ethics training and decision-making do they espouse? The web has lots of available examples. And going out to personally interview some ethics leaders and managers is a terrific way to get some great ideas. Relying *only* on other companies, however, is risky because too many of them have (it seems) hastily put together an approach that lacks rigor and comprehensiveness.

The trouble-shooting strategy that follows is a product of my years of study of not just the theorists and writers but the best (and worst) practices of many companies. As you take a look at it now, remember that it is a *generic* blueprint. In working in any particular situation I always help companies to adapt these ideas to their *particular* context and needs. There are some common themes in the best practices, but there is no one-size-fits-all template that can be imposed everywhere. Building something organically, in a concrete business context, is always the only way to go.

A Five-Step Trouble-Shooting Method

Five basic stages (let's call them steps) need to be part of a company's decision-making and trouble-shooting method. The details will vary, but all five steps need to be taken. First, we must have a way to *recognize* whether we are facing a potentially serious ethical problem (or not). Second, if a serious ethical issue has been recognized, we must then *strategize* about what to do. Third, if we cannot simply hand off the issue to someone else, we must know how to carefully *analyze* the issue and figure out our best options in terms of responses. Fourth, we must know how to *resolve* the particular issue. And fifth (often forgotten), we should step back and ask what kinds of ways we could *reform* our organizational structure, policies, reward systems, accountability, recruiting, and training to reduce the likelihood of this problem happening again.

Step 1: Recognizing Serious Ethical Dilemmas.

How can we determine whether a particular question, issue, or action is of serious ethical importance? It may be that our concern is really a matter of taste and manners rather than ethics and morality. It may be a question of technical competence or managerial preference rather than ethics. There are many business dilemmas and decisions that are not really moral or ethical in nature. In these cases, of course, wise and good decision-making is still critical, but our concern here is focused on detecting problems of ethical importance.

Is this a potentially serious ethical issue that I should not ignore? How would I know when something important comes along?

As we said in Chapter One, six test questions will help us recognize ethical problems serious enough to take to the next step:
- *Does it violate the law or applicable regulations?*
- *Does it violate our company or professional ethics?*
- *Does it violate people's consciences and personal values?*
- *Does it violate the "Golden Rule"? (i.e., we wouldn't like it done to us or our loved ones)*
- *Would it create an uproar or scandal if it was publicized?*
- *Could someone be seriously and irresponsibly harmed?*

All six ethics test questions are helpful, but none of them is all-sufficient, all the time. Exceptional circumstances can occur. Interpretation and discernment are always necessary. Some moral community and consultation are usually essential. But if we use these six tests and start getting either some intense red lights or a number of blinking yellows, we had better take the next step and strategize about what to do.

Step 2: Strategizing About Ethical Dilemmas: What Do We Do Next?

If it looks like we have a potentially serious ethics problem, the next step is to strategize: What should I do about this problem I see? With whom should I share this information? What should I do next? What are the things I must be especially careful about as I move forward on this? This is no time to be reckless. After all, if ethics is about protecting from harm, we do not want to react in a way that harms careers and companies and communities—including our own career and the well-being of those who depend on us.

Managers and organizational leaders can do a great favor to their company and its employees if they think about this strategy and create some guidelines and channels for response. Some companies specify clear guidelines and give several channels to raise questions or report possible violations. And some companies do nothing.

The appropriate strategy depends, first, on what your own role and responsibility may be. Maybe you should take responsibility and handle it yourself. Or maybe you should take it directly to your supervisor. . . or to HR or legal. In some smaller companies the president or a vice-president is the point person. In bigger companies it might be a compliance and ethics officer, an ethics committee, an ombudsperson, or even an outside consultant or ethics service. Using an outside consultant has its virtues and its place, especially if the company is not big enough to afford its own ethics officer. My view is that these things are best handled internally, if at all possible, and that consultants should help companies to move toward independence. A suggestion/question box might be provided. It is good to have an option to be anonymous, though anonymous complaints must be handled with special care not to tar the reputations of the accused, who may turn out to be innocent.

> *Strategy is critical. We could make an ethical problem much worse just by responding to it in the wrong way. Whistle-blowing must be the absolutely last resort, when the threat is grave and all other options have proven ineffective.*

Some bigger companies contract with an outside agency to handle an "ethics hotline"—though this is usually just to receive complaints or questions and forward them to the appropriate person or office; most company ethics hotlines do not give any advice. There may be some gains (anonymity, freedom, safety?) in outsourcing the ethics reporting process, but these must be weighed against the benefits of a hands-on, internally managed ethics and values process (more personal, better customized to our specific company).

Whatever strategy is chosen, it needs to be well-publicized and implemented. The extreme strategy of whistle-blowing needs to be addressed and precautions taken to protect both whistle-blowers and the accused, both of whom become especially vulnerable to unfairness in these situations. Nothing is more obvious, though, than the importance of getting questions raised early, before the problems escalate to whistle-blowing, major crisis proportions.

Here is the scheme I developed with and for Harris & Associates (covering both the "Recognize" and "Strategize" phases and adding some clarity about what happens to ethics questions and reports). It is always attached to the company code of ethics (at its end):

HARRIS & ASSOCIATES   (Concord, California)

What to do if you have an ethics question—or need to report a possible violation

Step #1: Reflection: Is your concern important enough to take any action?
If you become aware of a possible ethics issue in our company (or on the part of a client or business partner we are working with), here are five test questions to help you determine if you should take action. If the answer is "Yes" to one or more of these five test questions, you should take action and make an inquiry or report. *It may not turn out to be a serious problem—but it is important to take action to find out.*

1. Is it illegal?
Any time you see something that might be breaking a legal or regulatory standard, report it.
2. Does it violate our company values and ethical guidelines?
Any time something may be in contradiction to one of our core values or in violation of one of our ethical guidelines (or of a relevant professional ethical guideline, e.g., the code for civil engineers), report it.
3. Does it violate the Golden Rule or your internal sense of right and wrong?
If you wouldn't want it done to you, we probably shouldn't do it to others. If it really bothers your personal conscience and values, it probably would bother others. Report it.
4. Would we be doing this if it was the lead story in the news?
Individuals and companies doing wrong things usually try to hide what they are doing. If you wouldn't feel good about having the public know and see what we are doing, report it.
5. Could someone be seriously and irresponsibly harmed?
This is a bottom line question in ethics. If anyone could be seriously and irresponsibly harmed (physically, financially, reputationally, etc.), report it.

Step #2: Action: How should I report a question or possible violation?
If possible, start with the first three steps (below) to report and resolve ethical questions and challenges. If these steps seem dangerous, unwise, or unproductive, or you are not satisfied after pursuing them, move to any of the final three steps:

1. Speak to the offender(s).
It is not always possible to take your concerns to the (apparent) offender doing an unethical act. When possible, however, this is the place to begin.
2. Ask a trusted colleague for advice or help.
Sometimes ethical questions can be answered and problems resolved by simply discussing the matter with a colleague or two.
3. Report it to your supervisor.
Your supervisor is responsible for ethical as well as business matters. Unless the ethics question concerns your supervisor personally, or you remain unsatisfied by your supervisor's response, you should take the matter to him or her.
4. Report it to any supervisor or manager with whom you feel comfortable.
All managers and supervisors at Harris are available to all employees for ethics matters.

5. Report it to the Human Resources Manager.
The Human Resources Manager will always be available to provide help with your ethics questions and reports.
6. Report it to the President.
The President of Harris & Associates always has an open door for anyone who wishes to raise a question or make a report on any ethical matter.

You may submit your question or report anonymously by letter if you feel it necessary.

What happens to your ethics questions and reports?

• All ethics questions and reports of possible violations are taken very seriously by the company.

• There will be no retaliation for raising ethical questions or reporting possible violations; it is the obligation of every employee to report any violations and to protect the ethical health of the company.

• If your question or report is not anonymous and is submitted to a supervisor or manager (including the Human Resources Manager and President), it will be acknowledged in an appropriate and timely manner.

• If the issue can be resolved by the supervisor receiving the question or report, it will be addressed and resolved as quickly as possible and you will be informed of the decision and action.

• If the issue cannot be resolved quickly, easily, or satisfactorily by that supervisor you may be contacted for further discussion of the specific issue. The supervisor will consult with others on the management team, taking it as far as the President and Board of Directors, if necessary, until a satisfactory resolution can be found.

• A decision will be made by management, subject always to the approval of the Board, and corrective action will be taken to address the specific situation and those involved in it—and to reinforce or improve the policies, standards, and procedures of the company so as to minimize the possibility of such problems recurring.

• Unless the report was submitted anonymously, the reporting individual will receive a report on the company's resolution of the issue.

Some companies do not advise going to offenders first with an ethics concern or question. Perhaps they are concerned about lawsuits or retaliation. This may be the only way to go in some companies. But others, like Harris, ask "How would I want to be treated in similar circumstances, where a colleague had a problem with what I did? Would I want them to go first behind my back or over my head? Or come to me first?" The answer is obvious.

Step 3: Analyzing Ethical Issues.

If it turns out that it is on you to handle the ethical dilemma—you can't just hand it off to someone else—what, then, is involved in analyzing the case? Three basic aspects of the problem need clarification and study before a resolution can be chosen.

First, we must *clarify the relevant facts* of the case. What happened exactly? When? Where? Who was involved? Who were the players, what did they do, and who was affected? Document these facts. Get witnesses. Make sure you get this part straight. *Many* apparent ethical dilemmas actually disappear at this fact-gathering stage. What appeared to be wrong, or what appeared to be a forced choice between two terrible options, turns out not to be so.

Second, we must *clarify the decisive values and principles* at stake and in conflict. This is where the six test questions come up again: What law is being broken? What company or professional ethical guideline is being violated? What personal value or principle of ours is bring threatened? What value or principle would provoke a public outcry if they knew what was going on? Name the values and principles. That gets us to the core of the problem. It is in terms of these values that you raise the issue . . . and it is in terms of these values that you will later justify your response and can explain you are now in compliance.

Third, and finally, *clarify the action-options* that are available—and their possible and probable consequences. No one can fully guarantee or predict the consequences of our actions, but that does not excuse us from being as careful as possible to think about what might happen if we do this or that. By the way, this is the place where imagination plays an important role. Invent creative and workable options to minimize damage and maximize good outcomes. Think win-win rather than "zero sum."

> *Clarify the facts of the case. Clarify the ethical values and guidelines relevant to the case. Clarify the action-options and their possible/probable consequences. Be creative, collaborative, and careful: a lot may be at stake.*

Step 4 : Resolving Ethical Dilemmas.

The fourth stage is the immediate goal of the process: finding the best possible resolution of the particular ethical dilemma or crisis. Following our careful analysis and best possible, most imaginative, thinking we must choose the best, most responsible option we can come up with. How will we know our proposed resolution is the best we can do and is acceptable? We return to the earlier six test questions and to the core values and principles we clarified as being at stake in the dilemma (i.e., our proposed resolution should be legal, in compliance with our ethics codes, respectful of our consciences, something we could live with ourselves, something we could defend in public, and something that does not serious or irresponsibly risk harm to others). With our eye on the specific values and principles that were in jeopardy (e.g., safety, honesty, fairness), our resolution honors and observes them as well as we can under the circumstances (our resolution is as safe, honest, and fair as we can make it right now).

We decide and then we act. Unfortunately, too much ethical case resolution does not go further than assigning blame—and punishing the offender. My recommendation is to seek voluntary reform by the offender(s), to the extent possible and wise. If the offender is willing, he or she should step forward, acknowledge the problem (the breech of ethics), take responsibility, and agree to make appropriate amends and improvements. This could possibly save the offender's reputation and job—while correcting the problem the company had because of his or her actions. Of course, in some cases, this may not be enough and further disciplinary action (even firing or legal action) may be necessary. The point is to try for as much win-win outcome as possible. A complete resolution also requires follow-through on those injured (employees, customers, whoever was harmed by the breech of ethics).

> *Choose the option that best passes the initial six-question test and is as close to a win-win solution as we can get. Carry it out with courage. Follow through on both the offender and the injured as well as you can.*

Step 5: Reform.

Finally, we must carry through with organizational, structural, and procedural reforms to minimize the chances of recurrence of this kind of ethical dilemma. This fifth step is rarely mentioned, but it is utterly critical in ethically healthy organizations. What weaknesses in our company, our culture, our leadership, incentives, training, and so on, were contributing factors to this ethical breakdown? What organizational changes, structural and procedural reforms will minimize, if not prevent, recurrence of this problem? Maybe our compensation and reward system is actually providing incentives to *unethical* behavior. Maybe better management would lessen the temptation to get into trouble. Maybe we need better communications, more transparency, and better accountability. Maybe it is about hiring better people with better ethics and character. Maybe we need to upgrade our code of ethics code and our ethics training? If we don't take this fifth step, we are just asking for more crises of the same type.

It can be helpful to summarize the decision-making, trouble-shooting process in a worksheet, case-analysis format, like the one that follows:

Gill's Ethical Case Analysis Form
CASE DESCRIPTION (Give a brief outline/summary of the ethical problem)

Step One: RECOGNIZE (Is this case serious enough to take to Stage Two?)			
	YES	MAYBE	NO
1.1 Does it violate a law or regulation? *Name/describe it:*	❑	❑	❑
1.2 Does it violate company or professional ethical standards? *Name the ethical guideline/standard violated.*	❑	❑	❑
1.3 Does it bother your (and others') personal values and conscience? *What value/principle seems to be threatened/violated?*	❑	❑	❑
1.4 Does it violate the "Golden Rule" ("Do unto others what you would want done to you")? *Why wouldn't you want this done to you and yours?*	❑	❑	❑
1.5 Would there be a controversy, scandal, or uproar if it was made public? *Why? What is it that would bother people?*	❑	❑	❑
1.6 Could someone be seriously, irresponsibly harmed? *Who? How?*	❑	❑	❑

DECISION-TIME: If you get one or more "Yes" or "Maybe" answers, take it to Stage Two. Be sure you have documented, good evidence and are not depending on gossip, hearsay, and guesswork.

Step Two: STRATEGIZE (think carefully about what you do with this problem)			
	YES	MAYBE	NO
2.1 What is my role and responsibility with this case?			
2.2 Should/can I speak directly with the (apparent) offender(s)? *Why or why not?*	❑	❑	❑
2.3 Should/could I approach a third party (or two) for advice and collaboration? *Who could I approach/collaborate with?*	❑	❑	❑
2.4 Should I speak to my immediate supervisor/boss? *If not, why not?*	❑	❑	❑

Gill's Ethical Case Analysis Form (cont.)

	YES	MAYBE	NO
2.5 Should I report it through normal company channels (hotline, HR, ethics, office, etc.)? *If not, why not?*	❑	❑	❑
2.6 Should I "blow the whistle" (go outside normal channels)? *To whom do you blow the whistle (inside/outside company)?* *How will you release the information?*	❑	❑	❑

Step Three: ANALYZE (carefully figure it out)

3.1 Clarify the critical, central facts of the case.
What happened & when:

Who are the key stakeholders?

3.2 Clarify the key ethical values/principles at stake (consult Step One answers).
Describe them:

3.3 Clarify the options you can see (and invent/imagine)—and their probable/possible consequences.
In some (but not all) cases, this could include "buying time," delaying a decision for more study, etc.

Option 1:

Option 2:

Option 3:

Option 4:

Step Four: RESOLVE (choose the best option and carry it out)

4.1 Choose, as wisely and collaboratively as possible, the best option you have.
My choice and recommendation; this is what I will do:

4.2 Follow-through actions (indicate with whom & what you will do).
With the offenders/perpetrators:

Step Five: REFORM (organizational improvements to prevent/minimize recurrence)

5.1 What weaknesses in our mission, culture/structure, systems/policies, values, guidelines, recruiting, and/or training gave rise to, or allowed, this problem to happen?
Describe them:

5.2 What changes and improvements will I recommend (or make):

Educating & Training for Wise Decision-Making & Crisis Management

How do companies make sure that everyone knows how to respond to an ethical question or problem? The method and process must be communicated effectively at all levels through the organization. Orientation and training sessions, staff meetings, print and electronic descriptions and explanations (company newsletters, brochures, handbooks, web pages, etc.)—these are the unsurprising ways it is done. In addition to my suggestions here, look at other company web sites or visit other companies to get ideas on how to present the ethical decision-making and trouble-shooting method.

We always learn best, of course, by *doing*—not just by hearing. Thus, practical exercises such as case discussions and analyses are an essential part of the education process. Of course, cases can be analyzed by individuals, even in online formats. Some systems require the employee to check off the appropriate response to a case, or go back and re-think it until the correct answer can be checked and one can finish the online course. While this has its merits and its place, the benefits of small group or team discussions of ethical cases are even higher.

> *Ethical case studies can provide some great training opportunities. Remember that actual business ethics problems in the trenches deserve or even require serious collaborative discussion and response—not just individualistic responses to multiple-choice computer simulations.*

The cases that are used in one setting or another must be designed with care. Their subject matter needs to be chosen so that it (a) illustrates successfully the point of the lesson (for example—that clarifying the facts can be a critical stage in analyzing and resolving dilemmas), (b) is relevant to the actual work lives of the employees (e.g., less to be gained *usually* in having grocery store workers discuss at length the Three Mile Island nuclear accident), and (c) is manageable within the educational time frame (difficult sometimes to do justice to very complex problems in a two-hour session). It is also very important not to get lost in the details of the method. Use a case analysis format such as the sample above—but always simplify the overall structure of the "takeaway" lesson: i.e., *Recognize* if it is a serious problem . . . *Strategize* how best to respond . . . *Analyze* carefully and creatively . . . *Resolve* the immediate problem . . . *Reform* the organization as appropriate. Five basic steps (one for each finger!).

Here are eight brief ethical cases that can be used to practice the case analysis and decision-making method.[3] I will defer my own commentary to an appendix at the end of this book.

Sample Case One: Under the Influence?

Your boss has been great to work for these past three years. But on a recent occasion you smelled alcohol on his breath when he arrived back at the office after a long lunch at an off site location. He has been such a great boss; he is scheduled to retire in two years; his personal life has brought him terrible pain recently.

Do we have an ethics problem here? How should it be handled?

Sample Case Two: Google in China

Google has agreed with the Chinese government that it will censor its web site to comply with Chinese policy. In a widely debated example, a search of "Tiananmen Square" outside China gives photos and info about China's violent suppression of a free speech demonstration—but in China such a Google search deletes these negative images and facts. CEO Eric Schmidt defends the decision as necessary to reach the lucrative market of 111 million Internet users and argues that it is arrogant to walk into a new country and tell them how to operate. (*SF Chronicle*, 13 April 06).

How do you figure out what's right and wrong in this global business case?

Sample Case Three: Executive Compensation at Sun

Sun Microsystem's Board Chairman Scott McNealy's compensation rose from $4.2 million in 2005 to $16.5 million in 2006. CEO Jonathan Schwartz's compensation rose from $3 million in 2005 to $22.8 million in 2006. Meanwhile, in the past five years Sun has experienced annual layoffs, declining revenue, and a stock price decline of 93 percent.

Do we have an ethics problem here, or is this just a market reality? If it is ethically problematic, who should take responsibility? What should be done?

Sample Case Four: Legal but Unethical?

You are a sales representative for a new synthetic fiber that has excellent properties in every respect but one. To this point no one has been able to treat or process it so it will be flame-resistant or flame-retardant. It has therefore been outlawed in the USA as a fiber for apparel. Sales have dropped drastically since the fiber is now legally permitted only in certain industrial products. Hundreds of jobs are at stake if this company fails to find a way to market its product soon.

Your customer surprises you by asking you to quote prices and delivery schedules for a large order of your fiber. When you remind her that the fiber is not legally useable in apparel, she says, "The law only prohibits selling such apparel in the USA. I'm going to manufacture it here but sell it in South America where there are no legal restrictions on this material."

Will you quote her a price? [Discuss the case without reading the next paragraphs; then move on]

You find out that many children in the proposed market have inadequate clothing. The alternative may be between sleeping in cold, inadequate clothing—and sleeping in your warm, inexpensive but non-flame-resistant clothing.

Does this change your mind? [Discuss how this discovery might affect the case without reading the next paragraph; then move on]

Then you find out that most of the prospective buyers of your product use open fire ovens and fireplaces for cooking and heating in their living quarters—a more dangerous environment for accidental fires and burns than the typical American home.

Does this affect your decision?

Sample Case Five: Engineering Standards: Who Decides?
You are an engineer, widely respected in the whole industry for your expertise on tunnel design and safety. Six months ago you accepted a lucrative job offer to move from headquarters in Chicago to a booming branch office in San Francisco and serve as lead engineer on a new tunnel being built in a controversial, earthquake-prone area.

Now, six months after moving your family and deep into the project, you have reached an impasse. You believe that the California engineering standards have not caught up with the latest discoveries on tunnel earthquake safety. Your San Francisco boss, who recruited you from headquarters for this move, has rejected all of your arguments and insists that, for project budget reasons, the tunnel must be built in conformity with exist-ing regulations, not at the more expensive, newer engineering level you believe that will better provide earthquake safety.

You have concluded that you may be fired if you push too hard. The job market is tight in your specialty area. The kids are just now getting comfortable in their new schools.

What are the central ethical values and principles at stake here? How will you sort through the facts, values, and options and find the best, most ethical response?

Sample Case Six: Blow the Whistle?
Jane, a recent college graduate, has accepted a great job as a scientist at a leading high tech research and development company. She will be involved in exciting research right in her interest area. The job pays very well—her old classmates are a little envious of her great opportunity—but she is mainly grateful for the salary so she can make life a little better for her ailing, aged parents.

Jane has been given a security clearance and is deeply involved in a research project which is expected to save thousands of lives around the world if it is successful. The stakes are high and she is excited to be involved. Her boss has emphasized over and over to her how important this project is and how critical it is to maintain loyalty, integrity and mutual trust on the research team.

While walking past a van parked on the street just outside the compa-ny parking lot one morning, Jane unintentionally discovers that Joe, the key genius on the research team, is sexually involved with the boss's wife.

Jane asks you, her friend, what, if anything, she should do about it. And you say . . .

_____

Jane decides to hold off, at least for the time being (but was she right to do so?). She then is amazed one day when Joe tells her (and she later confirms from her own observation) that their boss has a serious cocaine habit (using even in his office some times), and that he appears to be spending government grant money on his drug habit.

She asks for your advice again . . .

Sample Case Seven: Big Pig Waste Management

Will is the financial vice president of a community hospital. He is under heavy pressure from the president and board of directors to reduce the operating deficit. His job may be on the line if he fails.

The hospital has a long-standing policy of providing basic care to all in need. A huge list of uncollected and perhaps uncollectible bills for such services is part of the financial problem. But no one wants to abandon this Good Samaritan policy.

Will could balance the books by giving the contract for disposal of medical wastes to Big Pig Waste Management. But Big Pig is widely suspected of dumping medical wastes in unsafe ways and illegal places.

What are the ethical values and principles at stake here? What is the best way to work toward an optimum ethical outcome?

Sample Case Eight: Who Is the Boss?

Laura has been promoted to a supervisory position at her company and is now responsible for managing a department with a dozen other employees. Several of these workers are significantly older than her and have worked at the company many years longer than she has. But she recently finished her MBA and was very effective in leading some recent projects.

Unfortunately, three of the veterans (generally viewed as high performers) under her supervision are having a bad attitude about her promotion. They are regularly, it seems, going behind her back to her boss (an old friend and golf partner of theirs) with complaints and questions. They are late or inattentive at staff meetings she calls.

Laura has tried hard to be supportive of them and has gone out of her way to praise their work. She has asked them repeatedly to come to her with whatever issues they have. They just ignore her and complain to other workers about reporting to someone her age.

What are the ethical—and managerial—issues here? What is your recommendation?

Discussing cases is a great way to educate ourselves in a decision-making, trouble-shooting method. You might solicit discussion cases (hypothetical or real) from the employees themselves. Another idea is for staff leaders to call in an ethics question directly to the appropriate channels during a staff meeting (phone or e-mail the recommended person or office right then, during the meeting, in front of everyone, with the ethics question). Submit it, and then watch (and discuss) what happens. Leaders can also reinforce the reporting/trouble-shooting method by inaugurating a regular "Ethics Q&A" column in the company newsletter or blog. Seed it, if necessary, with a few interesting cases or questions, write your advice on how to handle the situation, invite further comment from the workforce. Then put these real-life cases, questions, and commentaries in an easily accessible archive online or in print or both.

Implementing Our Method: Putting It into Practice

Implementation is the third critical phase in building the components of an ethically healthy organization. Put the method into practice. Implement it, do it for real. Business leaders and managers must show a good example in using the trouble-shooting method as often as they find opportunity (trouble shoot the *little* things, practice on the *possible* problems . . . then we will be ready for the *actual* and *big* things). In addition to setting a good personal example, leaders should recognize, encourage, thank, and praise those who submit ethics questions and reports.

Evaluation: Have We Got It Right?

The fourth process is *evaluation*: Are we doing what we need to do? Do we have a good trouble-shooting method? Does everyone know it and understand it? Are we practicing what we preach? Focus groups and staff meetings can discuss its helpfulness or lack thereof, and make suggestions for improvements. Employee evaluations can include reference to employee handling of ethical challenges, when appropriate. Employee and management ethics and values audits (sample below) can ask the hard, direct, evaluative questions about the company as a whole and its management. If we don't invite honest and regular feedback, our ethical health may be gone long before we even realize it.

As in the case of ethical motivation, in the previous chapter, what follows is a "generic" audit of a company's trouble-shooting method. It is always best to create an organic, customized format for each particular organization and not simply adopt or impose a one-size-fits all template like this.

Gill's Company Ethics Trouble-Shooting Audit

Does our company have an effective <u>method</u> for trouble-shooting and managing <u>ethical crises</u> and dilemmas?	Strongly Disagree 1 2 3	Strongly Agree 4 5
1. Our people all know how to <u>recognize</u> an important ethical problem when they see one.	❑ ❑ ❑	❑ ❑
2. Our people know what to do (how to <u>respond</u> and <u>act</u>) when they encounter an ethical question or violation in their work.	❑ ❑ ❑	❑ ❑
3. Our people who raise questions about ethics are encouraged, not punished, for bringing up their concerns.	❑ ❑ ❑	❑ ❑
4. Our company makes available a safe (confidential, if necessary) process for our people to report or discuss possible ethics violations.	❑ ❑ ❑	❑ ❑
5. Our company acts prudently but quickly to address ethical questions and problems.	❑ ❑ ❑	❑ ❑
6. While protecting privacy and confidentiality, our company is open, honest, and transparent—not inclined to create "cover ups" for its mistakes.	❑ ❑ ❑	❑ ❑
7. Our company does not end its response when the immediate ethical crisis passes but examines (and reforms, as necessary) the deeper structural factors that may have caused or permitted the crisis to arise.	❑ ❑ ❑	❑ ❑
8. Ethics failures and crises at our company are treated as opportunities for everyone to learn, not just to identify and punish those immediately responsible.	❑ ❑ ❑	❑ ❑

<u>Describe briefly an ethical dilemma or question that has come up in your work experience at our company. Was it resolved and handled well?</u>

<u>Comments on our ethical trouble-shooting and response systems and procedures:</u>

Afterthought: Broadening Our View of Ethics & Decision-Making

Beyond the ethical crises and dilemmas we face, a range of other decisions is also ethically very important. First, our day-to-day, mundane practices and decisions shape the long-term ethical health and performance of the organization. It is not just the big crises but the ordinary decision-making opportunities (how we greet and treat each other, how we decorate our spaces, how we respond to visitors and strangers) that are important.

Second, on a much broader plain, our decisions regarding the mission and vision, the core values, and the ethical standards of our organization are actually more fundamental and significant than our specific decisions about what to do in a given dilemma.

Third, our decisions about what kind of people we hire and what kind of corporate culture we build, have everything to do with our ethical health and performance.

We need to avoid a narrow "decisionist" approach and take a broader, deeper, richer standpoint toward organizational ethics. If we think of ethics and ethical decision-making only or primarily in the crisis/dilemma context, it remains little more than "damage control." We must move beyond this reactive "dilemma" ethics to a proactive "practice" ethics, from a negative, "boundary" ethics to a positive "mandate" ethics.

For Reflection or Discussion

1. What is your personal decision-making method for tough questions, including ethics?

2. What is the ethics trouble-shooting method or process at your organization? How helpful and effective would you say it is? How could it be improved?

3. Can you describe an ethical dilemma you or your company faced? How was it handled? How could it have been handled better?

4. What are the best ways to prepare yourself and your organization to handle ethical dilemmas and crises?

Exercises

1. Go on the web and check out a few competitors and admired companies to see what strategy or action-plan they recommend or require of their employees if they have ethics questions or want to report a violation. Would any of this be helpful if adopted in your company?

2. Interview a superior, a peer, and a subordinate: What are their usual methods for handling ethical questions or violations of ethical values and principles?

Resources for Further Study

Pick up almost any business ethics textbook and you will find a formula for decision-making, though often without a very thorough or comprehensive framework. Laura Nash's chapter "Ethics Without the Sermon" in *Corporate Ethics* (Harvard Business School Press, 2003) proposes twelve good, basic questions to explore in making a decision. Linda K. Trevino and Katherine A. Nelson, *Managing Business Ethics: Straight Talk About How to Do It Right* (John Wiley & Sons, 4th edition, 2007) devote two interesting chapters to ethical decision-making. Marvin T. Brown, *The Ethical Process: An Approach to Disagreements and Controversial Issues* (Prentice Hall, 3rd edition, 2003); Rushworth M. Kidder, *How Good People Make Tough Choices: Resolving the Dilemmas of Ethical Living* (Fireside, 1995), and Jeffrey L. Seglin, *The Good, the Bad, and Your Business: Choosing Right When Ethical Dilemmas Pull You Apart* (John Wiley & Sons, 2000) are three authors who contribute some helpful insight to this topic.

NOTES

[1] Woody Allen, *Side Effects* (Ballentine, 1975), p. 76.

[2] John Maxwell, *There's No Such Thing As "Business Ethics"—There's Only ONE RULE for Making Decisions* (Warner Books, 2003).

[3] Cases five and eight were inspired by similar cases in Clinton W. McLemore's *Street-Smart Ethics* (WJK, 2003). The others are either from news reports or were invented by me or others to highlight typical ethics challenges in business.

Moving Beyond Damage-Control

Ethics

Executive Summary

We have defined business ethics and six basic, share-able criteria for figuring out right and wrong (Chapter One). We have reviewed twelve good reasons to motivate interest in figuring out and carrying out the ethical, right thing in business (Chapter Two). And we have built a five-step trouble-shooting, decision-making, and crisis management approach (Chapter Three). These three tasks constitute Business Ethics 101—the critical minimum to keep our business ethically afloat. It is now time to move beyond this "damage control" approach to Business Ethics 201—a proactive, holistic, "mission control" approach that builds ethics and values into every part of an organization aligned and empowered for excellence and success. There are six components (motivation, trouble-shooting, mission/vision, culture/values, practices/principles, leadership/governance) and four processes (identify, educate, implement, and evaluate).

The corporate ethics meltdown manifested in Enron, Andersen, WorldCom, Global Crossing, Adelphia, and other companies, was a betrayal with still-unfolding, negative consequences that will be felt for years to come. What is perhaps most ominous about this business crisis is that it occurred from within, among reputable leaders of respected businesses, among friends of our highest political leaders, among the nice folks sitting over there in the church and the synagogue. This wasn't Al Qaeda, the Mafia, or the Ku Klux Klan. This was us.

It will not be enough to jail a few offenders and pass a few new regulations making certain accounting or compensation practices illegal. Both of those things may need to happen, but they are not a sufficient response to our business ethics challenge. Corporations must take serious, well-conceived steps to rebuild their own ethical health. This will not happen if we confine our attention to a reactive, narrow, and negative "damage control" approach to business ethics. What we need is a holistic "mission control" approach to ethics and values.

Six Components in Ethically Healthy Organizations

To build a successful, ethical, excellent business enterprise, serious attention must be given to six inter-related foci. We have reviewed the first two components in previous chapters.

1. Motivation. It is easy, but mistaken, to assume that everyone is eager to work and manage in an ethical manner. Despite all the news stories and warning flags everywhere, many businesspeople (and business students) remain apathetic, impatient, or unconvinced. But these attitudes are extremely dangerous, an invitation to disaster. To build an ethical, long-term, successful enterprise, everyone, from the board of directors through executive management to employees at all levels, must understand and embrace the strongest possible, most thoughtful and convincing rationale for taking ethics very seriously. Why should we—why must we—care about a sound ethics? What are the costs of ethical neglect? What are the benefits of sound ethics? Until this motivational challenge is addressed, little improvement can be expected.

2. Trouble-Shooting. We mustn't kid ourselves. Even in the best of circumstances, hard cases and crises in business are going to arise. An exclusive emphasis on crisis-resolution, "damage control" ethics is a mistake because it allows negative challenges and crises to set the ethics agenda and fails to move upstream to deal with the sources of these challenges. Nevertheless, ethical dilemmas and quandaries are inescapable, and ethically healthy companies must put in place a ready, effective trouble-shooting and crisis-resolution method.

3. Mission and Vision. What is the core purpose, the mission and vision of the company? Why do we exist? Where are we going? We focus so intensely on core mission because it is the mission that best leverages ethical behavior. An inspiring and shared mission and vision can mobilize people toward ethics and excellence. Each company must identify and articulate its own distinctive core mission, one that inspires people to bring their best, most ethical and talented selves to work each day. Without clear linkage to such a mission, codes of ethics become little more than abstract, arbitrary, boring legalisms. Ethical values and principles must be understood as integral aspects of all strategies and plans to achieve the company mission.

4. Culture and Values. Organizational culture refers to what the company "is" (not so much what it "does" in this or that circumstance). Culture is about context and capability. What are the characteristic traits, habits, and customs that (ought to) define the organization? What is the style and atmosphere of the company? What are its virtues and vices, its characteristic potentialities, skills, and inclinations? Without a healthy "value-embedded culture," ethical decisions and practices are imperiled. Just as a physically weak, out-of-shape sports team cannot successfully carry out even the most brilliantly conceived set of plays, so an ethically weak company culture cannot live up to its stated principles and its code of ethics. Each company must identify and articulate the cultural values and traits that are essential to carrying out its particular mission. The culture must align with, and enable, the mission and vision.

5. Practices and Principles. When a company has addressed its mission and culture, it is time to ask what the company specifically "does"? What are the basic practices of the company? What are the primary activities, behaviors, and processes undertaken as the company pursues its mission and vision? Here is where companies need action-guiding rules and principles—often stated in the form of codes of ethics. Without robust, reliable "principle-guided practices," companies are liable to fail in their quest for excellence and wind up dealing with far more crises than necessary. When principles have a nice "fit" with basic business practices and activities, when they are clearly rooted in the company mission and culture, ethics is not experienced as an abstract, negative restraint but rather as a "set of plays helping us get into the end zone."

6. Leadership and Governance. As with anything of importance in an organization, gifted, effective leadership is essential in the ethics domain. If no one has the leadership responsibility, training, and resources, the best ethics and values statements and ideals in the world will rest dormant and useless. Ethically healthy companies make sure that from the board of directors on down, through the whole organization, good ethics leadership is in place and in training. They strengthen and improve their governance systems and structures from top to bottom.

Four Processes in Building Ethically Healthy Organizations

Attention needs to be given to the six components in four ways. These are not one-time efforts; all four processes must be revisited on a regular basis. Often, the place to begin is with a review of the company's ethics experience and its current strengths and weaknesses (process 4 below).

1. Identification. At each of the six focal points—motivation, trouble-shooting, mission, culture, practices, and leadership—companies must identify *what* they have and are, and why it is important. This is a process of self-examination, identification, description, articulation, and explanation. A company has to "figure it out"—identify, describe, and articulate the six components. Through study of company documents and statements, surveys, focus groups, interviews and discussion, the goal is to arrive at clarity and confidence.

2. Education. When the six components are clearly identified and articulated, the challenge is to ensure that they are known from top to bottom of the organization. *Who* are the target audiences and what are the particular emphases they must receive? (boards of directors, marketing, manufacturing, sales, customer service, executive leadership, human resources, new hires, veterans, other stakeholders). *How* should the ethical content be communicated and reinforced? (documents, coffee cup inscriptions, posters, classes and seminars, online and interactive information, awards, recognition, etc.). Companies must review and strengthen their ethics education programs with the goal of thorough knowledge throughout the organization.

One concern to be noted here is the impact of the educational method on the learning. As discussed earlier, if ethics training consists of sitting individuals in front of computer screens, the trainees may be indoctrinated into (a) a highly individualistic approach that doesn't know how to find the ethical wisdom of colleagues and teams, and (b) an arbitrarily neat notion of ethical dilemma resolution because of the incapacity of computer-based Q&A to represent the "gray" and ambiguous nature of real business ethics and the way we must try to responsibly "muddle through" at times.

3. Implementation. It is still not enough to identify and educate. The third process is to implement. Implementation means that the mission actually guides the organization. Activities that do not fall clearly within the mission are rejected. Core cultural values are not just identified but are expressed in everything from architecture to employee review and compensation. Principles are "on the table" when decisions are made. Dilemmas are routinely put through the resolution method. Any organizational values, principles, programs, and processes that are not clearly implemented will breed cynicism. Implement them or eliminate them. It's about "walking the talk" and "practicing what we preach."

4. Evaluation. The ethical health of organizations must be reviewed on a regular basis. How is the company doing on each of the six focal concerns? In each of the four processes? What are the areas of strength and weakness? What can be changed and improved? How can the ethics aspect of the business be kept fresh, alive, dynamic, and interesting? Individual employees need to be evaluated on their performance and contribution to the values and ethics of the company. The organization itself needs to be evaluated by its employees (and other stakeholders), often centering on a company values and ethics audit (review, assessment) tailored for each company's particular needs and desires (longer or shorter in duration, this emphasis or that, etc.).

Throughout this book I include sample sections of a generic company ethics and values audit I have designed. Remember, though, that no single, generic template is going to be appropriate to every company or situation. Resist anyone who tries to say otherwise and wants to bring in some standardized form. Instead, tailor a form to fit your organization and which will tell you what you need to know.

Another recommendation for ethics auditors: Invite responses ranging from (1) strongly disagree to (5) strongly agree. Having these five options is important. Some test-makers push for "forced choice" yes/no answers (e.g., the popular Meyers-Briggs temperament analysis). But a moment's reflection tells us that this yields neat but bogus results. If someone feels right in the middle (3 on a 5-point scale) they should be able to say so; so too, a 3-point scale is still too extreme (positive, middle, negative). Give your people a chance to express how they feel. No forced choices or over-simplifications, even if your poll-takers are frustrated by the messy numbers. Hey, that's life.

Ethics audits should also always have some open, general questions with spaces to write feedback. Again, the psychologists and test-summarizers may not like it, but an accurate survey of employee attitudes must allow people to express their own opinions. Someone has to have the option of scrawling "This is all BS!!"—or "I love this place!" More often, they may make helpful suggestions or give us insights that the questions and numerical responses just can't capture.

The entire ethics audit (putting all the sections together from this book, for example) may be too much to administer every year. It may be better to audit the motivation, trouble-shooting and core values aspects this year; then audit the mission, ethics code, and leadership pieces next year. If it is broken up like that, the responses may be more thoughtful and complete.

Putting It All Together: Blueprint & Job List

The following schematic shows vividly the architecture of an ethically healthy organization:

The Blue Print

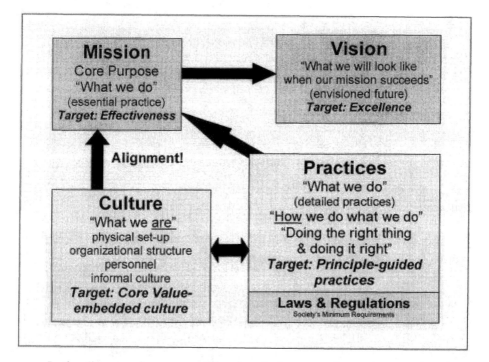

In the diagram above, everything is pointing toward carrying out the mission (effectively) and achieving the vision (excellently). There is an interplay back and forth between culture (what we are as an organization) and practices (what we do from day to day in our organization). Both are in service of the mission and vision. Alignment is a critical concept in the relations of the parts to each other.

Without self-consciously, intentionally building an organization this way, we may be left with the "laws and regulations" category as our only real guidance—maybe with just a big $ symbol at the top of the page as the business goal. We do want the $—and we do plan to respect the law. But the richer, fuller, more complex blueprint is the way we want to "go for it" in our business.

The next chart shows how the six components and four processes relate to each other and how the job list is created.

Gill's Job List for Building Ethically Healthy Organizations

4 Processes → 6 Components ↓	Identification What is it? How does it work? Identify it. Figure it out. Describe it. Explain it.	Education How do we teach it throughout the company? To do it, everyone must first know it. How do we train on this?	Implementation How do we make it part of our basic structures, policies, and practices? How do we practice all that we preach?	Evaluation How are we doing? How can we improve? What needs to change?
Motivation *Why we care.* A deep, thoughtful, convincing rationale for taking ethics seriously.	Why should we be concerned about our ethics? What is at stake? Consequences?	Activities and initiatives to keep everyone awake, alert, and motivated.	Instructing, praising, rewarding, disciplining to maintain the motivational edge.	Organizational Ethics Assessments; Focus groups; Internal/external research; Personnel evaluation.
Trouble-Shooting *How we manage crises and make decisions about dilemmas.* A ready, effective trouble-shooting and crisis resolution method.	What is our method and strategy for dealing with crises, dilemmas, and quandaries?	Ethics training case analyses online and in classroom; staff discussions. Newsletter Q&A	Get people involved in using the tools to research questions, discuss actual problems and find/invent resolutions.	Organizational Ethics Assessments; Focus groups; Internal/external research; Personnel evaluation.
Mission & Vision *Where we are going. Purpose, core business, and envisioned future.* An inspiring, shared core mission/vision.	Why do we exist? What are our core purposes, our overarching basic goals?	Statements posted everywhere; invoked, explained frequently.	Mission and vision brought up at strategy and planning meetings.	Organizational Ethics Assessments; Focus groups; Internal/external research; Personnel evaluation.
Culture *Who we are. The core values that shape our physical plant, policies, structures and atmosphere.* A healthy, value-embedded culture.	What are the basic, defining, core characteristics of our organization? Our habits, our atmosphere, our style, our traits?	Values posted everywhere, explained, illustrated by management.	Create & strengthen concrete exhibitions of each core value; smash all misalignments.	Organizational Ethics Assessments; Focus groups; Internal/external research; Personnel evaluation.
Practices *How we do the things we do. The principles and guidelines for our activities.* Robust, reliable, principle-guided practices.	What are the guidelines that keep our primary activities on track ethically? What is our code of conduct?	Ethics training on line, in print, in class.	Bring up guidelines in new employee orientation and mentoring, staff meetings, bring activities into conformity.	Organizational Ethics Assessments; Focus groups; Internal/external research; Personnel evaluation.
Leadership *Who makes it happen. What systems sustain it?* Gifted, effective leaders and systems in place and in training.	How is responsibility for organizational ethics distributed? Personnel, process, systems?	Make plain the organizational structure, lines of communication, accountability.	Set the example, inspire the people, hold people accountable. Encourage, reward, educate, discipline.	Organizational Ethics Assessments; Focus groups; Internal/external research; Personnel evaluation.

Chapter 4

What Do You Love?
Mission-Control Ethics

Executive Summary

*The foundation of ethical, excellent organizations is a clear, inspiring mission and vision. The great philosophers and leaders of the past understood and taught this, the best business literature of recent years (e.g., **Built to Last, Good to Great**) argues for it, and our own common sense and life experience insist on it. Mission/vision motivates good ethics; mission/vision actually guides the content of company ethics. The best mission/vision taps into and calls upon, in some way, (1) human creativity and innovation and/or (2) human helpfulness and caring for others. Nine research questions can take us where we need to go to determine our mission and vision. Lots of examples of mission and vision are followed by a model of a mission/vision audit form to help evaluate this crucial aspect of our organization.*

What is the foundation of an ethical organization? Contrary to some common thinking, it is not the company code of ethics. Nor is the key step to hire an ethics officer, or to schedule some employee ethics training. The foundational step is not to create a list of common ethical infractions and start doing some case studies on them.

None of the preceding steps will have much power to leverage or guide behavior unless they are intimately linked to a compelling overall organizational mission and vision. First get the mission and vision straight. That's where healthy organizational ethics begins.

Think about an athletic team: Only when a team is truly gripped by an intense, shared vision of winning a championship will they sacrifice and suffer through extra workouts. Only then will the players subordinate their individual egos to team interests. Only then will the players study the play book with total seriousness. Only then will they follow the exercise and nutritional guidelines for exceptional fitness. Only a compelling mission changes team behavior.

Negative feedback can have some impact on human performance, of course. Threats of punishment, insults, and shaming can motivate some behavioral improvement in both sports and business. Such negativity, though, makes for a generally weak foundation for ethics (most sexual harassment employee training is of this negative type). Positive, shared vision is much more powerful over time (in raising children, coaching athletes, building nations, or leading organizations).

> *Negative threats and consequences can change behavior, of course, but positive, shared hopes, purposes, and visions are much more powerful and enduring sources of change.*

Part of what happens in organizational ethical life is grounded in individual moral identity and conviction, of course. A passionate individual Muslim, or Christian, or feminist or libertarian (to give but four examples) will usually live out the ethical values embedded in their identity even when surrounded by others who don't share their values. But individualistic ethics like that is just not enough for today's high performance team needs and challenges. We need a shared ethics, not just a bunch of strong individual moral "athletes."

So this brings us to the question of a common mission and vision. The message of this chapter and this book is simple: First get the mission and vision straight. The organizational ethics rules and principles can then be understood, figured out, and implemented as strategic guidelines helping us achieve our ultimate goals and purposes. Ethics statements, training programs, ethics officers, and other structures and processes all follow from that crucial starting point. Any other way of pursuing organizational ethics is doomed to fall short.

We can recognize a sound ethics the way we recognize a good map. A good map will guide us to our chosen destination (not lead us astray). If we get off track we can study the map and find our way back. We accept a map because "it works for us" and because we know that it has worked for others. Ethics "works"—in all kinds of crises and circumstances—or it is wrong.

What does a good ethical map work "for"? Where does it lead us? The first question in ethics is, "What is our ultimate destination or goal?" What are our ultimate values, our purpose, our mission, our end? *The appropriateness and validity of moral virtues, principles, and rules lies in their relationship to an End, a mission and vision.* Character virtues are those traits, capacities, and dispositions that help us to achieve our ultimate ends, our mission. Moral principles and rules are the guidelines that help us make decisions and act in ways that lead to our ultimate goal.

Organizational codes of ethics are like maps. Their power to capture our attention and compliance only begins when we see they are necessary to make our way to some desirable destination. Their legitimacy and authority comes from their capacity to actually get us where we want to go.

Thus it is essential that we choose our mission carefully and articulate it clearly and persuasively. If we do not, our ethics will have little or no persuasive force. If we are not clear about the mission, we can't actually evaluate our ethics very well, because it is the mission that, in an important way, drives and justifies the ethics. If we are careful and intentional about it, a positive, shared mission can lead to a sound ethics. A good statement of mission and vision serves as a guide not only for current but prospective employees, business partners, clients, investors, and the public. The mission and vision statements tell both insiders and outsiders what the company stands for, why it exists, and where it hopes to go.

Jim Collins and Jerry Porras's bestselling study of great businesses, *Built to Last* (1995), argues that all great "built-to-last" businesses have been dedicated to a yin/yang dialectic of (1) preserving their core purpose and values while simultaneously (2) "stimulating progress." Collins and Porras define core purpose (what I'm calling "mission") as "the set of fundamental reasons for a company's existence beyond just making money. Purpose is broad, fundamental, and enduring; a good purpose should serve to guide and inspire the organization for years, perhaps a century or more. A visionary company continually pursues but never fully achieves or completes its purpose—like chasing the earth's horizon." (p. 77). Collins and Porras argue that mission-driven, visionary companies have experienced greater business success, over longer periods of time, than companies that were not mission and vision focused.

What Is "Mission"?

To be as precise as we can be, *mission* is a summary of the organization's *core purpose.*[1] Our mission is our basic, essential business. It is the umbrella phrase describing the essence and core of all our business activities. What does the company want to accomplish? What is the target out there? What is its business in the most basic sense? Sometimes, let's face it, a business starts up for not much more reason than that there is an opportunity to make some money. But think about this carefully: The core business is not just to "relieve people of their money." Some kind of service or product is being delivered—or that money will not be transferred. Only beggars and thieves can have "relieve you of your money" as an authentic, stand-alone mission. A successful business depends fundamentally on delivering some product or service well enough to keep customer cash flow coming in. What, in a brief phrase or sentence, is that core product or service? What is the change your business makes in the lives of its customers that warrants their paying you? That is your mission.

> *The mission cannot simply be to "relieve customers of their money." Only thieves can have that core mission. There must be some basic product or service we are delivering in light of which people will part with their money. It is that essential product or service, that change we leave behind in our customer's life, that is our core mission. So, what is it? This "thought experiment" is sometimes the best way to help get at a definition of a corporate mission.*

The Cisco mission is inspiring but a bit vague about what differentiates them from other IT companies: "Shape the future of the Internet by creating unprecedented value and opportunity for our customers, employees, investors, and ecosystem partners." Genentech's mission is inspiring and clear: "Using human genetic information to discover, develop, manufacture, and commercialize biotherapeutics that address significant unmet medical needs." Google is ambitious: "To organize the world's information and make it universally accessible and useful." For Kaiser Permanente the mission is "To provide high quality, affordable health care services and improve the health of our members and the communities we serve." At KCSM-FM Jazz 91 the mission is to "Craft extraordinary jazz programming, delivering the music and its related history to inspire and enlighten jazz listeners and artists worldwide."

The mission statement shouldn't be so big, broad, and inclusive that *anything* could be done under its flag (e.g., "providing great products to our customers"—ok, but *what sort* of products? Cars? Grilled chicken? We need some better focus here). What works best is to have a brief statement (like the examples above) followed by some fine print detailing out what we mean. At Harris & Associates, for example, the basic mission statement ("Helping clients, employees, and communities succeed through industry-leading management and consulting services") is followed by a sentence each for clients, employees, and communities, explaining the mission concerning them.

The Harris & Associates Mission
Helping clients, employees, and communities succeed through industry-leading management and consulting services.
• We serve our clients as their partner and advocate, bringing our expertise and dedication to their projects from start to successful finish.
• We provide our employees with opportunities for creativity, growth, and career success in a supportive, fun, and rewarding team environment.
• We protect and improve our community and environment through responsible stewardship of our shared resources.

What Is "Vision"?

The organizational *vision* is related to its *mission,* and the two terms are sometimes used (or confused) interchangeably. Vision and mission are both about the broad picture, the big goals and purposes. But vision is more about what the company will *be*—and mission is about what the company will *do*. Vision is a picture of what the company will look like when the mission is accomplished. It is a statement of aspiration (and expectation) of what the company will look like, of how it will be viewed not just by insiders but by all who see it.

Mission is the core business, what the company "does"; Vision is the desired, envisioned future, what the company "will be"—and how it will be seen—as the mission is accomplished.

Here are some examples: At Charles Schwab the vision is "To become the most useful and ethical financial services firm in the world." For KCSM, "We will be the first choice in public television and jazz radio." Chevron's vision is "To be *the* global energy company most admired for its people, partnership, and performance." For Washington Mutual, the vision is "To be the nation's leading retailer of financial services for consumers and small businesses." Levi Strauss's statement combines vision and mission elements: "People love our clothes and trust our company [*vision*]. We will market the most appealing and widely worn casual clothing in the world. We will clothe the world [*mission*]."

For Harris & Associates, the vision is to be "the excellence and integrity leader among management and consulting companies." Again, Harris details out what this means for three of its audiences: customer/clients, employees, and communities.

The Harris & Associates Vision
The excellence and integrity leader among management and consulting companies.

The Harris Vision is to be not the biggest but the best in our regions of operation. We want to continue to grow our company in a sustainable manner that does not compromise our core mission and values or the health of our company culture.
• We want to be the first choice of clients seeking management and consulting services, with a reputation for exceptional ethics, expertise, and client focus.
• We want to continue to attract and retain great people at Harris & Associates, drawn by our reputation for innovation, opportunity, and a fun and satisfying work environment.
• We want to be valued as model corporate citizens by all the communities in which we operate, with a reputation for generosity, responsiveness, and wise stewardship.

In effect, the mission and vision are the "boss" of the organization. They are the criteria by which actions are accepted or rejected. They are the foundation and goal of the business plan. Jim Collins draws a set of three overlapping circles in a Venn diagram in which one circle stands for "Marketability" (can it be sold?), one for "Competence" (do we have the skills and resources to do it well?), and one for "Core Ideology" (mission and values fit?). Only when a proposal or plan is in the overlap of all three circles is there a green light. Getting the mission and vision straight is thus a critical strategic task.

When I first got behind the wheel of a car as a young teenager (on an Oregon back road while on a family vacation) I scared my family to death by the way I steered. The car jerked back and forth, left and right. My dad grabbed the wheel and advised, "look farther down the road as you drive." I did and soon everyone was breathing more easily. I had thought I should drive by looking at the center line just in front of the car's left front fender, but I needed a longer range perspective to steer us smoothly forward. To drive well we need good peripheral vision and good reactions to immediate crises (deer runs across road, muffler and debris in lane, etc.). But the longer range perspective is basic and essential. That's not unlike the way mission and vision help organizations to steer their way safely and smoothly forward.

Here is how Toyota watcher and management expert Jeffrey K. Liker describes the first principle of the "Toyota Way": "Base your management decisions on a long-term philosophy . . . Have a philosophical sense of purpose that supersedes any short-term decision-making. Work, grow, and align the whole organization toward a common purpose that is bigger than making money." Liker goes on: "Throughout my visits to Toyota in Japan and the United States, in engineering, purchasing, and manufacturing, one theme stands out. Every person I have talked with has a sense of purpose greater than earning a paycheck. They feel a great sense of mission for the company and can distinguish right from wrong with regard to that mission. . . Toyota's strong sense of mission and commitment to its customers, employees, and society *is the foundation of all the other principles* and the missing ingredient in most companies trying to emulate Toyota."[2] I think we all know which auto company leads the world in innovation, quality, and (soon, if not already) in sales.

We want to build a mission-driven, vision-pursuing organization—not just a backward-looking, trouble-avoiding one. To recall the earlier metaphor, organizational ethics relates to mission and vision the way maps and directions relate to destinations. The map isn't just about staying away from the city jail (negative) but about guiding us to our destination (positive). If we want to motivate drivers to use and follow the map, first turn them on to a desirable destination (a great restaurant, a music club, etc.), then give them the map. Here is the mission and vision of Paradise Foods, a great supermarket that gets it right:

Paradise Foods, "A Classic Market" in Corte Madera, CA

Our Mission: *To provide high quality food in a pleasant atmosphere where employees enjoy their work and customers enjoy their shopping.*

> *Our Vision: Paradise Foods will be the best market in Marin County. As measured by:*
>
> • *Sustainable profitability and wise growth*
> • *Employee satisfaction and growth*
> • *Loyal customers who promote us to others*
> • *Significant contributions to our community*

Sound Ethics Depends on Mission and Vision

For the business to achieve its mission, what kind of value-embedded corporate culture and what kind of principle-guided practices are needed? What guidelines will get us from here to there with excellence? Business writer Douglas Sherwin explained how ethical values relate to mission and purpose in a classic essay several years ago: "The values that govern the conduct of business must be conditioned by 'the why' of the business institution. They must flow from the purpose of business, carry out that purpose, and be constrained by it."[3] Ethics is essential to fulfill the "why" of business. If the ethical guidelines are not integral to the company's purpose and mission, they will fail.

Costco explicitly links its mission to its code of ethics. Here is how they put it:

> ### Costco
>
> *Our Mission: To continually provide our members with quality goods and services at the lowest possible prices.*
>
> *In order to achieve our mission we will conduct our business with the following Code of Ethics in mind:*
>
> *Our Code of Ethics*
> *1. Obey the law.*
> *2. Take care of our members.*
> *3. Take care of our employees.*
> *4. Respect our suppliers.*

> *If we do these four things throughout our organization, then we will achieve our ultimate goal, which is to:*
>
> *5. Reward our shareholders.*

The argument for mission-control ethics has common sense and business experience on its side. It also happens to be the way ethics has been understood, taught, and practiced for millennia (how did we get off track and fall in love with damage-control, reactive ethics?). Aristotle began his *Nichomachean Ethics* with "The good is that at which everything aims." Ethical/moral goodness is about "Ends," and means to those ends. An Aristotelian approach asks "How would we describe a *good* horse?" Well, first of all, "What is the *purpose* of a horse?" Answer: "to carry heavy loads." And if that is a horse's purpose, then the virtues of a good horse will be strength, durability, sure-footedness, tame-ability, etc. Or "What makes for a *good* knife?" Well, "What is the purpose of a knife?" Answer, "to cut things." Therefore the virtues of a good knife are things like sharpness, safety, durability, etc. If the purpose of a knife was to be displayed in a museum, things like shininess and color might be among its core virtues; if the purpose is to cut, then sharpness tops the list. Identify the purpose first, then detail the characteristics necessary for excellence in carrying out or achieving that purpose.

The Ten Commandments, ostensibly the core ethical principles and guideline not only for Jews but also Christians and Muslims, are also structured in a mission-control way. The rabbis pointed out that what they really are is *one* commandment followed by *nine* implications or corollaries. First get your god straight: "I am the Lord your God . . . you shall have no other gods before me." If the god Yahweh is on the throne, so the argument goes, *then* we will speak to others by name with respect, honor our elders, protect life, avoid theft, and so on. It is the God who determines the good. First get your god straight, then work on the ethics of good and bad. There is an integral relationship.

> *Mission-control (teleological, "end/telos-oriented") ethics is implied by the studies of great contemporary businesses by Jim Collins in* **Built to Last** *and* **Good to Great***. It is also the way ethics was approached by Aristotle and Moses, to name just two ancient luminaries.*

By contrast, most of today's business ethics has been "damage control" ethics, focused on containing harms from problems already spinning out of control. It concentrates on the messes at the end of a process that has gone awry. It is crisis oriented. We are confronted by various moral dilemmas or quandaries and have to choose how best to "muddle through." Certainly, "damage control" is an important activity (hence, Chapter Three). But if we think of ethics *only* as a matter of damage control of agonizing quandaries, we will never get to a major source of these dilemmas: a defective or weak mission and culture.

Think about the Mississippi River. If there is a problem of dead fish and polluted water around New Orleans, we could focus our energy down there on trying to filter the water and decontaminate the fish. That's damage control. Wouldn't it be smarter to go upstream to St. Louis and even up to St. Paul, start our clean-up efforts at the headwaters, and move downstream making sure that stuff isn't getting into the river that is inconsistent with the health of the river from its very starting point? That's mission control.

> *"Damage control" ethics is like trying to purify the water and decontaminate the fish at the end of a long river; "Mission control" ethics is like moving upstream to concentrate on what goes into the river that eventuates in it being clean or polluted at the end.*

Mission and Vision Motivate and Leverage Our Ethics

Our mission and vision persuade and convince us to use appropriate means to our chosen ends, to behave in ways that will get us where we want to go. That's the logical structure of the Costco statement above. *If* ethics, *then* missional success. A positive motivation takes over from the negative reasons to be ethical (staying out of jail, avoiding bankruptcy, disgrace, etc.). We alluded to this in the discussion of fear and love as motivators in Chapter Two.

Think of how a person's bad habits and long-entrenched behavior sometimes change radically. This doesn't happen very often, but when it does it is often because that person fell in love and wants so badly to please or win another person that they will change their ways. And think of how in an era of epidemic childhood obesity we see an impressive band of super-fit kid athletes (gymnasts, skaters, basketball players). What makes these kids behave so differently from their peers? A major factor is their vision of getting a gold medal at the Olympics or playing in the NBA. Mission and vision motivate and leverage behavioral change like nothing else.

Any business or organization that wants to motivate ethically healthy behavior should begin by giving employees a mission and vision that they can be passionate about, one that taps into and engages the best aspects of our human nature.

> *If we want to motivate our employees to be ethical, give them a mission and vision to be passionate about, whose achievement requires ethical behavior.*

Ethical Value Choices Flow from Mission Choices

Mission and vision don't just motivate ethical behavior, they indicate the *content* itself of good ethics. By analyzing what it will take to achieve the mission and fulfill the vision, we can figure out the appropriate values and guidelines. The mission of "cutting things" logically leads us to conclude that the first virtue must be "sharpness." After a business gets its mission and vision straight, it then (and only then) figures out the core values it must embed in its culture and the basic principles that must guide its practices in order to achieve success and excellence. This is, by the way, a common mistake made by many businesses and other organizations, i.e., separating and treating as independent the mission and vision, on the one hand, and their core values and ethical guidelines, on the other.

It is hardly a surprise that an absent, unclear, or inauthentic mission/vision will normally be accompanied by weak ethics, perhaps even by unethical behavior. Let's recall the map and driving metaphor: If you give someone a car but your destination is vague ("let's just drive around town"), don't be surprised when your driver doesn't bother to look at the map. Or, if you say you want to get to some shopping center, but you clearly don't care (you are really just driving around killing time, avoiding a meeting), your driver will sense the inauthenticity of your "destination" and the map will not have any power over him. If you don't know (or care) where you are going, just about any road will work.[4] Unclear, absent, or inauthentic mission and vision cannot lead to an ethically healthy organization.

If your company has a clear purpose but it is a bad or negative one, be prepared for the ethical consequences. For example, if the mission is really all about maximizing short-term financial pay-offs (perhaps especially for a handful of executives), the characteristics that are generated may include ruthlessness, greed, selfishness, cunning, and willingness to step on others. The fall of

Arthur Andersen (described in detail in *Final Accounting: Ambition, Greed, and the Fall of Arthur Andersen* by Barbara Ley Toffler) offers a clear case study of how a mission turned bad rapidly led to behavior turned bad and unethical. To return to the football analogy, if the players' real mission is to set individual records and get drafted by a professional team, their behavior will be very different from the players at a team-championship-oriented competitor school.

> *If your company has a clear purpose—but it is a bad or negative one—be prepared for the ethical consequences. For example, if the mission is really all about maximizing short-term financial pay-offs (perhaps especially for a handful of executives), the characteristics that are generated may include ruthlessness, greed, selfishness, cunning, and willingness to step on others.*

Characteristics of Good Mission and Vision Statements

What makes for good mission and vision statements? There is a good deal of flexibility and variety possible, but there are four basic characteristics:

First, the mission and vision statements must be *authentic*. These statements must describe *what actually* is the purpose and aspiration of the organization. Of course there is an element of aspiration beyond current achievement; it is not a mere status report recalling the past. But the statements must be genuine. They must accurately represent what the company truly is about and how it is distinguished from other companies. An outside consultant or wordsmith cannot just invent a mission or vision for an organization. Nor can the CEO normally just write the mission and vision all by himself/herself. It falls to the leaders and veterans, but this is a critically important task that requires a careful effort. Authenticity is the first criterion.

Second, the mission and vision statements must be *clear*. If the vision and mission statements are to do their job effectively they must be conceptually clear, sharply stated, easily communicable, and quickly comprehended. Brevity is almost always a virtue here—ten to fifteen words, perhaps, although two or three words have sometimes done the job. Nike's mission was once simply "Crush Reebok." Pepsi's was "Beat Coke." During the fall at my two alma maters, Cal Berkeley and USC, we often chanted just two words "Rose Bowl" to articulate our mission and vision (sadly unfulfilled for longsuffering "Old Blues" at Cal).

In any case, mission and vision statements should use pithy, pregnant, succinct phrases where every word counts. Get to the point. Often the basic mission and vision statements can be accompanied by brief paragraphs which elaborate key aspects of the basic statement.

Third, the mission and vision statements must be *inspiring*. The mission and vision should be capable of drawing people forward, of stimulating their passion and energy, of engaging them, not just informing them. "Love" and "passion" are not often used in the business vocabulary, but they communicate the right idea here. The mission and vision need to be gripping, exciting, inspiring.

Fourth, the mission and vision must be *unifying*; that is, they describe a challenge that invites teamwork and cooperation, not individual greed and ego. Ask about a proposed mission and vision if it will be a flag that we will all really want to march under.

Effective mission and vision statements must be:
- *authentic—this really is what we are about*
- *clear—we can all see immediately what we are about*
- *inspiring—it invites passion, excitement, and commitment*
- *unifying—it invites and challenges us to work together*

Two Great Themes in Inspiring Missions

Such inspiring (and unifying) mission and vision statements often tap into one (or both) of two basic aspects of human nature. The first of these is human *creativity*. When a company challenges its people to innovate, create, and build in some way, it connects with something profoundly human. People are rarely inspired by jobs that have no space for creativity, that ask just for repetition, compliance, and maintenance. There are some classic psychological and anthropological studies of this human characteristic (Latin, *homo faber*, "man the maker"). But it is also common sense and personal experience: Think about how good it feels to take on a challenge and have the freedom and responsibility to carry it out. Think of how good it feels to finish the project and be able to look back on it. Getting a book published, finishing a deck building project, running a marathon, completing an acquisition project at work, etc. Human beings are builders by nature.[5]

Great companies tap into that creative "build something good" characteristic in all of their workforce. Try to express that theme in your mission and vision statement if you want to more fully mobilize the best in your people. Again, Toyota is a model: "Central to the Toyota Way is innovation . . . from the small workplace changes made by plant workers on the shop floor to fundamental breakthroughs in production technology and vehicle engineering."[6] Toyota's development of both the Lexus and the Prius are expressions of creativity and innovation unleashed by a mission-driven organization. 3M is another company whose success has been creativity/innovation driven.

The second great theme is human *helpfulness*. People are inspired by organizational missions and visions that help those in need, heal the sick, liberate those in various kinds of bondage, and overcome hunger, ignorance, or oppression in some form. Again, there are academic studies of this "herd instinct" and altruism, but the evidence of common sense and observation is powerful enough by itself.[7] Think about how people respond to disasters and human cries for help; there is something in us (most of us, most of the time) that makes us want to help others. When a tsunami, earthquake, hurricane, or terrorist assaults our neighbors, most of us join together to help. When a child falls down or an older person struggles to carry something, most of us step up quickly to help. It actually makes us feel good about ourselves to be able to help others. We dehumanize ourselves when we could help someone in need and we selfishly turn away (we never brag to our friends about these episodes of selfishness and stone-heartedness).

To summarize the point just a little glibly, a viable, inspiring mission and vision either helps people "fulfill their dreams" or it helps people "overcome their nightmares." Tapping into one or both of these themes is really about aligning the organizational mission with the best aspects of human nature.

The mission of Walt Disney has been a good example of the inspiring potential of the "create something beautiful" theme: *To bring happiness to millions.* While some recent events may give us pause, the broader Disney story has been one of mission-driven, ethical business success. Who wouldn't be inspired to work for a company whose mission is "to bring happiness to millions"? As might be expected, the great pharmaceutical companies have (in the past at least) tapped primarily into the "help somebody" theme. Johnson & Johnson's mission has been: *To alleviate pain and disease.* Merck described its mission as: *the business of preserving and improving human life.* As long as, and to the extent that, these phrases really focus the mission and vision of these companies (assuming of course a reasonable financial success), employees and investors find these companies inspiring places to be associated with.

Sony's older mission statement was an inspiring statement of creativity with a secondary "help somebody" theme: *To experience the sheer joy that comes from the advancement, application, and innovation of technology that benefits the general public.* Hewlett-Packard's "H-P Way" also picked up both the creativity/innovation and helpfulness themes. Some of its key elements: *To make technical contributions to fields in which we participate . . . To make a contribution to the community. . . . To provide affordable quality for customers. . . . To provide respect and opportunity for H-P people including opportunity to share in H-P success.* Baxter Health Care emphasizes the innovation side of its mission to care: *We will be the leading health-care company by providing the best products and services for our customers around the world, consistently emphasizing innovation, operational excellence, and the highest quality in everything we do.*

The Two Great Themes in Inspiring Mission/Vision Statements
The most inspiring and positive missions and visions will tap into one or both of two basic aspects of human nature:
(1) our desire to build (create, innovate) something good and/or
(2) our desire to help those in need (solve a problem, heal a sickness, fix what is broken, etc.).

In its most dramatically stated form, an inspiring mission and vision challenge our people to help others "fulfill their dreams"—or "overcome their nightmares."

Building a Mission-Driven, Vision-Pursuing Organization

Now that we understand what mission and vision are, and why they are so centrally important to organizations and their ethical health, the first action item is to *identify* our company mission and vision. If such a statement already exists, the task is to review it and perhaps revise and strengthen it. The mission and vision need to be figured out, clarified, described, and articulated in understandable language. In some cases it may be sufficient (or somehow more appropriate to the circumstances) to confine the effort to a mission *or* vision statement. But since mission and vision provide two complementary lenses for viewing the company, creating both statements is usually the wisest course.

Who is best positioned to drive this process of identifying, figuring out, the mission and vision? Since the mission and vision are the overarching "boss" of everything in the organization, it is crucial for the top executive leadership of the organization to be fully involved in creating, reviewing, modifying, and guarding the mission and vision. The whole organization must buy into the mission and vision—and good ideas and suggestions must be welcomed from everyone. But the top leadership (including the board of directors) has to carry the primary responsibility here. If they are not fully and enthusiastically involved, if they are not passionate and inspired by their company's mission and vision, the process is doomed to fail.

Whether outside consultants or inside project leaders facilitate the process of identifying the company mission and vision, the heart of the project is first to *listen* to what the leadership understands as the overarching, fundamental purpose of the company's business activities (its mission)—and as its aspiration, ambition, and dream (its vision). Interviewing founders, leaders, and any other primary "definers" of the company vision and mission is the first step; reviewing company publications, recruiting material, web sites, and archives provides additional insight. Press coverage and outside analysis of the organization should be consulted if available.

> *With or without professional writers or consultants, with or without an active, broad-based participation in the early stages, it is the top executive leadership of an organization that must carry the ball on mission and vision because the overall, company-wide perspective is both their responsibility and their capability.*

As suggested above, connecting the mission and vision to the basic human nature of employees, customers, and other stakeholders is an important way to create an inspiring statement. Tap into the "creativity/innovation" side of human nature; tap into the "help somebody/fix something" side of human nature. Another link to keep in mind is the history of the organization. Values and ethics are not just related to human nature and instinct but to the human narrative. We are story-telling creatures. Our sense of meaning, purpose, and direction is related to where we came from, our significant experiences, and where we are going.

Depending on time, personnel, and resources available for the project, the identification and articulation of the mission and vision can be pursued partly as an inductive group exercise. In any case, drafts of the emerging mission and vision statements should be discussed not just in one-on-one communications but in a leadership group setting (more than one if appropriate and necessary). It is essential for the researcher/author/editor(s) to be articulating what is in fact the authentic expression of the mission and vision of the whole company. The leadership must truly own the company mission and vision, whatever the nuances of the process that give it final expression.

When I am helping an organization get its mission and vision straight, here is my agenda. Questions one to three are about process; four through seven are about mission; eight and nine are about vision:

Gill's Mission/Vision Research Questions

1. Who are the key founders, current leaders, and key "old-timers" we can interview to find out what this company is really all about? (Action: careful interviews)

2. What are the key pieces of literature—introductory statements, company history and reports, press coverage, policy statements, marketing pitches, etc.—we should study to really understand this company? (Action: collect and study)

3. Who are the main competitor companies in this industry—and which ones do you admire most? (Action: study their mission, vision, values, and ethics)

4. In a brief phrase or sentence describe this company's business (make every word count). What key words are the best umbrella description covering all our products/services?

5. What key words are essential to differentiate our business purpose from a "generic," overly inclusive statement?

6. What key words set our mission/business apart from our competitors in our industry?

7. Other than relieving our clients/customers of their financial payments to us, what have we done to/for them by the time we leave them?

8. How would you describe this company if and when we are the success we dream about?

9. How, in a brief phrase, would you like others (our customers, competitors, journalists, et al) to describe us when we succeed in our basic business mission?

As the statement(s) near final form—but before final adoption—it is important to circulate the proposal widely among the workforce, invite comment, and take such comment seriously before freezing a final statement for a period of time. Drafts of the mission and vision statements need to be bounced back and forth, floated out to the workforce, reviewed by skilled writers, marketing and communications experts, revised and then adopted.

It is not good if the mission and vision jerk wildly around from year to year (like a road trip that starts for San Francisco and changes abruptly to go to Las Vegas … and then again to Boston). On the other hand, the occasional "tweaking" and sharpening of mission and vision after careful review and evaluation should not be feared. Maybe every two or three years, company leadership should take an especially careful look at a corporate mission/vision audit (see below) and devote some time to a mission/vision review.

Educating for Mission-Control

Once the mission and vision are figured out and articulated, the second process is to *educate (train)* all the organizational stakeholders. It is not enough to write a fine statement of mission and vision—and then have it filed away and remain little known (or unknown) in the organization. Everyone needs to know the company's vision and mission. This helps build unity in the organization, and it clarifies the direction of the company. Outside business partners and stakeholders need to know your mission and vision as well.

"Constant exposure" is the primary requirement in this educational process. Using (at least in short form) the mission and vision statements in company presentations, publications, web pages, and business cards, framing and posting them on office walls, providing coffee cups, sweatshirts, and other paraphernalia imprinted with the mission or vision statements—these are some of the ways to create constant exposure. Company leaders can write (in company newsletters, e-letters, etc.) and speak about the vision and mission, their meaning and implications. The Harris & Associates president recently wrote three successive monthly columns in the company newsletter discussing three angles on the mission and vision and giving examples of individuals in the company who lived out those aspects of the mission and vision in exemplary ways.

> *Constant exposure and frequent explanation are the keys to mission/vision training. It has to start at the top—and it has to permeate down through all organizational leaders and levels.*

Implementation: Making the Mission the Boss

The third process is to *implement* the mission and vision. It is not enough merely to identify and describe the mission and vision. Nor is it enough to educate everyone about it. If a company does not *implement* the mission and vision, in other words, *put it into practice*, it is actually better never to begin the mission and vision project at all. Hypocrisy creates cynicism; cynicism corrodes cultures and makes leadership and high performance impossible. If the mission statement is really just "high-sounding, idealistic, b.s. for marketing purposes"—believe me, the employees will think of it and refer to it in exactly those terms.

Implementation of the mission and vision means *walking the talk*. The mission and vision are implemented when a project is rejected because it didn't fit within the mission, didn't contribute to the achievement of the vision. It means not hiring someone with a great skill set but an incompatible personal career mission. Implementation means a fierce loyalty to the mission and a ruthless commitment to alignment: If something doesn't fit, we don't do it. Positively, implementation means constantly challenging one another in the company to find new and better ways (projects, products, and services) for living out and expressing the company's vision and mission. Jim Collins and Jerry Porras discovered that visionary, mission-driven organizations always adopted "big hairy audacious goals" ("BHAGs") as ways of making the mission concrete in the organization. As we saw earlier, developing the Lexus and Prius were two BHAGs for Toyota. Implementation also means recognizing and rewarding mission-keepers and vision-achievers in the organization.

> • *Implementation means aggressive, creative development of projects that carry out the mission—"big, hairy, audacious goals" that are integral to the mission and vision.*
> • *Implementation means ruthless, relentless alignment—including termination and rejection of any projects or operations that are not integral to the mission and vision.*

Evaluating Mission & Vision in Our Organization

The fourth process is to *evaluate* the mission and vision of the organization. Typically, the mission and vision are the most stable, enduring element in the company, serving for decades as the organizational compass. Nevertheless, nothing can be taken for granted in an uncritical way in our world of change and challenge. At least every two or three years, a careful evaluation of the mission and vision should take place. The executive leadership should carefully review the description and wording of the mission and vision statements and their paragraphs of elaboration. Should any of the wording be "tweaked" to modify an emphasis? to sharpen a point? The review process could invite suggestions from throughout the organization as long as the impression that "the mission and vision are up for grabs" (or uncertain) is avoided.

Part of the evaluation process is to evaluate individual (and team) performance in terms of its contribution to the company mission. A complete review process also entails an audit of the organization from top to bottom to find out if the mission and vision are clear, if they are well understood, and if they are implemented/practiced (in the opinion of the respondents). None of this can be taken for granted. An employee (and board) survey (with opportunity for written comments, not just a fill-in-the-dots form to complete) can be supplemented with focus group and staff discussions. The research questions listed earlier in this chapter should be pursued again. And an ethics audit like the following can elicit valuable feedback from the whole employee base.

Gill's Company Mission and Vision Audit

Does our company have a clear, strong, inspiring, and unifying core mission and vision?	Strongly Disagree 1 2 3	Strongly Agree 4 5
1. Our company has a clear and authentic purpose beyond just making money.	❏ ❏ ❏	❏ ❏
2. Our mission and vision statements are inspirational and memorable.	❏ ❏ ❏	❏ ❏
3. Everyone at our company knows and understands our mission and vision.	❏ ❏ ❏	❏ ❏
4. When important business decisions are made, our mission helps decide what should or should not be done.	❏ ❏ ❏	❏ ❏
5. There are many examples of our organization living by its purpose ("walking the talk")—even choosing not to do something because it didn't fit with the mission.	❏ ❏ ❏	❏ ❏
6. Our most successful leaders and managers focus the organization on pursuing its core purpose and vision.	❏ ❏ ❏	❏ ❏

Briefly summarize the core mission and vision of our company:

Comments on our mission and vision:

Afterthought: Relating Personal Mission/Vision and Company Mission/Vision

It should not be lost on us that serious problems emerge when someone's personal career goals are not in sync with what the company sees as its mission and vision. This is the problem of "alignment" that comes up throughout this book.

To individuals my counsel would always be to think through your personal calling and your career goals in the big, lifetime sense. What do you really want to accomplish in your career? What do you want to be your legacy, the impact you have made on those around you? It is worth getting away and spending some time thinking this through—so as to avoid wasting time, making bad career moves, spinning your wheels, bumping up against bosses whose interests are totally different than yours. In interviews be sure to articulate an outline of your career mission and vision and ask your prospective employer how that aligns with their company mission and vision. Make your decision with open eyes about whether this is a good context for your growth and progress in your desired career trajectory.

To companies, managers, and human resources directors, I would always urge that career mission and vision questions play large in interviewing prospects for jobs. Be clear about the company's mission and vision and ask job prospects to describe not just their own background, but their desired "foreground," where they want to be in five or fifteen years if they could describe their dream. Ask them how they see their personal goals relating to the company's mission and vision. If their career vision is not in alignment with that of the company, don't hire them, no matter how good they look in other respects.

It is worth noting that a company with a robust "build something great" and/or "help somebody" orientation, a company that wants to truly unleash its employee creativity, innovation, and altruism, will probably find that lots of great people will want to come on board and be part of their team.

For Reflection or Discussion

1. Have you thought through your personal career mission or vision (overall goals and dreams). Has this influenced your choices and behavior in any way?

2. How important have mission and vision been in the organizations you have worked for? How would you explain and evaluate these experiences?

3. Is it important to recruit employees partly for their missional fit? (i.e.,

people whose personal career vision and mission is compatible with the company's core purpose?)

4. If an intelligent, observant stranger were to spend a couple weeks just looking at what your organization does (without reading your PR material), how do you think they would describe your mission?

Exercises

1. Go on the web and take a look at the mission and vision statements of your competitors and of a few companies you admire. What are the "take-aways" that can be helpful in your company?

2. Ask three or four top company leaders—and a couple long-time, veteran employees—how they would describe the real, authentic mission and vision of your company if it was up to them. How does this compare with official company statements?

Resources for Further Study

There is a growing literature about mission, vision, and purpose in business. As mentioned already in this book, *Built to Last: Successful Habits of Visionary Companies* by Jim Collins and Jerry Porras (HarperBusiness, 1994) studies some of the most successful businesses of the past century and argues that their clear sense of purpose, beyond just making money, was a major factor in their success. The twelve essays by business leaders, collected in Frances Hesselbein & Rob Johnston, editors, *On Mission and Leadership* (Drucker Foundation, Jossey-Bass, 2002) are a great read. Jeffrey Abrahams, *The Mission Statement Book: 301 Corporate Mission Statements from America's Top Companies* (Ten Speed Press, 1995) is a helpful resource. C. William Pollard's reflections on his tenure at ServiceMaster, *The Soul of the Firm* (HarperBusiness, 1996) shows what one *Fortune* 1000 mission-control organization looks like. Two recent books which take the study of business mission/vision/purpose to a new level are Richard R. Ellsworth, *Leading with Purpose: The New Corporate Realities* (Stanford University Press, 2002) and Nikos Mourkogiannis, *Purpose: The Starting Point of Great Companies* (Palgrave Macmillan, 2006).

NOTES

[1] Nikos Mourkogiannis, *Purpose: The Starting Point of Great Companies* (Palgrave Macmillan, 2006) prefers to distinguish purpose from mission (and vision). His view of purpose is akin to the "great themes" I discuss later in this chapter. While I am very enthusiastic about his book, my view is that organizations need to articulate and emphasize a more substantive and precise mission than one of the (more general) human "purposes" provides by itself. For example, "Create something great" isn't focused enough to help us choose our map or know how to plan. "Create affordable mass transit for today's megacities" has the kind of focus that can inspire and direct an organization.

[2] Jeffrey K. Liker, *The Toyota Way* (McGraw-Hill, 2004), pp. 37, 71-72. Emphasis in the original.

[3] Douglas Sherwin, "The Ethical Roots of the Business System," *Harvard Business Review,* Nov-Dec 1983, p. 186.

[4] Anne Erler reminded me that when Alice (in Wonderland) asked the Cheshire cat which way to turn at a fork in the road, the cat replied, "Well, where do you want to end up?" When Alice said that it didn't matter, the cat said "Well, then it doesn't matter which direction you take."

[5] Nikos Mourkogiannis describes this as "discovery," one of four basic core purposes grounding great companies. See *Purpose: The Starting Point of Great Companies* (Palgrave Macmillan, 2006), pp. 30-31.

[6] *The Toyota Way*, p. 42.

[7] Mourkogiannis also highlights this theme, calling it "altruism," one of his four basic core purposes. He suggests "Excellence" and "Heroism" as the third and fourth core purposes undergirding great companies. There is no single way to describe our topic, but, in my view, excellence and heroism are more about *how we approach* "creating good and useful products and services" and "fixing broken things and helping hurting people" (my "two great themes") than separate thematic purposes. See *Purpose: The Starting Point of Great Companies*, pp. 32-37.

Chapter 5

Building Ethical Muscle:
Value-Embedded Corporate Cultures

Executive Summary

> *Missions and visions don't fulfill themselves. Nor do codes of ethics apply themselves automatically. Ethics and excellence are radically dependent on culture. Culture is what we "are"—more than a list of what we "do." Culture is about our organizational "muscle," our capability, our potential to carry out our mission and live up to our ethical principles. Culture has four levels: (1) physical buildings and equipment, (2) organizational systems, policies, and procedures, (3) personnel, and (4) informal rituals, traditions, habits, and cultural atmosphere. A worksheet and process is provided to show how organizations can identify the core values which must be embedded at all four levels of their culture, along with lots of examples and a model of a culture and values company audit.*

In the previous chapter the case was presented for viewing the corporate mission and vision as the starting point, the foundation for building an ethical and excellent organization. Now, in this chapter, the argument is, in a sports metaphor, "If you want to win that championship (mission), you've got to get into good shape (culture)." No matter how inspiring your goal, you must build the capacity to achieve it. In sports, it's about physical fitness, mental preparation, and habits of teamwork. In business, it's about the kind of personnel, structures, and policies you have in place. Do they empower you to achieve your business mission? Do they enable your business to "leap high"? Or is your organization toxic, weak, and like a weight keeping your business from leaping up above the rim?

In business we call this "corporate culture." In a word, culture is what you *are*—more than what you *do*—even though, in the end, being and doing are inextricably related.[1] On a personal or individual level we call this phenomenon "character"; on a corporate, group or organizational level we call it "culture." This has been a topic of growing conversation, study, and attention for the past couple decades. Louis V. Gerstner, who led a turnaround at IBM during the 90s, said that changing the culture was critical. "Culture isn't just one aspect of the game, it *is* the game."[2] Jim Collins and Jerry Porras devoted a full chapter of *Built to Last: Successful Habits of Visionary Companies* to a positive description of "cult-like cultures."[3]

Comparisons have been noted among company cultures such as IBM (traditionally conservative, male, regimented, strong), Hewlett-Packard (open, warm, innovative, egalitarian), and Apple (hip, chaotic, creative). We want to go deeper than just the "feel" of a culture, but you can see the kind of thing we are talking about. Obviously, too, all three of these companies have been major business successes, so there is not just one way to build a culture.

As for ethical health, we can say that people respond to ethical challenges partly based on "internalization"—that is, based on their internalized, personal values, character, and interior moral compass. (Lesson: Pay attention to this when hiring your people). But we also respond based on "socialization"—that is, the influences of other people around us, and the influences and pressures of systems of rewards and penalties. (Lesson: Pay attention to your culture).

Cultural/organizational systems can be formal (IBM) or informal (Apple), strong (IBM and Apple) or weak (organizations with little self-conscious "identity" or distinctiveness), healthy (empowering ethics and excellence) or unhealthy (toxic relationships, unethical behavior, unmet standards). *Alignment* (between the mission/vision and the culture) is critical—enabling and reinforcing or disabling and undermining ethics and excellence.

Culture is what you are, what kind of company and organization you are building, your capabilities, habits, structural strengths and weaknesses, "feel," etc.

Corporate culture (like personal "character") can't be overlooked or taken for granted. It needs to be intentional, carefully crafted and aligned with the mission and vision.

Four Components of Corporate Culture

Sometimes the term "corporate culture" is used only to refer to the "feel" of a company, its "folkways" and rituals. That is certainly important (part of the fourth characteristic). But we should look at culture in a broader way, like an anthropologist would do on discovering a new group of people in some remote area. In this larger, more complete sense, a culture has four basic components.

1. The Physical Set-Up and Infrastructure. The first component of an organizational culture is its physical set-up, the architecture, decoration, and maintenance of its buildings and its equipment. How are the offices laid out? What kind of hardware and software do we have? Do the windows have views? Who gets them? Values are embedded here, whether they have been examined or not. Is this physical aspect of the culture about beauty . . . or about ugliness? Usefulness and efficiency . . . or waste and impracticality? Does it scream "hierarchy" . . . or "equality"? Is it about openness . . . or closure? Individuality . . . or community and team?

Every organization doesn't have to be the same, but it is important to be intentional about these matters. The Ph.D. ethics program community I was part of many years ago at USC had a truly marvelous sense of community, shared ideas, lively intellectual debate, and social acceptance and camaraderie across traditional barriers of gender, age, race, religion, and politics. But when I returned for a visit years later it was pretty much all gone, even though much of the personnel was the same. Why? Originally the program operated in a very modest suite with faculty offices in cubicles around the sides, all opening up into a central common area with a couple reception and administrative support desks, couches, a coffee machine, etc. The office layout "threw" us together into conversation.

Sadly, following a gift of several million dollars, the space was redesigned, refurbished, and redecorated into "proper" offices—all of them now dumping their inhabitants out into hallways leading them inconspicuously away from colleagues and students. Architecture carries values! Hewlett-Packard was one of the first companies to address this side of culture in an intentional way. H-P eliminated traditional private offices (even for executives) and built an open, cubicle environment in which people would find it nearly impossible to avoid interacting and sharing ideas. Private meetings could be held in offices set aside for such uses. Of course, cubicles can, Dilbert-style, serve in negative ways also. The point, I repeat, is to recognize that these choices of physical setting and equipment are not neutral; they are deeply embedded with values. Make sure they are the ones you really want.

Tools and equipment are part of the picture also. Some offices and organizations allow employees to use whatever software packages they prefer. Others are intentional about building IT platforms that facilitate file-sharing, communication, and teamwork. Some companies provide their employees cell phones or automobiles or trucks to facilitate the kind of travel and communication they value in their organization. Other companies have similar expectations but don't provide an infrastructure that carries and promotes these values.

> *The building, office set-up, furnishings, IT system, software, landscaping, decoration, and so on, all carry and proclaim core values, whether we like it or not. This material infrastructure empowers—or undermines—our mission and our ethics.*

2. Structures, Policies, and Procedures. The organizational chart along with company policies and procedures comprise a second aspect of culture. Do the org chart and compensation system shout "hierarchy, elitism, and class division"—or "equality, collegiality, and team"? Do our policies say that ethics and human values are important—or just the financial bottom line? What behaviors do they reward? Are all rewards and compensation given to individuals—or is teamwork and group accomplishment encouraged by our system? Are power and responsibility highly centralized—or widely distributed? Do our policies (on hours, monitoring, reporting, etc.) say "trust"—or "distrust"? If someone just looked at our budget, what values would it say to them?

The old Hewlett-Packard, followed by several other companies, pioneered a flexible hours approach where employees had latitude to come early, leave early or come later, stay later, as their lifestyles, commute patterns, and work requirements all combined to suggest. Lincoln Electric has been very egalitarian, communitarian even, in physical setting (no perks for executive offices, etc.) . . . but individualistic on compensation (bonuses for individual production, penalties for defective motors returned, traceable to you). A college I served had a policy of all faculty committees rotating membership and leadership at least every three years. Democratic, perhaps, but random, incoherent, and ineffective by assigning people to positions in which they had little interest and no particular, relevant ability. Structures, policies, and procedures are deeply value-laden aspects of an organizational culture.

> *Organizational charts, structures, policies, and procedures, including compensation and budget patterns, express concretely to everyone what and who is valued.*

3. Personnel. The third component of corporate culture is the people in our company. This refers not just to executive leadership but to boards of directors, mid-level managers, and all other employees. Of course, the educational backgrounds, intellectual skills, and work experiences play large in defining the company culture. But so too do our varied personalities, cultural, social, ethnic, national, sexual, linguistic, religious/philosophical, and age characteristics. These characteristics of our personnel, our varied attitudes and temperaments, and (most profoundly) our personal character and values are critical factors in building a corporate culture. In *Good to Great*, author Jim Collins urges the importance of "getting the right people on the bus" (and the wrong ones off).[4]

For example, if your business mission requires scientific and mathematical brilliance—or great diplomatic, persuasive people skills—or a generous dose of humor, joyfulness, and a positive attitude—we had better recruit for these characteristics. If a core value of our company is "fun" (like at Southwest Airlines), it will not happen if we hire mostly sour people, no matter what our architecture or reward systems! A manager might get an honors grade in an MBA program—but be totally ineffective as a leader of people. It's not just about grades and degrees and head knowledge. Personal character and temperament are a critical component in building an organizational culture.

> *Personal character and temperament are a critical component in corporate culture. Hiring for "cultural fit" is critically important.*

4. The Informal Culture. Finally, we come to the "informal" culture of the company. For some commentators it seems like this is all they mean by "culture." I urge a more comprehensive perspective that pays attention to the preceding three aspects as well. But we must not fail to notice how important this fourth aspect is. It includes the "atmosphere" of the company, its habits, "style," rituals, folklore, and tradition. How are meetings conducted, decisions made, visitors greeted, communications given, disagreements handled, successes celebrated, and personal tragedies supported? Every organization develops a sort of informal culture around these activities and passages. Some companies sing, others exercise. Some joke a lot, others are pretty straight-laced and controlled.

Hewlett-Packard used to have company picnics where Bill and Dave flipped burgers for everyone. Harris & Associates has a "Harris Fest" every year-and-a-half or so, bringing together as many of their 500 employees from around the Western USA as possible. It's fun, it's great to learn what others are doing in the company, it's got an educational component. Most of all it is a distinctive company ritual and a cultural festival. Gill's Fitness in San Diego pays great attention to the way its personal trainers dress on the job and the way they speak to their clients—there are important values embedded in these choices.

Four Aspects of Corporate Culture
1. *Physical (architecture, office set-up, decoration, equipment, etc.)*
2. *Organizational (structures, systems, policies, etc.)*
3. *Personnel (skills, backgrounds, character, temperament, etc.)*
4. *Informal (rituals, traditions, atmosphere, etc.)*

How Culture Relates to Mission and Vision

Remember the basics: A company or organization comes together in order to carry out some common *mission* (purpose) and achieve together a *vision*. The culture (physical, organizational, personnel, and informal aspects) either enables and empowers the achievement of that mission and vision—or it undermines, impedes, and frustrates that mission. Having an inappropriate (or ugly) office or laboratory set-up, idiotic policies, divisive and incompetent personnel, and a toxic atmosphere are the kinds of things that undo the best of purposes.

So the critical question is, What traits, habits, capacities, and "style" will help us achieve our mission? What structures and traits will impede or frustrate mission? A careful study of our company mission will tell us what we need. As Aristotelian philosophy says, if the purpose of a knife is to cut, the primary trait of a good knife will be sharpness (not shininess or some other irrelevant trait). And if the purpose of our team is to win football games, the core traits we need to build into our people and systems will be things like speed, power, durability, flexibility, team spirit, coachability, and so on (not physical cuteness or good table manners).

What is our company's mission and vision? Then, what are the handful of key traits needed throughout our culture in order to achieve these objectives? That's the question.

Two kinds of value-challenged cultures are often seen in today's business world. The *accidental* culture is one that has not been intentionally created, but has haphazardly evolved. It is weak, adrift, patchwork, thoughtless, and unintentional. The *misaligned* culture is one that may be strong but is in conflict with the mission and core values. For example, the reward systems may all focus on individuals—while teamwork is critical to the success of the company. Or the computer systems or office set-up may be inadequate for the sort of information sharing that is essential to achieve the vision. Or the environmental stewardship commitment is undermined by our gas-guzzling company auto fleet.

What we are looking for is a *value-embedded culture*. This is a culture where someone is paying attention to the physical set-up to be sure the building, the office set-up, the computer system, etc., is going to empower the activities central to the mission. Systems, policies and procedures empower and encourage mission-fulfilling behavior. Personnel are recruited for their missional fit, where their personal career ambitions and dreams align with the company's mission and vision. And leaders pay attention to the atmosphere. Jim Collins and Jerry Porras use the phrase "cult-like cultures" to describe what they found in the exemplary companies of their *Built to Last*.

Three Possibilities for Our Corporate Cultures
1. *Accidental cultures*—*ignored, haphazard, thoughtless; irrelevant to mission*
2. *Misaligned*—*strong but toxic and out of sync; undermines mission*
3. *Value-embedded*—*healthy, intentional, empowering, aligned*

Core Values and Culture

We will use a common term—values—to describe the most basic, core, fundamental traits needed in a successful mission-controlled organization. In moral philosophy it is more precise to call these "virtues" or "traits," but we'll stick with the common terminology of "core values." Our core values are the essential characteristics, habits, and orientations, the basic capacities and inclinations we want to see embedded in our culture, in all four of its components. "Values" are things having "worth"—the things worth embedding in every part of our company (not just some parts, some times). Our values are our standards for evaluating our office set-up, compensation policies, hiring decisions, and atmosphere. If our company culture is thoroughly guided and permeated by values that are key to helping us achieve our vision and fulfill our mission, we will be on our way to ethics and excellence.

Here are three great examples of well-chosen core values in alignment with their respective corporate mission/visions—from an upscale, local grocery store, to a venerable global clothing merchant, and a successful young Silicon Valley hi-tech firm. In the previous chapter we saw that the mission of Paradise Foods is "to provide high quality food in a pleasant atmosphere where employees enjoy their work and customers enjoy their shopping." Their vision is "to be the best market in Marin County." Here are the six pairs of core values they embed in every part of their organization and operation in order to achieve that mission/vision. Notice that certain values are especially critical in a food-handling business.

<u>Paradise Foods: Our Core Values</u>

1. Respect & Care. Employees, customers, and all others we interact with deserve to be treated with respect. Taking the next step and showing care and service to others lifts us beyond the competition.

2. Excellence & Quality. Not mediocrity but excellence and superior quality in all of our products, services, and operations is our standard.

3. Honesty & Integrity. Telling the truth is always our policy. Taking responsibility for our products and actions and acting with complete integrity is essential.

4. Cleanliness & Aesthetics. Cleanliness everywhere in our store and among our staff, with special concern to maintain the highest standards in sanitary food storage and display are critical requirements. A beautiful, enjoyable shopping environment is a distinctive we pursue.

5. Safety & Security. The safety and security of our customers as well as our employees is a non-negotiable requirement.

6. Family & Personal Life. Human life is more than working and shopping. Our policies and business practices encourage balanced, healthy lives with time for family, friends, and personal interests.

Levi Strauss's mission and vision are inspiring and challenging: "People love our clothes and trust our company. We will market the most appealing and widely worn casual clothing in the world. We will clothe the world." The popularity of Levi's blue denim jeans and their Dockers line of casual clothing are good evidence that their mission and vision have worked. But it is not easy to figure out what people want to wear and then work in the manufacturing, political, social, and ethical minefields of today's textile industry. You can see why the following four core values are precisely chosen to enable their missional success.

> **Levi Strauss Core Values**
> *Empathy—Walking in Other People's Shoes*
> *Originality—Being Authentic and Innovative*
> *Integrity—Doing the Right Thing*
> *Courage—Standing Up for What We Believe*

Finally, consider Xilinx, a "best place to work" Silicon Valley powerhouse. The mission of Xilinx is "to help our customers attain the fastest time-to-market and flexible product life cycle management through programmable logic solutions consisting of software, silicon and support." To help all Xilinx people remember them, these core values have been arranged so that they build the vertical acronym "Creative" to the left—a critical aspect of their mission.

> **Xilinx Core Values**
> **Customer Focused.** *We exist only because our customers are satisfied and want to do business with us . . . and we never forget it!*
> **Respect.** *We value all people, treating them with dignity at all times.*
> **Excellence.** *We strive for "Best in Class" in everything we do.*
> **Accountability.** *We do what we say we will do and expect the same from others.*
> **Teamwork.** *We believe that cooperative action produces superior results.*
> **Integrity.** *We are honest with ourselves, each other, our customers, our partners and our shareholders.*
> **Very Open Communication.** *We share information, ask for feedback, acknowledge good work, and encourage diverse ideas.*
> **Enjoying Our Work.** *We work hard, are rewarded for it, and maintain a good sense of perspective, humor and enthusiasm.*

Two Special Challenges to Today's Culture Builders

Two important new factors are challenging—and assisting—today's corporate culture builders. The first has to do with the changes to our work lives brought by technology, especially information technology. Books titles like "culture.com" describe the replacement of face-to-face relationships with electronic ones. Information (and other) technology has ratcheted up the speed and intensity of life (making it harder to establish trust as well as tradition). The sheer scale and amount of information we must confront sometimes undermines our culture building. Quantity can trump quality. Impersonality, transience, and novelty deeply affect our work lives.

On the other hand, technology also allows us to stay in closer touch, via e-mail, cell phones, teleconferences (to say nothing of air travel, mass transit, etc.). Technology provides access to rich troves of insight and information. Technology enables those who can't make a certain face to face meeting to have the next best thing—instant access to distance learning or an asynchronous discussion. On balance it seems the pros outweigh the cons, and in any case there is no turning back. The critical caution is to ensure that there is at least enough deep (usually face to face) contact to build trust and context in support of the other more extended electronic communications and to never forget that time, reflection, silence, nuance, personal conversation, rest, and the like (i.e., non-technical aspects of relationships and communication) are essential components of life and work. We want wise strategy, human health, relational success, etc.—not just quantifiable technical progress.

The other new factor, enabled by technology, is globalization. Globalization means that our corporate cultures are now far-flung and extended over vast distances. *Globalization* means that our businesses are spreading out around the whole world. The counterpart is *diversity*: The whole world is coming to our office and town. People are brought together with huge differences in language, culture, and personal values. Often this is a challenge to overcome—e.g., working with people who believe in restricting women to certain roles and no other, clashes over manners and dress, different concepts of property and compensation fairness, etc.

But diversity also has a huge potential upside. Multiple perspectives help illuminate problems. Al Erisman used to tell me that as Director of IT Research at Boeing he (and his colleagues) discovered that even when it came to technical and mathematical problems, a roomful of men and women from different nationalities and cultures, different ages and experiences, could solve problems better and faster than a roomful of only bright guys from Harvard (I'm not sure that was his exact phrasing, but you get the idea: Diversity is an asset in technology and mathematical problem solving as elsewhere).

Pay attention to these cultural challenges, work hard on communication, be careful to mitigate or avoid misunderstandings and damages, and exploit their upside potential in a mission-controlled, value-embedded fashion.

Drawing the Blueprint for a Value-Embedded Culture

As with each of the six components of an ethically healthy organization, there are four basic processes here. The first phase of the culture-building process is to identify—figure out, describe—what the core values are that will best enable our company to fulfill its mission. For this process to succeed, it is essential to involve the actual culture-builders and culture-tenders of the company. That means not just top executive leadership but managers of functional units, branch offices, and teams. These are the culture-tenders of the company. Top executive leadership always remains the guardian and herald of the mission and vision. But the core values clarification and culture-building challenge cannot be defined and executed by top management alone. The task must be carried by management at all levels.

> *Managers—the culture tenders of the organization—need to be involved at every step of the core values and corporate culture-building process. They need to own it. The company needs their experience and wisdom. No top executive or outside consultant can do the managers' job on this project.*

Through a combination of in-person meetings, discussions, and intensive individual communication (probably mostly by e-mail in our era), managers need to be presented with the project to identify (and later implement) the handful of core values. First, roll out the mission and vision to them—and then ask what are the four to eight key values that will help achieve that mission and vision? What are the basic traits and characteristics we should embed in our architecture and physical set-up, equipment, organizational structure and policies, hiring practices, and informal traditions and rituals?

If your company already has a statement of core values but it is time for a review, I would still pose the question a similar way: "In light of our mission and vision, is this current set of core values really on target? Or should we modify or strengthen it in some way?"

My preferred way of identifying the core values at a company is for executive leadership to bring most or all of their managers to one location for a two-hour or so values clarification exercise (possibly as part of a larger management meeting or off-site strategy session). After the CEO or meeting chair draws attention to the corporate mission and vision, and after hearing a brief explanation of what culture and core values are all about, the managers present are given the worksheet below (or some customized version of the same).[5] They are then asked to review individually, for ten (or so) minutes, a list of fifty (or so) commonly stated corporate cultural "values" and circle a few that seem to be especially characteristic of their company—or truly *ought* to be if the company is to achieve its vision.

130   *It's About Excellence*

After this solo work, they are asked to compare lists in groups of four or so, for twenty minutes, and try to come up with a consensus list of four to eight core values. Finally, in a large group setting, a member of each small breakout group rises to share briefly their consensus list and perhaps a brief thought on the topic of core values in the company. The consultant or coordinator of the values identification process collects the consensus statements, takes notes on the discussion, and then drafts a working statement of core values. When similar concepts and terms are widely affirmed (e.g., lots of votes for "excellence" and "quality"), one of the two words might be used as the key term and the other in a descriptive phrase used to define that term.

The emergent working list of core values needs to be bounced off a committee of managers and executives (with some additional committee members chosen for their wisdom, language skills, and other potential insights). The values committee reviews and amends the working document until it is confident that it is getting very close to what is required. Then it is circulated out to all managers with a request for their affirmation and/or suggested changes. Their feedback goes into a near-final revision. It is important not to go public until the company at large has a chance to respond and make suggestions—but it is the managers (culture builders and tenders) who drive and own this process.

Gill's Core Values Worksheet

In order to carry out its mission with excellence . . . in order to pursue and achieve its vision . . . what are the four or six or eight core (central, defining) characteristics/traits that must be embedded in every part of our organization, every geographic area, every person hired, every project, every policy? What have been our defining characteristics and values up to now, that have helped us become what we are? What are the most important characteristics to have in the people we hire?

First, take about five minutes to circle any of the values listed below that seem to be of core importance for our company as you have come to understand and know it? Add some terms at the bottom if the list is missing something important.

Second, compare your choices with those of the others in your breakout group and then come up with a "top four" or "top six" company core values list you can all agree on.

loyalty	passion, dedication	commitment
openness, receptivity	humility, service	teachable, learning, listening
responsibility	accountability	
freedom	creativity, innovation	responsiveness
opportunity	entrepreneurial	growth
integrity	fairness, justice	flexibility, originality
excellence, quality	effectiveness, efficiency	ethics
wisdom	stewardship	reliability, dependability
profitability	stability	environmental concern
generosity	caring, empathy	security
honesty	trust, trustworthy	tolerance
teamwork	mutual respect, diversity	transparency
courage	persistence	collaboration
fun, happiness	excitement	adventure, joy
family	casual, informal	open communication

_____   _____   _____

_____   _____   _____

Our Top Six List of Company Values:

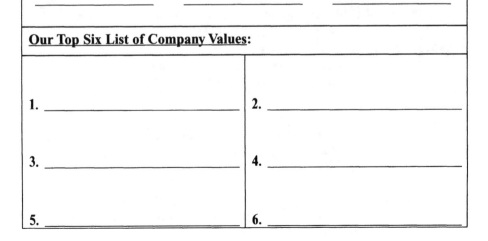

1. _____

2. _____

3. _____

4. _____

5. _____

6. _____

Part of the research process ought to also include a review of what other companies in the same or similar industries have articulated as their core values. Perhaps some admired companies in other industries should be studied also. We want all the help we can get, though in the end we must boldly choose what is right for our particular context. We cannot just adopt someone else's beautiful statement. Our core values must be organically related to our history, mission, and vision and created and owned by our culture builders.

Out of this kind of process, here is what the culture tenders came up with at Harris & Associates, the growing, successful, thirty-year old construction and project management firm based in Concord, CA, we have looked at in previous chapters. Harris's mission is "Helping clients, employees, and communities succeed through industry-leading management and consulting services." Their vision is to be "the excellence and integrity leader among management and consulting companies." As consulting engineers and project managers aiming for that mission and vision, here are the core values they identified in the company culture, and to which they commit themselves.

Harris & Associates Core Values
In carrying out our mission and pursuing our vision, we are shaped and guided by six core values:

Integrity: "Doing the right thing"
   We are about honesty, fairness, and responsibility, about consistently living out our values and principles with uncompromising integrity and ethics.

Quality: "Doing things right"
   We have a passion for excellence and high standards, for industry-leading innovation, expertise, and effective performance.

Reliability: "You can count on us"
   We do what we say—and we stand behind what we do—with accountability, responsiveness, and follow-through, from project start to project finish.

Respect: "Everyone is important"
   We value and respect every member of our team—whatever their role—and each of our clients, business partners, and communities.

> *Teamwork: "Working better together"*
> *We team with each other and our clients to meet challenges and then share the success. It's about collaboration, approachability, good listening, and sharing ideas.*
>
> *Fun: "More than just a job"*
> *We enjoy our work and our fellow workers, experiencing personal freedom, creativity, and growth in a "family" atmosphere of mutual support and celebration.*

The ethics consultant helped organize and push the process from start to completion, and strengthened and finessed the English expression. But the basic, core ideas came from the hearts, minds, and experiences of the managers. No surprise then that everybody at Harris loves the statement and says, "That's us!"

Basic Training: Building Cultural-Ethical Muscle

What happens next is to *educate* or train not just the managers but everyone in the company so that everyone knows what the core values are and how to define their meaning. After we draw the blueprint, we all study and become completely familiar with it. Like the mission and vision, the core values need and deserve constant exposure. In company literature, on wall posters, perhaps even on company stationary, put the core values (in their short form, not with all the explanation). Some companies make a little plastic card with the values imprinted for employees to carry around (maybe with a calendar—or some helpful phone numbers—or the mission and vision—on the other side). One of the best strategies is to put the core value terms on a coffee cup. Make sure it is a functional cup (not a decorative, useless item) so that employees will actually want to have it on their desk and use it. Give the cups away. In fact, giving them to business partners, clients and customers, with company logo and contact info also on the cup, could be a terrific way to publicize the company and to make sure everyone knows what you stand for.

A great way to teach the meaning of these core values is for the company president or CEO to write a series of short columns or articles in the company newsletter (or in a series of e-mails if there is no regular newsletter). Write a short essay on each value, defining the value term and then illustrating it with a story or two of how that value has been lived out by someone or some team within the company. Praise these company examples of living by the values. Employees, in general, look in newsletters for names they know, feel pride in their company and colleagues, and want management recognition and approval themselves. Harris & Associates recently invited employee-written limericks and short videos on company core values; the best submissions would be featured at the company-wide Harris Fest. The core values do no good unless everyone knows them and understands them.

Living It Out Consistently

The third process is to *implement* the core values in the culture. Practice what you preach—or stop preaching it. Teach those great values, then put them in practice. For every value, we must be able to point to various concrete examples of it being practiced. We must find ways to act out every value—or drop the value from our list. Implementation means making appropriate changes to our office set-up, equipment, our systems, policies, procedures, and rewards, our hiring and promotion practices (preferring those who exemplify the values), and creatively tweaking our informal cultural rituals and atmosphere. We must ruthlessly eliminate any misalignments and any unjustified or anti-core-value systems, personnel, and traditions.

> *For every value, we must be able to point to various examples of it being practiced. We must find ways to act out every value—or drop the value from our list.*

Regular Health Check-Ups Are Essential

The final process is to *evaluate* our core values and cultural health. If we don't pay attention and carefully audit or assess our cultural values and health, we can easily fool ourselves—and fooling leads to failing. Managers evaluating employee performance need to put in a category for values and ethics and assess how each employee has lived out or contributed to each of the core values of the company in the past year—and make an action plan for how to do even better in the coming year. Executives and board members need to provide each other such evaluation. Focus groups and discussions and an outside values audit by a consultant might help once in a while (if they understand the process and the company, which many will not). Every year or two, all employees should complete a survey like the following one, to evaluate the company itself and its leadership. Inviting such a frank assessment will do great things for morale and will provide great insight, on the basis of which reforms can be made.

Gill's Culture & Core Values Company Audit

Does our company have a strong, healthy, core-value-embedded culture and structure that aligns with our core mission and vision?	Strongly Disagree 1	2	3	4	Strongly Agree 5
1. Our organizational core values are clearly defined and explained and are well-known within our company.	❑	❑	❑	❑	❑
2. Our core values are right on target about who we are—and who we need to be—to fulfill our mission and achieve our vision.	❑	❑	❑	❑	❑
3. Our company does a good job of orienting/training its people in the cultural values and style of the company.	❑	❑	❑	❑	❑
4. Our architecture, office set-up, and equipment are good expressions of our core values, and they help us achieve our mission and vision.	❑	❑	❑	❑	❑
5. Our organization chart, systems, procedures, and policies (including our compensation system) are good expressions of our core values and help us achieve our mission.	❑	❑	❑	❑	❑
6. Our company selectively recruits and hires people with a "tight fit" to its core values and culture—and eliminates those who don't fit.	❑	❑	❑	❑	❑
7. Our work environment and informal atmosphere conform to our core values and contribute to the success and fulfillment of our core mission.	❑	❑	❑	❑	❑
8. Our most successful managers are good at building up a healthy organizational culture that exhibits our core values.	❑	❑	❑	❑	❑
9. Our culture helps both employees and managers to operate in an ethical manner, i.e., to stay within the law, to treat one another right, and do the right thing.	❑	❑	❑	❑	❑

Can you list the core values of our culture?:

1. _____

2. _____

3. _____

4. _____

5. _____

Comments on our company culture and core values:

Afterthought: Core Values, Ethical & Otherwise

When we defined ethical right and wrong earlier (Chapter 1), a distinction was made between "harm" and "offense." Ethics is about potential and actual harm; offense is about manners, customs, and etiquette. This is a very important distinction and criterion for ethics.

However, when we turn to the core values of an ethically healthy culture, we have to think more broadly than just about narrowly ethical, traditional concepts like integrity, honesty, fairness, and safety. The core values also may include things like teamwork, balance, imagination, precision, and even fun. Why is the conceptual net thrown out more broadly at this point?

The answer is that the culture provides the capacity, the "muscle," the ability to do what is (more narrowly and precisely) ethical. For example, without imagination and creativity we may fail to see an opportunity to apply our ethical principles in an optimum way. Without teamwork and some fun, we may suffer from "ethics fatigue" and bail out on an ethical obligation.

Aristotle's ethics—and the ethical teaching in the book of Proverbs—both show this pattern of weaving together narrowly ethical values and counsels with challenges to have a good sense of humor, work hard, take some time off, etc. It all fits together. And in our own ordinary experience we know that being a successful parent or coach is more than just a matter of sticking narrowly to some plan and strategy—success in these domains requires a sense of humor, creativity, and other virtues.

Thus, our core values as individuals and as organizations need to be thought of in larger, more inclusive terms than just the traditional vocabulary of moral philosophy.

For Reflection or Discussion

1. If an outside observer were to study our company culture for a few days, what would be the five most important characteristics (or "values") he or she would detect in our operations and structures?

2. What are the *stated* core values in our company? What *should* be our core values in order to empower both business excellence and business ethics?

3. What are my most important, tenaciously held *personal values*? How do these complement—or contradict—the values of my company? How do I deal with any contradiction here?

Exercises

1. Go on the web and take a look at the core values statements of a couple competitors in our industry and a couple other admired companies. Any takeaways or lessons for our company?

2. Ask three or four managers in your company which of our stated core values are most clearly practiced and "embedded" in our company, and for some examples. Then ask which of the stated values are *least* practiced and embedded in the culture, and how things could improve.

Resources for Further Study

Ken Blanchard and Michael O'Conner's little fable-based *Managing by Values* (Berrett-Koehler, 1997) may look like light reading, but it is right on target and thick with good ideas and practical suggestions for building value-embedded business cultures. Jim Collins's *Good to Great* (HarperBusiness, 2001) offers some important help on culture, but his collaboration with Jerry Porras, *Built to Last* (HarperBusiness, 1994) is essential reading on this topic.

Terrence E. Deal and Allan A. Kennedy, *Corporate Cultures: The Rites and Rituals of Corporate Life* (Addison-Wesley, 2000) deserve credit for naming, highlighting, and analyzing "corporate culture" in a way that really changed the way we look at business organizations. This is still a valuable read, as is Deal and Kennedy's follow-up, *The New Corporate Cultures: Revitalizing the Workplace after Downsizing, Mergers, and Reengineering* (Perseus Publishing, 1999). John P. Kotter and James L. Heskett, *Corporate Culture and Performance* (Free Press, 1992); Rob Goffee and Gareth Jones, *The Character of a Corporation* (HarperBusiness, 1998); and Richard S. Gallagher, *The Soul of an Organization: Understanding the Values That Drive Successful Corporate Cultures* (Dearborn Trade Publishing, 2003), each add something to the subject. Peg Neuhauser, Ray Bender, and Kirk Stromberg, *Culture.com: Building Corporate Culture in the Connected Workplace* (John Wiley & Sons, 2000) addresses a critical change in the cultural challenge. Frankly, however, most of the books by the experts view culture too narrowly as an affair of values and beliefs expressed in rites and rituals, incarnated in heroes, and reinforced through stories. The material and structural/policy aspects of culture are underplayed or ignored, and yet these are integral to the phenomenon itself.

One of the best ways to get at organizational culture is to read about specific companies. A wonderful recent book is Raj Sisodia, David B. Wolfe, and Jag Sheth, *Firms of Endearment* (Wharton, 2007) which describes twenty or so, distinctively great and successful companies. Some other good resources are

David Packard's *The HP Way: How Bill Hewlett and I Built Our Company* (HarperBusiness, 1995); C. William Pollard's *The Soul of the Firm* (about ServiceMaster) (HarperBusiness, 1996); Kevin & Jackie Freiberg's *Nuts: Southwest Airlines' Crazy Recipe for Business and Personal Success* (Broadway Books, 1996); Jody Hoffer Gittell's *The Southwest Airlines Way* (McGraw-Hill, 2003); Howard Schultz & Dori Jones Yang's *Pour Your Heart into It: How Starbucks Built a Company One Cup at a Time* (Hyperion, 1997); Jeffrey K. Liker's *The Toyota Way: Fourteen Management Principles from the World's Greatest Manufacturer* (McGraw-Hill, 2004); Len Lewis's *The Trader Joe's Adventure: Turning a Unique Approach to Business into a Retail and Cultural Phenomenon* (Dearborn Trade, 2005); Dennis W. Bakke's *Joy at Work: A Revolutionary Approach to Fun on the Job* (about AES) (PVG, 2005); and Bo Burlingham's *Small Giants: Companies That Choose to Be Great Instead of Big* (Penguin/Portfolio, 2005).

NOTES

[1] In ethics, I have always reminded my students, it isn't just "do" (the right thing) or just "be" (a good person or company)—it's "do-be-do-be-do" This chapter is about the "be" stuff; the next chapter is about the "do" stuff.

[2] Louis V. Gerstner, *Who Says Elephants Can't Dance?* (HarperBusiness, 2002).

[3] Jim Collins and Jerry Porras, *Built to Last: Successful Habits of Visionary Companies* (HarperBusiness, 1994), Chapter Eight, pp. 115-139.

[4] Jim Collins, *Good to Great* (HarperBusiness, 2001), pp. 41-45.

[5] Ken Blanchard and Michael O'Connor inspired my version of a core values worksheet with theirs in their *Managing by Values* (Berrett-Koehler, 1997), p. 112.

Chapter 6

Playbook Genius:
Principle-Guided Business Practices

Executive Summary

Finally, in this chapter, we get to the code of ethics. It is easy to go wrong here, so we need to proceed carefully. The first thing to do is to map out the practices of the organization and its employees. How do we spend our time? What, specifically, do we do each day to contribute to the mission and the goals of this company? We must also note any areas of possible future temptation and past failure. Once that mapping is accomplished we must write down some basic guidelines for how best to carry out these tasks that occupy our time. What guidelines will keep us on track and get it done "our way"? What guidelines will warn us away from trouble in this or that activity? What guidelines apply to all employees? What guidelines are just for particular areas? How can we make sure our code feels positive, not scolding and negative? How do we get our whole workforce involved in writing, revising, and utilizing our code? Worksheets, code examples, and an audit form are part of the discussion.

Our practices are the basic things we do in our business. Culture is what we *are*; practices are what we *do*. One is about being, the other about doing. Of course, they are interdependent. "Mission" is the umbrella action term, the essential, common theme running through all of our activities, all of our "doing." Carrying out our business practices is the way we fulfill our mission. If any activity cannot be seen as a value-adding piece of the mission, it is a waste of time and resources. In a similar way, our culture is the present expression of our vision. It may be only a partial fulfillment of our vision, but it must align with, and be a sort of down payment on, or anticipation of, that envisioned future. Our culture and vision are about what we are and will be.

139

Back to our business practices. The first exercise is to map them out. How are we spending our time? Our general practices (that all of our people engage in) would include things like meeting, communicating, and decision-making; our specialized practices (that some of our people engage in) might include marketing, research, and accounting. Different companies, different practices. Our particular mission determines what activities or practices are appropriate.

Every employee and every business unit needs to map its practices and check its map for accuracy from time to time. All the roads on the map need to lead to the destination (the vision). Even aside from any particular concern about ethics, this mapping exercise is good management. We may find, for example, that our sales representatives are spending three-quarters of their time shuffling paper and one-quarter meeting with potential buyers—when we thought it was the opposite. Practice-mapping is an important exercise.

> ***The first task is to map out the practices of the organization: How do we spend our time? Let's develop a comprehensive description of what we do here.***

The ethics side of our practices is about providing guidelines for *how we do the things we do.* Several terms can be used for such guidelines; we will interchangeably use "rules," "principles," and "guidelines." A principle/rule/guideline here is a "process value"—an action-guide, indicating what to do. Such principles have two basic functions. First, they delineate "boundaries"—ways we should *not* act. "Do not go here," they tell us. "This is not how we do this activity." Second, principles articulate "mandates"—positive guidelines, ways we *should* act. "This is how we do it here." "Always do it this way," etc.

Company guidelines are usually gathered into a *code of conduct or code of ethics*—a comprehensive collection of the organization's guidelines on "how to do the right thing here." Company codes of ethics typically have some *general* guidelines or principles that cover all activities, practices and decisions. They also typically have some *specific* guidelines for certain business activities. Examples of such general principles would be, "Do unto others as you would like done to you," "Do what results in the greatest good for the greatest number (utilitarianism)," and "Treat everyone with respect." Examples of specific principles might be, "Do not take credit for the ideas of others," "Do not conceal negative product test results," and "Always acknowledge business-related e-mails in a timely way."

Let's think back to Chapter One in which we reviewed six basic criteria for figuring out what's ethically right or wrong. The second item on the list was "company and professional codes of ethics." The point of that list in Chapter One was to ask, "How can we get started on our ethics questions and concerns?" and "Is there any way we could find some common ground?" Now, in Chapter Six, we are asking how to build the best possible contribution to that second item on the list. What we will see is that a great code of ethics is pointed toward fulfilling the company mission with excellence, but it cannot do that job unless it respects the other five criteria for ethics (i.e., respecting the law, trying to honor people's consciences and personal values, observing the Golden Rule, passing the "publicity test," and avoiding serious harm to others).

> *Ethical principles (or "rules") are our guidelines for "how we do the things we do." Gathered into a coherent whole (a "code of conduct/ethics") they establish (negative) __boundaries__ ("Don't do it this way," "Don't go here")—and (positive) __mandates__ ("Always do it __this__ way"). A good code covers all the important operational activities— and is more positive than negative in tone.*

Mission + Culture + Practices: A Three-Legged Stool

A three-legged stool doesn't fall over. One or two legs won't do it. In business, mission, culture, and practices are the three-legged stool. Each one needs the other two. Let's go back to the football metaphor: The first and fundamental task is to get the mission and vision straight and to make sure it drives and controls the organization. Second, we ask, "What kind of people do we need to be (our character) and what kind of organization do we need to build (our culture) in order to succeed in that mission?" For football, the desired traits will include strength, toughness, teamwork, speed, flexibility, etc. The third task is to design the actual plays to stop the opponent and to advance the ball into the end zone (our code of conduct/ethics).

Believing you can win the championship and making that everyone's goal and focus is the first task of great coaches (and CEOs). The second task is to recruit good players and build a winning organization with the conditioning and character to achieve greatness. The third task is to design brilliant and effective plays for the offense and defense. If the coach is a great "rah-rah" inspiration but does nothing else, he won't last long and the team will be routinely slaughtered by opponents. If the coach works on conditioning but not the play book—or on the play book but not conditioning—the mission will still not be a success. Without good plays—just improvising as they go along—even the most inspired and best conditioned team will be slow and ineffective; without good conditioning, however, even the most brilliant plays cannot be run effectively. It's a three-legged stool.

The San Francisco 49ers were led by one of the greatest football coaches in history, Bill Walsh, for ten seasons starting in 1979. Walsh's 49ers won three SuperBowls, after the 1981, 1984, and 1988 seasons. Walsh and his team certainly got their mission straight and built a powerful organizational culture, with the right people on the bus, including stars like Joe Montana, Steve Young, Jerry Rice, and Ronnie Lott, but also dozens of terrific position players. But *a propos* to this chapter, it was in Walsh's "playbook genius" that his greatness became most obvious. Walsh's "West Coast" offense could defeat any rival, especially the "mad bomber" relics of the past.

The 49ers had some of the greatest players of all time but a few legendary players can't win Super Bowls all by themselves. Bill Walsh's playbook genius was the final key. So too in business, even a strong culture with an inspiring mission and vision cannot be successful if it has weak or ambiguous principles and guidelines. A weak ethics "playbook" means the company will be slow and inefficient when facing ethical challenges. Without good ethical principles, business decisions may be guided only by legal, financial, technical, traditional, or other considerations.

As suggested by the stool analogy, the code of conduct/ethics will be more persuasive if it is explicitly associated with the mission/vision, and core values "legs." Practically speaking, it is best to publish them together in one document and not let the Code of Ethics float off separately from mission/vision, and core values. An introductory letter from the CEO can outline the basic motivational argument (why we take ethics seriously here; see Chapter Two), and this can be followed by the mission/vision statements, the core values, and then the code of ethics.

The Code of Ethics is one leg of a three-legged stool. Without the mission/vision leg and the culture/values leg, it totters on its on. Try to keep all three together in company publications, training programs, and in management strategy.

Ethical Guidelines: General and Specific, Positive and Negative

In detailing out the ethical guidelines of an organization there is a lot of latitude. One cautionary note has already been alluded to: Be sure to "cover the field," i.e., be comprehensive in outlook. Some codes of ethics have long, detailed guidelines for office relationships and sexual harassment, with perhaps another big section on use of office equipment for personal reasons. But really, are those addressing and guiding the great, core activities of the company? Let us hope not. So think broadly and comprehensively about the coverage of the code of ethics,

A second suggestion is to move as much of the company's ethical guidance into a general area as possible, leaving the specialized areas smaller. Many of a company's guidelines will, in fact, apply to everyone, and it unifies us as a team to have a larger, shared set of mandates (and boundaries).

The third suggestion is to state guidelines not just negatively but positively,. Here is an example (taken from my "Gill's Ten Principles," Appendix B in this book) of a lead-in mandate, follow-up boundary, positive/negative framing of an ethical guideline for organizational communication:

Communicate to others by name with respect.
Never use or impose demeaning, trivializing, or derogatory names on others.

The reason for doing this should be obvious. A predominantly negative "Thou shalt not" set of guidelines gives company ethics a negative, scolding tone and feel. It's like making all of your cooking instruction of the nature, "Don't burn yourself," "Don't use too much salt," and "Don't leave the kitchen a mess." Such cooking advice would hardly make someone want to go in and try to delight you with an orgasmic, gourmet experience. Of course, we must state some boundaries and negative "Don't go there" guidelines, but keep the overall message tilted to the positive. In fact, for some companies with ethics codes, this may be the best next step in strengthening your approach—to rewrite or augment your message with a more positive tone.

Here is another good example of the positive/negative balance—a death and dying ethical guideline from Swedish Covenant Hospital (Chicago), which didn't want to go on record as just *opposing* physician-assisted suicide. Notice that the fourth line establishes their boundary, but all the rest is a positive set of guidelines.

Swedish Covenant Hospital (Chicago) Ethical Guidelines

- *We affirm life as a sacred gift of God and offer our best efforts to heal and preserve the lives of our patients.*
- *We provide the best palliative measures we can to relieve the pain, discomfort and suffering of our patients.*
- *We offer spiritual care and counseling to patients and their families and friends to cope with dying and death.*
- *We do not act in any way intentionally to cause, assist, or accelerate the death of patients.*
- *Within this policy we respect the freedom and wishes expressed by patients and their families, personally or by means of Advance Directives (including Living Wills and Durable Power of Attorney for Health Care).*

Four Sample Codes of Ethics

Let's take a closer look at four sample codes of ethics.

Example 1: The Hippocratic Oath

The famous Hippocratic Oath for ancient Greek physicians is regarded as the first great code of professional ethics. The whole oath/code makes for a fascinating study, even including the opening and concluding sections that may strike modern people as strange. At the heart of this code are guidelines for five specific practices of physicians, though the practices are often implied rather than explicitly stated.

Hippocratic Oath (6th Century B.C.)

I swear by Apollo Physician and Asclepius and Hygieia and Panaceia and all the gods and goddesses, making them my witnesses, that I will fulfill according to my ability and judgment this oath and this covenant:

To hold him who has taught me this art as equal to my parents and to live my life in partnership with him, and if he is in need of money to give him a share of mine, and to regard his offspring as equal to my brothers in male lineage and to teach them this art—if they desire to learn it—without fee and covenant; to give a share of precepts and oral instruction and all the other learning to my sons and to the sons of him who has instructed me and to pupils who have signed the covenant and have taken an oath according to the medical law, but no one else.

I will apply dietetic measures for the benefit of the sick according to my ability and judgment; I will keep them from harm and injustice.

> *I will neither give a deadly drug to anybody who asked for it, nor will I make a suggestion to this effect. Similarly I will not give to a woman an abortive remedy. In purity and holiness I will guard my life and my art.*
>
> *I will not use the knife, not even on sufferers from stone, but will withdraw in favor of such men as are engaged in this work.*
>
> *Whatever houses I may visit, I will come for the benefit of the sick, remaining free of all intentional injustice, of all mischief and in particular of sexual relations with both female and male persons, be they free or slaves.*
>
> *What I may see or hear in the course of the treatment or even outside of the treatment in regard to the life of men, which on no account one must spread abroad, I will keep to myself, holding such things shameful to be spoken about.*
>
> *If I fulfill this oath and do not violate it, may it be granted to me to enjoy life and art, being honored with fame among all men for all time to come; if I transgress it and swear falsely, may the opposite of all this be my lot.*

The basic mission of a physician is to "benefit the sick." The overarching general principle is to keep patients from harm and injustice (a "boundary" principle) and benefit them through dietetic measures (a "mandate" principle). Then follow five specific practice areas (and guiding principles): (1) caring for the terminally ill (guideline: no euthanasia or physician-assisted suicide), (2) caring for the pregnant (guideline: no abortion), (3) tending patients desperate for surgery (principle: leave that for those with surgical expertise and training), (4) making house calls to vulnerable patients (principle: no sexual involvement), and (5) acquiring patient information (principle: absolute confidentiality). On first reading, the Hippocratic Oath may seem a bit odd and obscure, but on a careful re-read we can see that the mission is clear, a community of accountability is recognized, and guidelines are given for five basic practice areas.

Example 2: American Marketing Association

As a second example let's look at the American Marketing Association, formed by marketing people in recent decades to provide professional education, link together those in the marketing arena, and set professional and ethical standards for their vocation. Their exemplary statement (see the complete statement on the web) begins with three sets of general guidelines:

Regarding the Marketers' Professional Conduct, four general principles:
(1) follow basic rule of professional ethics: not knowingly to do harm;
(2) follow all applicable laws and regulations;
(3) be accurate about training and experience; and
(4) actively support, practice and promote this Code of Ethics.

Regarding Honesty and Fairness, uphold and advance the integrity, honor & dignity of the profession by:
   (1) Being honest (to all stakeholders);
   (2) Avoiding conflicts of interest; and
   (3) Having equitable fee schedules.

Regarding the Rights and Duties of Parties in the Marketing Exchange Process ensure that:
   (1) Products and services offered are safe;
   (2) Communications are not deceptive;
   (3) All parties have good faith (and intentions); and
   (4) Methods are provided for adjustment/redress.

These general principles are then followed by specific guidelines for five basic practice areas that marketing professionals find themselves doing—(1) product development/management, (2) promotions, (3) distribution, (4) pricing, and (5) marketing research. Again, we see a code of ethics flowing from a mission and a community, we see the general followed by specific guidelines, and we see how practice areas are mapped out, then given ethical guidance. Take a look at the complete statement on the web. It is a best practice model.

Example 3: Levi Strauss
A third example comes from big business: Levi Strauss is one of the great American companies and has been a leader in corporate ethics and social responsibility. In earlier chapters, we looked at Levi's mission, vision, and core values. A clothing company these days is almost always dependent on labor in other countries. The situation is ripe for the exploitation of workers. As a result, Levi's goes into considerable detail on its *Global Sourcing and Operating Guidelines.*

First, they articulate several *Country Assessment Guidelines* having to do with Health and Safety Conditions, the Human Rights Environment, the Legal System, and the Political, Economic and Social Environment. These are their ethical guidelines for deciding whether to do business in a given country.

Second, to decide on prospective business partner companies (within those countries that meet their country standards), Levi's details out several *Business Partner Terms of Engagement* having to do with Ethical Standards, Legal Requirements, Environmental Requirements, Community Involvement, and Employment Standards. This last section on employment standards gets very specific about Child Labor, Prison/Forced Labor, Disciplinary Practices, Working Hours, Wages and Benefits, Freedom of Association, Discrimination, and Health and Safety. Codes of ethics need to be drawn up in relation to the specific practices (and challenges) a given company is concerned with.

Example 4: Harris & Associates

Finally, here is the complete code of ethics for Harris & Associates, the thirty-plus-year-old, five hundred employee construction and project management firm in the San Francisco Bay Area we have looked at in earlier chapters. Notice how it is introduced, how the twelve general guidelines are given in simple form, then explained in a few phrases, and how specific guidelines are given for practices among three groups of their stakeholders. Notice how the first few general principles embrace other components on our initial list of six criteria for ethics (in Chapter One). Notice also the predominantly positive way these guidelines are stated.

Harris & Associates: Our Ethical Guidelines

1. Introduction

Our mission and vision describe *where* we are going as a company. Our core values describe *who* we are, the kind of organization we are building. Our ethical guidelines describe *"how* we do the things we do." Every Harris employee is expected to be familiar with these guidelines and comply with their provisions. Ethics at Harris is everybody's business. It is the responsibility of every employee to carry out their own work in an ethical manner, to report any questions or possible violations, and to suggest ways of improving this code and, more generally, the ethical health of our company.

2. General Principles and Guidelines

In addition to the more specific ethical guidelines which follow below (section 3) the following twelve general principles guide ethics at Harris, in all of our relations with clients, business partners, fellow employees, or anyone else. These guidelines supplement the policies and procedures outlined in the *Harris Personnel Policies Manual*.

Never knowingly do harm.
• *Follow this basic, historic, first rule of professional ethics at all times.*
Comply with applicable laws and regulations.
• *Observe the legal ground rules of our society and marketplace (e.g., concerning copyright, building codes, environmental impact, taxes, etc.) at all times.*
• *Never compromise or violate a law even if a client or business partner asks for it and says they will take responsibility for it.*
Comply with relevant codes of professional ethics.
• *Observe the standard ethical guidelines espoused by professionals working in our vocational and business areas (e.g., the American Society of Civil Engineers, the Construction Management Association of America).*
Treat others as we would want to be treated, with honesty, fairness, dignity, and respect.
• *Use the classic "Golden Rule" as one helpful guide in figuring out the right thing to do.*
• *If in any doubt, ask some colleagues how they would want to be treated in a given situation.*

Protect life, health, and safety.
• *Rectify or report immediately any unsafe or threatening situations.*
• *Accept responsibility for any unsafe conditions we may have caused or contributed to and take corrective action.*
• *Pursue the highest standards in safety, whether on Harris property, in transit, or at a project site.*
• *Never compromise safety at any stage from project design, to execution, to final inspection.*

Fulfill commitments, contracts, agreements, and promises.
• *Follow through completely and reliably on agreements made with clients, business partners, and fellow employees.*
• *Make any changes in such commitments only by mutual agreement and in a transparent, above-board, manner.*

Maintain fairness in business and financial matters.
• *Avoid both the appearance and the reality of any kind of financial or business impropriety.*
• *Deliver the full value service that has been purchased from Harris.*
• *Compensate employees, sub-consultants, and business partners fairly for services rendered.*
• *Ensure that invoicing and billing practices are accurate and fully justified, whether dealing with clients, business partners, or personal expense reimbursements.*
• *Avoid real or potential conflicts of interest that could arise from giving or receiving gifts, dealing with relatives or close friends, or from any other source.*
• *Avoid improper tampering with the employees, operations, inside information, or intellectual property of other companies.*

Never compromise on truthfulness and accuracy.
• *Maintain clarity, consistency, and accuracy in all communications with clients, contractors, business partners, employees, governmental agencies, and the public.*
• *Never submit deceptive, incomplete, or inaccurate proposals, financial reports, or inspections.*
• *Do not over-promise on schedules, project outcomes, or personnel; disclose any contingencies and concerns.*
• *Correct mistakes, misstatements, and misleading communications immediately.*

Respect privacy and protect confidential and proprietary information.
• *Protect the privacy of individuals and their records, whether Harris employees or not.*
• *Protect the confidentiality of the proprietary information, business plans, and communications of Harris and its clients and business partners.*
• *Do not accept or misappropriate any confidential information or proprietary data from competitor companies; respect always the rights of the rightful owners of information.*

Maintain respectful and professional relationships.
• *Communicate (voice, written, e-mail, or otherwise) in a respectful and professional manner to fellow workers, clients, partners, contractors, competitors, and all others.*
• *Maintain a professional and inoffensive personal appearance and work environment*
• *Avoid behavior or communication that could come across as disrespect, harassment, or lack of courtesy or professionalism.*

Be open to criticism, admit mistakes, take responsibility, and take corrective action.
• *Take the initiative to improve your own performance.*
• *Do not hide from criticism, evade responsibility, or try to pass the buck.*

Address questions, criticisms, and admonitions directly and privately with the persons involved.
• *Take the initiative to address issues with others as soon as possible.*
• *Do not go behind people's backs with complaints.*
• *Do not risk humiliating people in front of others.*

3. Specific Guidelines

3.1 Clients

Developing Business

• *Market our services and develop our business by telling the truth, the facts about Harris experience, expertise, and client service.*

• *Build positive relationships with potential clients and demonstrate our collaborative style and orientation.*

• *Never engage in, or respond to, manipulative, unprofessional, or unethical business development tactics.*

Working with Clients

• *Provide loyal and competent representation of the client at all times during the contract.*

• *Inform clients fully and clearly about the risks, options, and possible ramifications of choices; provide fair and objective advice to enable sound client decisions.*

• *Protect the client's budget and best interests.*

3.2 Contractors and Business Partners

Choosing Business Partners

• *Choose business partners based on their qualifications and availability, and on client needs.*

• *Maintain openness, transparency, and objectivity in determining business partnerships.*

Working with Contractors and Business Partners

• *Partner with contractors to deliver excellent results to clients.*

• *Maintain open, honest, and adequate communications with contractors and other business partners.*

• *Encourage and facilitate open communication among clients, contractors, business partners, and managers with full disclosure of relevant developments, challenges, problems, and opportunities.*

• *Provide competent information and advice to clients on contractor issues and concerns.*

• *Never agree to any work that is substandard, out of compliance with codes, regulations, or cuts corners to save money or time.*

• *Ensure that inspections are carried out in an objective, competent, transparent manner.*

3.3 Employees

Employee Recruiting & Hiring

• *Recruit employees by honestly and effectively communicating the facts, opportunities, and benefits of employment at Harris.*

• *Seek a workforce characterized by a rich diversity in terms of age, experience, gender, ethnicity, and cultural background.*

• *Seek prospective employees whose values and purposes are in alignment with the mission, vision, and core values of Harris.*

• *Refer interested individuals to the Harris web site and to our Human Resources department. Do not engage in "raiding" of employees of other firms.*

Working for Harris

• *Treat all fellow employees with integrity, dignity, respect, and care, valuing everyone's role on the Harris team.*

• *Carry out individual assignments with competence, diligence, and pride.*

• *Build teamwork and healthy, open, honest communication.*

• *Contribute to the fun and family atmosphere at Harris, but do not violate basic norms of professional behavior.*

• *Use company equipment, resources, and assets appropriately and responsibly.*

• *Refrain from behavior away from work which could create a conflict of interest, tarnish the reputation of the company, or affect your ability to carry out your job at Harris.*

Blueprint for Principle-Guided Practices

Four processes here: identify, educate, implement, evaluate. First, how does a company figure out and articulate its basic ethical guidelines? Or, if the company already has some guidelines or even a code, how do they carry out a comprehensive review and upgrade. Since this affects the whole company, the code of ethics needs enthusiastic support and leadership from the top. If the CEO and top management yawn (or joke about) the process, we're probably dead in the water. Obviously, all managers need to be on board here as well. Some of them may be especially interested or gifted in this part of the process. Some large companies put a special, senior-level ethics (or ethics and compliance) officer in place, maybe even with some support staff. Other companies put HR or Legal in charge. All of these strategies can work, but think through the message and impact. For example, if the Legal Department is put in charge, the ethics program is likely to look and sound a lot like lawyer-speak and legal compliance (no offense intended, but let's keep our eyes open to how varied backgrounds, temperaments, vocabularies, and concerns can affect the result).

Outside consultants can sometimes help, but, again, be careful to look at what your consulting prospects have done and said (or written) before coming to you. There isn't just one school or brand of organizational ethics consulting and training. Some are really psychologists, others lawyers, others philosophers, others in many additional domains, and always lots of amateurs (admittedly, sometimes no worse than the pros).

In my view and experience, the most important personnel in creating a good ethics code are the practitioners themselves. For example, the best people to try to articulate ethical guidelines for company sales representatives, are the sales representatives themselves. They know best how they spend their time. They know best what works and doesn't work, and where the temptations as well as opportunities lie. They know best how to orient a new sales staff member about what to avoid and how to succeed. The practitioners can bring both quality and relevance to the table. And when they are the authors, they also become the owners and protectors of the territory. Of course, there needs to be outside review of what various employees come up with (just as employees and managers needed to review the executive management's work on the mission, vision, and core values before they are adopted company-wide). Someone from outside or inside the organization must help ensure both the overall comprehensiveness as well as the internal coherence of the code of conduct. But the basic work should come from the practitioners.

> *The best ideas for a practical set of ethical guidelines will come from the hands-on practitioners. No one knows where the ethical temptations and problems can arise in a particular area like those who work there day in, day out. Challenge the practitioners to write the guidelines for the sake of newcomers to their departments and activities.*

Clearly, if the company already has a code of ethics or conduct, or if it has some ethics-related policy statements in the company handbook (for employees, for engineers, for directors, et al) or elsewhere, that is where we begin our careful study. It is also important during this process to give some time and effort to a review of what the law requires, what (if anything) one's industry competitors have come up with, and the codes of ethics of relevant professional associations in various overlapping or relevant activity areas (e.g., in marketing, HR, engineering, accounting, etc.). This sort of research can provide some good ideas and can minimize any oversights in the company code of ethics.

It's best to have a committee oversee the project to draft the code of ethics, but remember that, in general, individuals do the work and committees are best at brainstorming and review. The drivers of the committee need to have organizational, research, and writing abilities. But putting some key people on the committee who represent the broader employee population will be all to the good.

My experience is that the best way to collect company-wide ethics input from the practitioners as well as the managers is to use a questionnaire like the one that follows. This sort of worksheet can be completed by individuals on their own time, but doing it as part of a group exercise is even better.

Gill's Ethical Guidelines Worksheet

In order to carry out its mission with excellence . . . in order to pursue and achieve its vision . . . what are the most important ethical guidelines about right and wrong that we need to commit ourselves to—from our newest hires to our veterans, our management, and our board of directors? This questionnaire is being distributed to all of our employees. Everyone's input is critical if we are going to have a meaningful, helpful code of ethics. Thank you for your help.

<u>First</u>, take about ten minutes to jot down your responses to the five questions below.

<u>Second</u>, compare your answers with those of the others in your breakout group, asking questions of clarification, and making suggestions for how to put things more clearly and helpfully.

<u>Third</u>, make a few changes and additions to upgrade your suggestions (try to write legibly, but don't worry about grammar or handwriting) . . . then turn in this page with your name and contact information so we can follow up with you if we need further clarification.

Name_____
Phone/E-mail:_____

1. What are the basic tasks that make up your job? (name them briefly)

2. On each of those tasks you have listed, what written guidelines should we give to help new employees avoid doing the wrong thing—and know clearly how to do the right thing? (jot them down)

3. What in your opinion are the most likely ethical temptations or challenges someone in your work area is likely to face? (describe them briefly)

---

4. What company guideline could help someone avoid getting into ethical trouble in each of those areas? (jot down some guidelines)

5. Are there any other ethical principles or guidelines that, in your opinion, really need to be part of our company code of ethics to make it strong and complete? (jot them down)

Building from this huge data input from the trenches, and the other research mentioned earlier, the project leader then drafts a provisional, working code of ethics which is then reviewed and improved by the ethics code committee, by management, and by the workforce that submitted the basic ideas in the first place. We might go through two or three revisions until there is widespread confidence that it is ready to be rolled out. We want buy-in; when all is said and done, we want to be able to announce to our workforce, "Thank you for your good work in writing our company code of ethics."

In Chapter Three, we looked at ethical decision-making and trouble-shooting. It is important to remember that for that process to be effective, there needs to be some advice appended to this Code of Ethics on how to use it— how to raise questions or report possible violations.

Guidance on Specific, Detailed Questions

We can't really provide detailed guidelines for every possible ethical issue or question in our companies. Organizations that try to address all possible cases soon become mired in a vast clutter of minute rules, distracting us from the "essence of the matter," and slowing us down. In any case, life always brings changes and new challenges, and we just can't keep up with all possible problems. One of the best ideas for how to address the applied complications is to have a section of "frequently asked questions" at the end of the code. In this expandable, archivable section, employees can raise questions about specific situations and receive guidance from managers. These are on the order of "examples of how to apply our principles and values," not heavy-handed laws. Especially by using company newsletters and then the company web site, such ethics questions can be welcomed and answered regularly and then entered into a company archive on the topic.

Here is how such matters are addressed in the Harris & Associates Code:

Harris & Associates: Frequently Asked Questions—Values and Ethics

It is both impossible and undesirable to try to write a rule or guideline for every conceivable ethical dilemma we might face. Acting ethically is a matter of making wise judgments about how to apply our values and principles to particular cases. In the following section, Harris leaders comment on cases and questions that have been submitted by Harris employees. Please submit any cases or questions you may have (to Human Resources Manager, *name and contact info given*) and you will receive a response as quickly as it can be prepared. Some cases, questions, and responses will be shared with the larger Harris community in our newsletter or at our web site. Published cases and questions may be edited for publication, and we will delete the authors' names from the published texts.

Employee Recruiting
Dear Harris:
I had a situation where I was working on a project with a sub-consultant who began asking me about what it is like to work at Harris—and whether we had any openings for someone like her. What should I say in a situation like that? She seemed like someone who would be a great addition to our company.

Dear Harris colleague:
These are difficult situations, but one of our basic ethical principles is to treat others as we would want to be treated. We do not want our employees poached by other companies and agencies when we send them out on a job—so we don't believe we should do it to others. Our specific guidelines for employee recruitment also direct us not to take advantage of such recruiting opportunities.
At most, what we think you can do ethically is say something like, "We have a policy against tampering with the employees of our business partners while we are on a project together. If you are still interested when our project is over, I would suggest that you check out our web site and contact our HR department to get more information." Of course, if this person badgers you with questions about how you like Harris, you can share your personal feelings and experience. But be careful not to cross the line and make any recruiting moves.
—*Marie S, Human Resources Manager*

Receiving a Gift from a Contractor
Dear Harris:
When on a job site out of town, one of our contractors paid our green fees for a weekend round of golf and then the cost of an expensive dinner at the country club. We did chat most of the time about our project, so it seemed like time well spent for our work relationship and the success of our project, even though we were also hitting golf balls. I tried to offer to pay for dinner, but he said visitors

can't pay at the club and he absolutely refused to hear of it. Oh yeah, and he also gave each of us in the foursome a sleeve of three golf balls with his company logo imprinted on them. Did I do the right thing here?

Dear Harris golfer:

Accepting the golf balls seems like a nominal gift unlikely to create a real or apparent conflict of interest (where your treatment of him and his company might be influenced by these gifts and favors). A nice touch is to reciprocate by giving him a Harris cap or something similar.

The green fee and expensive dinner is another matter. You should have made it clear beforehand that you would not join in for golf and dinner unless you could pay your own way. Always try to be aware of these situations before you get boxed into a corner that is embarrassing for everyone involved.

—Neil M, Director of CM & Northern Regional Manager

Booking Vacation Tickets on My Work Computer

Dear Harris:

I recently logged on to my usual airline company to book my tickets for a vacation trip next summer. I did this on my Harris computer at my desk in our office. I had to do it during day hours because I might need to speak to an actual representative at the airline, and they seem to be there only during day hours. I sometimes use my home computer to log on and do company work during evenings and on weekends, so I felt that things balance out. I want to get your opinion on whether I am being ethical.

Dear Harris traveler:

You have posed a very difficult question, given the fact that, for many of us, our personal and business lives are so intertwined. This is where judgment comes in, rather than trying to find the "letter of the law."

I personally would not feel comfortable booking a personal flight from the office and during working hours. It does not feel "right" for me. However, I understand the balancing-out concept, and you will need to do what is comfortable for you.

See, this ethics business isn't as easy as it sounds!

—Guy E, President

Company Ethics Education & Training

Once we identify (figure out, articulate) our Code of Ethics, how do we best *educate* all company personnel so that everyone knows it? A written booklet can serve a company well here. If a brief list of the key general principles can be edited out, it might serve the company well to have this abbreviated list on every employee's wall—or mouse pad. Regular columns and articles on ethics in the company newsletter help. A regular "Ask Dr. Ethics" type of column can invite and stimulate ethics learning and discussion. New and continuing employees need to be mentored, educated, and trained on the content of company ethics. Part of this can happen simply through requiring a reading and sign-off on the document at the point of hiring and annually thereafter. Some companies require completion of web-based ethics tutorials and refreshers every year; others use in-person training sessions.

The specific training challenge here is to help employees at all levels to know the code and how to interpret and apply it. Much can be accomplished by individual training exercises, but remember that ethics is a "team sport" in which discussion and group interaction is a critical factor in coming up with creative and wise resolutions to problems. If all the ethics training is individualistic, don't be surprised when in actual crises, individuals try to go it alone.

Ethics training is critical at all levels, from new hires to veterans, from employees to managers to executives to boards of directors, from corporate insiders to business partners, customers, and investors. It needs to be part of the "job description" of both official and unofficial mentors in companies to pass on the ethical convictions and guidance of the company. Unfortunately, ethics scandals are not limited to one part or another of an organization. As we see every day in the news, executives and boards of directors need ethics and values training as much (perhaps more, given their opportunity to do massive right or wrong) as anyone in the company.

Who will be responsible for ethics training? It hardly seems sufficient to make each person responsible for his or her own ethics education and let it go at that. In the same way as above, when discussing who should or could drive the identification process and get the code figured out and articulated, there are lots of possible leaders for ethics training—from special ethics officers, ombudspersons, and committees, to CEOs, VPs, HR Directors, managers, and outside consultants. It can be done in small group sessions (Harris & Associates asks for one annual, two-hour, face-to-face ethics and values workshop of every employee, usually in a group of 15-20; an electronic, online session is the back-up for anyone who, toward the end of the year, didn't get to one of the sessions because of schedule conflicts, illness, date of hire, etc.). Some companies require one or more online ethics training sessions every year. Others prefer face-to-face workshop settings. The size and nature of the company must be considered here and a customized program is the best way to go rather than some proposed "one size fits all" program.

Ethics training is an ongoing task that must be taken seriously throughout the organization. There is no "one size fits all" training program however. Build a program that fits with your company's needs and resources after studying how others do it.

Practicing Our Principles

The third process is to *implement,* or *practice,* the principles of company ethics. Practicing what we preach means *complying* with our own stated standards and guidelines, not breaking or trivializing or ignoring them. We need to rigorously and consistently apply our ethical principles to our daily practices. We will sometimes need to stop doing something one way, and start doing it another way to be in compliance. We will sometimes need to do some research and ask for help from our colleagues and managers to figure out how to carry out a mandate or stay within a boundary. Always remember that these are the "plays" that will get us into the end zone. If it doesn't seem or feel that way, if our ethical guidelines feel like a bunch of negative or abstract rules, then we missed something. Back to the drawing board, or at least to the discussion table, to figure it out and see things in their appropriate, positive light.

Use the code and the ethics reporting and inquiry processes—not just on your own, but in a staff meeting or alongside a colleague. Get used to it. Make it work for you.

Evaluating Individual & Organizational Performance

The fourth process is to *evaluate* our principles and practices. Employee (and manager, director, and business partner/subcontractor) evaluations need to include an ethics piece: Did this person comply with our ethical commitments and core values this past year (or during this project or contract)? Were they exemplary? Or borderline? Were they looking for exemptions and permission to suspend our ethical guidelines (Hello, Enron!)?

But the evaluation process must go the other direction as well: Employees (customers and business partners could participate here as well) must be asked every year or so to critique the company itself, its code of ethics—how helpful it is, whether it needs changes, whether it is being complied with, and so on. The audit form that follows is an example of how that might be done:

Gill's Company Ethics Code & Practices Audit

Does our company have a clear, robust, and effective set of ethical principles and guidelines that guide our practices?	Strongly Disagree			Strongly Agree	
	1	2	3	4	5
1. Our company has clearly identified ethical principles (rules, standards) that provide solid guidance for our daily work.	❏	❏	❏	❏	❏
2. Our ethical guidelines are not just about negative behavior to be avoided but positive behavior to be pursued.	❏	❏	❏	❏	❏
3. Our company does well at training its new employees in its guidelines on ethics and how the company wants its practices carried out.	❏	❏	❏	❏	❏
4. Our company makes sure that at all levels of responsibility and at all stages of experience its people know and understand the code of ethics and principles.	❏	❏	❏	❏	❏
5. Our company does a good job of keeping its code of ethics and principles up-to-date, so that there are no blind spots or unaddressed problem areas.	❏	❏	❏	❏	❏
6. Our statement of ethics and values is made readily available to clients, business partners, government agencies, and the public.	❏	❏	❏	❏	❏

How many of our company's basic ethical principles can you remember?:

General guidelines & ethical principles:

1. _____
2. _____
3. _____
4. _____
5. _____

Guidelines specifically for your area of our business:

1. _____
2. _____
3. _____
4. _____
5. _____

Notes on our company code of ethics:

Afterthought: Personal, Organizational, & Global Ethical Principles

Earlier in this book I argued that we must distinguish between our personal ethics and those of our company. But some degree of alignment of personal and corporate ethics is desirable and even necessary so that our success and our company's success can be mutually reinforcing. So the question is: What are your own bottom-line, foundational ethical principles? In Appendix B I share my own list and a little questionnaire I sometimes use to push people toward self-conscious reflection on these things. Don't undervalue this process. You have something to bring to your company and industry and to the marketplace—your ethical muscle and wisdom, not just your technical skills.

At the other end of the spectrum are global ethics statements like the Caux Round Table principles of international business (www.cauxroundtable.org) and the United Nations Declaration of Universal Human Rights (www.un.org/rights). Take a look at these statements and compare them to your own personal principles, and the ethical guidelines of your company. You may decide to augment yours or your company's or bring them into closer alignment after doing so.

For Reflection or Discussion

1. In your own personal code of ethics, what are your two or three most basic, bottom line principles or rules as you think about right and wrong? Can you describe a situation in business when you consciously applied these personal principles?

2. As you think about your own professional life and work, what are the most significant temptations for you and your colleagues to do something ethically wrong (or at least "ethically questionable")? Can you articulate an ethical principle/rule/guideline that you could give to new colleagues coming into your work area that would keep them doing the right thing and avoiding the wrong thing? State it.

3. What do you think about the argument in this chapter that it is the practitioners themselves who are best positioned to carry the ball on the ethics code? Could there ever be a problem of "writing the rules to give myself a break"? If so, what would be the best response?

Exercises

1. Go on the web and find the codes of ethics of a competitor or two and compare them to your company's code.

2. Sketch out a rough outline of an optimum code of ethics for your organization, including some general principles first, then some specific guidelines. Share this with a colleague or supervisor and see if they think your company could use some attention to this matter.

Resources for Further Study

Patrick E. Murphy's *Eighty Exemplary Ethics Statements* (Notre Dame, 1998) is a good resource. Many (though not all) business ethics textbooks give some advice on creating a code of ethics. See also the web sites of the Ethics Resource Center (www.ethics.org), the Institute of Business Ethics (www.ibe.org.uk), Business for Social Responsibility (www.bsr.org), and the Ethics & Compliance Officer Association (www.theecoa.org).

One of the best ways to improve your knowledge of business codes of ethics is to visit company web sites. Many company codes are posted and available to all visitors.

Chapter 7

The Market for Ethical Leadership

Executive Summary

In Chapter Two we argued that nothing good will happen without adequate motivation. Now we will say that nothing good will happen without adequate leadership. We can all think easily of times when poor leadership undermined constructive activity in organizations. Leadership starts with a strong and visible commitment to ethics at the top of organizations. Ethics officers and ethical personnel up and down the line can have a real impact, but without a commitment at the top, without "tone at the top," ethics will suffer. Leadership can be pursued on six fronts: (1) working for better legal and regulatory standards and oversight, (2) creating or strengthening industry and professional influence, (3) reforming and improving corporate governance at the board and executive suite level, (4) building organizational systems and processes to promote ethics and values, (5) recruiting, building, and training good people throughout the organization, and (6) communication, mentoring, and modeling by company leaders themselves.

The final component in ethically healthy organizations is leadership. Earlier in this book we saw how top management must take charge and make the case for why ethics is important, and that they must be enthusiastic in support of the whole ethics program, from beginning to end. We noted that *top executive management's* particular focus had to be on the overarching mission and vision. We noted that *all managers* at all levels are the "culture-builders" and "culture-tenders" of the company, so their leadership on the core values and culture side of the ethics program was especially necessary. And we noted that *all employees* must show some ethical leadership, not just in their own particular job responsibility but in mentoring others, especially new hires, and that they play the key role in writing the code of ethics for their work area.

None of the ethics and excellence we have been describing in this book will happen by itself. It takes leadership. David Vogel, author of the recent study of corporate social responsibility, *The Market for Virtue* (Brookings Institution, 2005), has concluded that the key factor in determining whether or not a company commits to social responsibility and virtue is their CEO. Some of the Triple Bottom Line literature comes close to making the argument that the realities of limited resources, growing transparency, and demands from stakeholders will drive improved ethics and sustainable business practices. I would love to believe this, but human experience cautions us that greed and rationalization are recurring problems, even in the best of times, even in the face of logic and evidence. So leadership is going to have to be a self-conscious choice.

Any business leader today is going to face some special challenges. Globalization (and extended enterprise in general) requires leadership to be effective over broader distances—a challenge even with the help of communication and transportation technologies. Cultural diversity means that our varied basic languages and value systems provide fewer points in common on which to build. Speed and mobility put us in constant motion, including movements from one company (culture, values, principles, etc.) to another. Competition and economic pressures restrict our time and energy for ethical leadership concerns. Finally, a growing cynicism and loss of trust among many people in society and in the workplace make it harder to lead. People have trouble believing in ideals and ethics when they have been disappointed or betrayed before and are treated to a daily diet of news stories of unethical leadership.

Nevertheless, the other side of the situation is that there is a great hunger and opportunity for creative, ethical leadership. Good leaders will find lots of people who want to work on inspired, ethical teams. Diversity itself brings great resources; change brings great opportunities when it comes to building ethical and excellent organizations. So we need not give up the fight.

Before examining some key characteristics of good leadership, I want to look a bit more broadly at five larger strategies for promoting more ethical business.

Helping Big Brother Lead Us

One of David Vogel's points in *The Market for Virtue* is that if some business activity is really unethical and harmful, the most responsible thing for business to do is to get a law or regulation in place to prohibit it. Why allow one business to gain a market advantage over another by doing something that is actually wrong? Isn't this what laws are for—to even the playing field for everyone and to protect all citizens? Vogel has a good point, and it is an argument for business leaders to get involved in government policy and regulatory reform. The logic here is similar to our calling on employees to help write their own ethics code. The practitioners know the temptations, problems, and positive potentials better than anyone else. So too, business knows better than some professional politician how best to make the playing field fair and how to protect consumers and citizens.

The flip side of this argument has to do with the sometimes negative influence of industry lobbyists from domains as varied as pharmaceuticals, automobiles, agriculture, mass communications, and entertainment. Powerful business interests can buy influence and corrupt the political and regulatory process. The practitioners cannot always be counted upon to forego self-interest and write fair laws and regulations. Of course, it doesn't take business involvement to corrupt politicians; they often enough figure out how to do it on their own. Political and regulatory corruption and ineptitude come from more than one source.

Still, this is not sufficient grounds to abandon the process of political and regulatory reforms. Clumsy and costly though it may be, Sarbanes-Oxley regulation has helped clamp down on unethical business. The "Do Not Call" regulations reining in the telemarketers were a godsend. The Food and Drug Administration, National Highway and Traffic Administration, and other agencies have sometimes protected us and the environment in important ways. The Small Business Administration and other agencies have sometimes been a source of positive encouragement; government is not just about restraining evil but about promoting good business development.

> *Government regulatory standards and oversight agencies can be ham-fisted and moronic—but business cannot operate without some rules and referees to keep the game clean and fair. Leadership will mean getting involved and helping to improve the process. Griping and dropping out is not leadership.*

"Cowboy capitalism" without government oversight and the rule of law translates into the strong plundering the weak to the extent they can get away with. Some government is necessary and desirable, but it is usually very slow and a bit late in responding. Government regulations are also written in large generalities and are not so good at dealing with small, exceptional circumstances. For these and other reasons, calling on "big brother" for ethical leadership can only be one of several leadership strategies. We cannot wait for government to get it right before we try to make business more ethical by other means.

Industry and Professional Associations

Another potential source of leadership is non-governmental industry and professional associations. The Caux Round Table is an association of business and political leaders who articulated a set of ethical principles for global/international business and who try to persuade businesses to sign on publicly and commit to these principles. The Sullivan Principles exerted significant pressure on South Africa and helped that country move past apartheid. Professional groups like the American Marketing Association or American Nurses Association also have this kind of potential for ethical pressure and accountability. On the downside, the accountancy profession, once known for its commitment to ethics, failed to stem the tide of unethical practice of its members involved in the downfall of Arthur Andersen (and others). Still there is leadership potential in this strategy.

One way for a business to deal with an unethical competitor is for the business to convene an "industry" summit, calling together all of its competitors (and perhaps some relevant NGOs and other stakeholder representatives) to study the issues they face in hiring, client-acquisition, dealing with government, etc. Put the tough issues on the table (e.g., the pressure to hire low-cost, undocumented workers). Collaborate in setting some industry standards and creating a framework to ensure transparency and compliance among each other's companies. Then get all your competitors to sign on and create wide public awareness of the problems, the new standards, and the identity of companies signing on (or not, as the case may be). Now you have a means of embarrassing and leveraging industry-wide improvement. It's not perfect. There are no guarantees, but it is an example of a non-governmental strategy for exerting ethical leadership while remaining competitive. In *The Triple Bottom Line,* Andrew Savitz describes how a consortium of Asian logging companies joined together with community and environmental activists to set voluntary standards that saved companies and jobs while also saving a sustainable forest.[1]

> *Leadership means taking an active role in developing and supporting*
> *voluntary professional and industry standards and accountability.*
> *Some of the time this is a better leadership strategy than referring*
> *things to the governmental Big Brother.*

Corporate Governance

Many students of the temptations and business ethics scandals of recent decades argue that the answer is better "corporate governance." Sometimes this elastic term includes a call for better government oversight and for government-mandated reforms. The primary focus is usually placed on the structure and operation of the board of directors and the executive leadership appointed by the board. If companies do not improve their leadership and governance at this level, the argument goes, nothing else will really have much effect.

The corporate governance problem today is usually a lack of accountability, transparency, and democracy in many boards today. The Chairman of the Board is often also the CEO and President of the company (not so in European corporations or in the non-profit world, but justified by claims of efficiency in American corporations). Who sets the agenda and runs the meetings? The CEO. Whose hand is most significant in choosing the membership of the Board? The CEO. And the CEO returns the favor by serving on a few boards for this same elite band of corporate executives. Small wonder that they approve each other's compensation packages, to say nothing of working in close harmony on political lobbying and policy influence.

Who is going to call the CEO on the carpet? Who can hold the board accountable? Many voices are now accusing boards and executives of failing in their fiduciary responsibility to manage corporate affairs in the true interests of the owners/investors. Stock option grants may be out of sync with actual performance and end up diluting the value of stock held by investors. And beyond the investors, who can speak for employees? Or for the community that granted the corporation the right to exist? And which shoulders the cost of schools, roads, air and water clean-up for the corporation?

Of course, there are corporations which choose to pay rather than evade their fair share of the tax burden, give back to the community, and pay careful attention to employee, customer, investor, and community concerns. But the bad guys are still making out like gangsters. Former Home Depot CEO Robert

Nardelli drew some criticism even from the *Wall Street Journal*, for his rude and high-handed refusal to hear investor comments and complaints (about Home Depot's performance compared to that of competitors like Lowe's, and about Nardelli's Olympian compensation package) at a meeting. The investor activist movement is growing, but it remains very difficult to penetrate the security walls constructed by corporate elites. Journalists like Gretchen Morgenson write exposés all the time about high-handed and corrupt behavior by corporate boards and CEOs—but what happens then? This is why corporate governance is such a hot topic: Something needs to be changed.

Meanwhile, we also have great governance and leadership examples provided by Costco (CEO Jim Sinegal), Southwest Airlines (CEO Gary Kelley), and many other companies. One can only hope that enough customers, investors, and employees will vote with their feet and pocketbooks to get the attention of the bad guys and force some changes. I know I now avoid shopping at a major grocery chain where I have spent thousands of dollars each of the past thirty or forty years, and I no longer fly a couple major airlines on which I have flown hundreds of thousands of miles over the past thirty or forty years. I have been careful to make sure my retirement investments in mutual funds do not include these companies. I don't care what kind of deals any of them may offer me; they have lost my business to their more ethical competitors. If I see some governance improvements, I might come back, but not otherwise.

> *Leadership requires steps to improve the effectiveness, accountability, transparency, democracy, and ethics of corporate governance at the board of directors and executive decision-making and strategy levels.*

Why would any business want to risk aggravating customers, employees, investors, politicians, journalists, and communities like the "bad guys" to whom I refer? It is essential to be proactive and take the initiative for governance reforms now. Push for accountability at the top (not just one Olympian leadership post, reviewed perfunctorily by cronies who owe a lot to him or her), transparency (e.g., full disclosure and justification of compensation, full disclosure of meeting agendas and minutes to at least the primary stakeholder groups), democracy (giving stakeholder groups a voice and a vote on the board), and justice/fairness in all of the company's activities, policies, and decisions.

Internal System Building

Leadership is also about internal system building. Obviously, corporate governance board reforms fit here, but now we want to think more holistically about the whole structure of the company. In his pioneering studies of organizational development, growth, change, and leadership, the German father of modern sociology, Max Weber, describes how charismatic leaders who start movements must be succeeded by systems and procedures. Weber called this the "routinization of charisma."

A good example of this process is Hewlett Packard. For many years the vision, values, and ethics of HP were embodied personally in Dave Packard and Bill Hewlett. They were the walking, working incarnation of a set of values and a philosophy of work. They could "manage by wandering around" and even grill and serve burgers to all employees at the annual picnic. Any questions about how to do things or how to respond to an ethical dilemma, they could be asked personally. But after some decades of growth there were too many employees, in too many locations, to stay connected in the same way with everyone. Bill and Dave went off and wrote the summary statement of their core beliefs, goals, and values: "The HP Way" was the beginning of the "routinization" of their charisma.[2]

Harris & Associates offers a similar story. Carl Harris started his company in 1973 with two other people. Harris & Associates became a great company, clear on its values and vision, deeply ethical. All this happened with no mission statement or code of ethics. But by 2005, Carl Harris was living in semi-retirement in Idaho; still providing leadership on the board of directors, but no longer hands-on present everywhere. Guy Erickson, the President, and a few other old timers in leadership positions recognized that they too might be thinking "retirement" in the coming decade. Meanwhile the company was now operating out of twelve locations (no longer just the Concord headquarters), and the workforce was nearing 500, double what it was just ten years ago. Business was booming and more hires were on the horizon.

What happens when someone from Bechtel or Halliburton gets hired on at Harris & Associates? Do they bring their former company's values and culture with them? Of course, their experiences with these companies can be a great contribution to Harris & Associates, but there may be other old habits and patterns that Harris would not want to import into its culture. Harris & Associates needed to decide what it wanted to be about, and not just drift toward an accidental mission, culture, and ethics. Old time company leaders can travel a lot, but an extended enterprise culture is harder to lead than a centralized one.

So, in a similar way to Hewlett Packard, Harris & Associates decided to invest some serious energy in clarifying and articulating their mission, vision, core values, and ethical guidelines. This was no cosmetic, PR effort; it was a careful, thorough self-examination and construction project. They put in place some training and orientation structures and programs to be sure that everyone in the company will know what the company is about. Recruiters can't always call Carl Harris and ask for his opinion—or introduce new prospects to him before hiring decisions are made—but they can internalize the mission and core values of the company so that, in effect, the same objectives are achieved, the same core values that brought the company to its current level of success will be preserved into the next generation.

Without repeating the details again, a holistic and effective systems approach requires attention to six components (motivation, trouble-shooting, mission, culture, practices, and leadership) and four processes (identification, education, implementation, evaluation).

> *Leadership is not just about individuals in top positions of power, it is about creating systems, policies, processes, and the components of an ethically healthy company.*

People Building

Leadership means recruiting and training good people in an organization. Recall Jim Collins's metaphor of "getting the right people on the bus" and "getting the wrong people off the bus" in his *Good to Great*.[3] What makes someone a good hire? Collins argues that the good-to-great companies find people who can learn and adapt to new circumstances, people whose character and values are as important as skills and training. It is about recruiting and training good *individual* personnel, and it is about building effective, value-driven *teams*.

Good leadership means training others. It is a priority to identify, mentor, and train other leaders. Leadership can fail for many reasons—bad systems, bad governance structures among them. But the people component is certainly a critical piece of the leadership puzzle. It's about recruiting and training the right people with the right stuff. An executive or manager who creates an impressive organization which then falters badly or collapses as soon as they leave for lack of able successors has been a bad or at least a "deeply flawed" leader. Whatever flaws he had, Jack Welch was a good example of leadership training. Not just his successor at General Electric but the executives at several other companies were products of his leadership training (we'll forgive him for Robert Nardelli). Collins and Porras's *Built to Last* has a chapter on "Home Grown Leadership"—showing how great companies think ahead in training future leaders from among their own people.

<u>Five Strategies for Leading Companies Toward Ethics and Excellence</u>
  1. Help government to create sound, ethical regulations and oversight.
  2. Participate in voluntary industry and professional associations
     promoting ethics.
  3. Reform your board and corporate governance for accountability,
     transparency, democracy, and justice/fairness.
  4. Build systems in your company which support sound ethics.
  5. Recruit and train an ethical workforce and future leaders.

The Marks of Good Business Leadership

Looking at leadership in a more personal sense, how should we define it? One of the stupidest definitions known to man was in a bestselling book about twenty years ago, *Megatrends* (called "megabaloney" by an insightful reviewer). "Leadership," the author wrote, is "finding a parade and getting in front of it." This is, of course, "followership," not leadership. Unfortunately, some people seem to buy this sort of approach. They justify their behavior with lame excuses like "everybody else is doing it" or even "the market made me do it." Whatever this is, it is not leadership.

True leadership *creates* parades behind it. Leadership is about setting directions, mobilizing people, and bringing about positive change. We are not going to find the leadership we need by checking out who's riding the latest wave. We are looking for wave-makers, not wave-surfers. I don't think we can improve on the leadership description of James Kouzes and Barry Posner in their great study called *The Leadership Challenge*.[4] Kouzes and Posner describe five leadership practices, each of which is empowered by two action commitments by the leader. Let's review them briefly.

True leaders are wave-makers, not wave-surfers. True leaders don't justify their actions by saying "everyone else is doing it" or "the market made me do it."

Practice #1: Model the Way. Leaders lead by setting an example. They walk their talk. Kouzes and Posner urge two commitments: (1) Find your voice by clarifying your personal values, and (2) Set the example by aligning actions with shared values. Certainly part of this is what Jim Collins describes as "Level Five" leadership in *Good to Great*.[5] "Level 5 leaders embody a paradoxical mix of personal humility and professional will. They are ambitious, to be sure, but ambitious first and foremost for the company, not themselves. . . . They set up their successors for even greater success in the next generation. . . are fanatically driven . . . are resolved to do whatever it takes to make the company great . . . They look out the window to attribute success to factors other than themselves. When things go poorly. . . they look in the mirror . . . taking full responsibility." You can't have a passionate, teachable workforce if you as a leader don't model the way.

Leaders lead not just by what they say but by what they do. The personal example of "walking the talk" by a leader has tremendous impact. Much of the ugliest side of business today is the self-serving, "robber baron" behavior of some executives. It is unseemly and unfair, and the chickens will come home to roost (and are already). Why shouldn't an employee or business partner just grab for everything they can get, legally or otherwise—when that is exactly what their CEOs seem to be doing?

One thing to model here is the capacity to say "No." Leadership is not just gorging myself "because I can." The great French sociologist Jacques Ellul often said that the first act of a free person is to say "No."[6] If leaders expect their subordinates to say no to opportunities to rip off the company, they had better think about the example they are setting and the message their actions are sending. Could a CEO be worth ten times their lead engineer or salesperson? Are they ever worth 400 times an employee's wages? Arguments to that effect seem obvious to the circle of the blessed in many of today's executive suites. Somehow CEOs of some outstanding companies, like Gary Kelly of Southwest, John Mackey of Whole Foods, and Jim Sinegal of Costco, don't get on board, so maybe the logic isn't so inexorable after all. Being wealthy and powerful does not provide one with a moral right to take everything we can get our hands on, even shaking down the poor to add to our wealth and luxury.

Compensation is obviously not the only issue here. Leaders need to be models of good communication, a great work ethic, teamwork, excellence, and other core values. But money and compensation are critical indices of our values. Financial decisions send messages with impacts. We need to be sure we are saying what we want to and need to in this area. We simply cannot overstate how important personal example is in effective leadership.

> *Leaders must "walk the talk" with integrity and enthusiasm. If they do not believe and practice the mission, values, and principles of the organization, both the leader and the ideology will be running on three cylinders. The corporate Grim Reaper is at the door.*

Practice #2: Inspire a Shared Vision. The two commitments recommended by Kouzes and Posner are (1) envision the future by imagining exciting and ennobling possibilities, and (2) enlist others in common vision by appealing to shared aspirations. Remember how we looked at the importance of mission and vision in an earlier chapter. In his great study of business leadership, *Leading Change: The Argument for Values-Based Leadership* (1995), James O'Toole says that "Leadership is about ideas and values. It is about understanding the differing and conflicting needs of followers. And it is about energizing followers to pursue a better end state (goal) than they had thought possible. It is about creating a values-based umbrella large enough to accommodate the various interests of followers, but focused enough to direct all their energies in pursuit of a common good. In practical business terms, it is about creating conditions under which all followers can perform independently and effectively toward a single objective."[7]

One of the most important things that leaders do is act as the heralds and guardians of the core ideology—"preserving the core mission and values," as Jim Collins and Jerry Porras describe it in *Built to Last*. Closely connected with this is telling the company story, within which the mission and core values emerged. Stories ("narratives" is how social philosophers talk about them) form the essential texture and background for a believable, inspiring mission and vision.

> *Leadership need not be loud, but it must be powerful and moving, focusing our thoughts on a future situation that is inspiring, challenging, and doable. It is that vision that leverages both ethics and excellence.*

Practice #3: Challenge the Process. Kouzes and Posner say this entails commitments (1) to search for opportunities by seeking innovative ways to change, grow, and improve, and (2) to experiment and take risks by constantly generating small wins and learning from mistakes. "Built to Last" companies "try a lot of stuff and keep what works," Collins wrote with his co-author Jerry

Porras about America's great companies. They commit themselves to "big, hairy audacious goals." Leadership is about inspiring your people to stand up and do things differently, to take pride in scaling a mountain no one else will attempt, to go against the flow, to attempt the impossible, to go where no man has ever gone before, etc. Some authors distinguish management from leadership by saying that the former are consumed by what is, while the latter focus on what could be or ought to be.

Part of this is the "creativity/innovation" mission theme we talked about in Chapter Four. Making sure that the company mission taps into the human instinct to innovate, create, invent, and build, is critical. People are by nature innovators and status quo challengers. For its part, ethics itself is about "what ought to be"—about pursuing standards that we do not always live up to for one reason or another. Challenging the process goes with the ethics territory.

Leadership, in contrast to management, challenges the status quo and pulls us toward a possible better future . . . better not just in business terms, but in terms of our ethics.

> *Leadership, in contrast to management, challenges the status quo and pulls us toward a possible better future . . . better not just in business terms, but in terms of our ethics.*

Practice #4: Enable Others to Act. The commitments are (1) foster collaboration by promoting cooperative goals and building trust, and (2) strengthen others by sharing power and discretion. Whitworth College President Bill Robinson describes a critical characteristic of good leadership as "leading from the middle."[8]

His argument is that leading from "on high" or "out front" do not work these days—and maybe never worked as well as some command-and-control proponents claim. "From the middle" means from among the people you are leading. Effective, ethical leadership will be best attempted as the CEO or other leader walks where the people walk. It is about being present, open, and accessible. It is about paying some dues where the people are. Bill Hewlett and David Packard called it "management by wandering around" (MBWA) at HP. Bill Pollard, former CEO of ServiceMaster, described in his *The Soul of the Firm* how he and all other managers at the company were required to put in some days cleaning hospital rooms or other tasks that their employees did. It is not surprising that this kind of thing results in trust and loyalty to leaders.[9] Think about the best and worst leaders you ever worked for. Did you enjoy working for that micromanaging, control freak? Did that bring the best out of you?

Leaders enable others to act by giving them responsibility and authority, by giving them access to tools and training, by giving them freedom to learn, make decision, make mistakes, learn and grow. Systems and policies as well as colleagues and teams empower our action. Taking the initiative and taking responsibility when confidence is placed in us intensifies our bonding to the values themselves. Max DePree reminds us that one's leadership achievements are to be measured, not on paper, not in what the leader says or does per se, but in the actions of the "followers."

At Harris & Associates, the message is always "Ethics is everybody's business. You wrote the code; you execute it; you help us reform it whenever it needs it." When ethics is seen as the responsibility of management, or of the ethics and compliance office, or of our supervisor, it will inevitably be weak and incomplete. It is crucial to get the entire organization involved in the creation, ownership, training, implementation/application, and evaluation of the ethics and values of the company.

> *Good ethical leadership is measured not in the leader's actions alone, but in the ethical performance of those led. Good ethical leadership is not about micromanaging and controlling what others do; it is about freeing others, empowering, inspiring them to act ethically on their own. It is crucial to get the entire organization involved in the creation, ownership, training, implementation/application, and evaluation of the ethics and values of the company.*

Practice #5: Encourage the Heart. The commitments Kouzes and Posner identify are (1) Recognize contributions by showing appreciation for excellence, and (2) celebrate the values and victories by creating a spirit of community. Max DePree has written that the last duty of a leader is to say "thank you." Lots of managers out there are clueless about this and never thank others for anything. Many workers will never make much money, but they live for the occasional word of thanks and encouragement. I was impressed with Harris & Associates when I discovered that their company-owned vacation condos were for all employees, not just for the top executives. As they have added employees they have added condos so that every employee can have one week each year in one of the vacation condos. What do you think that does for the spirit of the Harris & Associates workforce? David Gilmour, proprietor of Paradise

Foods, takes great care of his employees, giving lots of thanks and recognition. But he went a step further and decided to send a $25 gift coupon to all the school teachers in his area, "just to say thank you to these public servants who rarely get thanked much." He had no hidden agenda and there were no catches; come in and redeem your coupon when and how you wish. It didn't surprise me to find out recently that Gilmour was voted businessman of the year by people in the area. Leadership encourages the heart.

Kouzes & Posner's Five Leadership Practices
 1. Model the way
 2. Inspire a shared vision
 3. Challenge the process
 4. Enable others to act
 5. Encourage the heart

Identify . . . Educate . . . Implement . . . Evaluate Company Ethical Leadership

What we have seen is that ethical business leadership can be—and must be—expressed in many different ways. Every company needs to consider these leadership strategies and make some decisions about where to put the focus. Almost certainly this must be a board of directors and executive management agenda item. How much effort will be given to working with government or industry and professional groups to improve the level of ethics? Who will be assigned to the chosen tasks and priorities? Big companies may have entire departments working on these strategies. Smaller companies need to be active in the ethics process but very careful about the allocation of their time and talent.

The leadership structure of both the board and executive management deserves careful review. What is our best structure now and for the years to come? How will we recruit and train our leaders? At this point we are moving from identifying our leadership (structure and personal) to questions about educating and training them and about implementing our leadership plans. And finally, we need to evaluate our leadership. Part of that is from the top down (e.g., board committee evaluations of the CEO and supervisor evaluations of employees). But part of the process needs to be from the bottom up (i.e., inviting the workforce to evaluate the leadership and its ethical performance). What follows is my generic leadership audit questionnaire.

Gill's Company Ethical Leadership Audit

Does our company have gifted, effective ethical leadership in place and in training?	Strongly Disagree			Strongly Agree	
	1	2	3	4	5
1. Our current leaders and managers clearly know the values and ethics of our company and they "walk the talk" with integrity.	❏	❏	❏	❏	❏
2. Our company leaders and managers frequently remind each other and employees of the core mission, values, and principles as planning takes place and important decisions are made.	❏	❏	❏	❏	❏
3. Our company is committed to continuity of ethical leadership, and it actively identifies and mentors/trains future leaders within the company.	❏	❏	❏	❏	❏
4. Compatibility with our mission, culture, values, and ethics is an essential qualification for all prospective management and leadership candidates.	❏	❏	❏	❏	❏
5. Our employees understand and carry out their responsibility to keep our company ethically healthy and set a good personal example of ethics.	❏	❏	❏	❏	❏
6. Our company has in place systems, procedures, and policies that will help keep our ethics on track and healthy even during leadership transitions or failures.	❏	❏	❏	❏	❏

Describe one positive example of ethical leadership at our company:

Comments on ethical leadership at our company:

Overall assessment of our organization's ethical health.	Strongly Disagree		·	Strongly Agree	
	1	2	3	4	5
1. Overall, our company is ethically healthy—with clear values and principles, good leadership, and a commitment to do the right thing.	❏	❏	❏	❏	❏
2. By comparison to its main business competitors, our company is stronger in terms of its ethics and values commitments and practices.	❏	❏	❏	❏	❏
3. By comparison to other places I have worked, our company is stronger in terms of its ethics and values commitments and practices.	❏	❏	❏	❏	❏

The ethical strengths of our company are:

The areas where our company could improve its ethical health are:

Afterthought: If You Are Not the CEO

We may be tempted to think that in the end only the CEO can really make changes in the ethical health of an organization. David Vogel's careful study of socially responsible businesses led him to observe that what made the difference among companies was primarily whether the CEO was personally interested in CSR. No doubt this is true and is an argument (a) for choosing your CEO with careful attention to ethics and values matters, and (b) for ethical people to aspire to top executive positions where they might have greater influence.

At the same time, we need not despair if we are in a small company—or perhaps leading a small part of a big company—that seems uninterested in ethics. Collins and Porras in Built to Last *argue that their principles and findings are applicable for leaders in almost any environment—small businesses, non-profits, departments of big business, or even government bureaus.*

The phrase "Think globally, act locally" (attributed variously to Jacques Ellul, Mohandas Ghandi, Rene Dubos, and Buckminster Fuller) has some merit here. While we may not be able to act "globally," we can nevertheless think in big picture terms—and then find a place to live out what we have come to think is important. Many of the important and lasting changes in the world actually began in small groups with little fanfare, so we must not be paralyzed by our lack of large scale power and influence. Grass roots movements among workers have organized and demanded change—sometimes successfully. Customers have brought about changes in companies through boycotts, protests, demands, and other tactics. Journalists and politicians can exert pressure on companies. Investors have sometimes been successful in demanding improved performance.

Our challenge is not just to denounce the evil but to show the way to the good. The alternative to greed and appalling ethics is new leadership that creates living examples of how to do good and do well at the same time. Ethics is still about excellence. A new generation of leaders embracing that truth and reality can bring the business renewal we eagerly look for—whether they are big-time CEOs who come alive, or relatively unknown workers and managers creating small but vibrant examples of another way.

For Reflection and Discussion

1. What are/were the most impressive characteristics of a good leader you have known or worked for? Did ethics have anything to do with it? What made them good leaders?

2. In your own leadership experience, describe a successful—and a less-than-successful—experience. What factors contributed to—or undermined—your leadership effectiveness in these cases?

3. In your view, what are the three or four key ethical characteristics desirable in good leaders?

Exercises

1. Read up on a couple business leaders named as "Best CEOs" or some other designation recognizing their above-average leadership. What has made them great or successful or admirable? How do ethics and values factor in (if at all)?

2. Have a conversation with an admirable leader from some domain other than business (e.g., a coach, priest, pastor, principal, et al). Ask them what their leadership secrets are—and how they view business leadership today.

Resources for Further Study

The leadership "library" is huge and growing all the time. The leadership secrets of Attila the Hun, Machiavelli, Moses, Jesus, Ulysses S. Grant, Robert E. Lee (who lost to the previous guy on the list), and hundreds of others, including lots of sports coaches as well as more conventional business leaders—these sit alongside an equal number of books from leadership "experts" and consultants. Some of the latter is platitudinous nonsense, and some is common sense. Careful what you buy!

Here is some of the best material out there: James M. Kouzes & Barry Z. Posner, *The Leadership Challenge* (Jossey-Bass, 4th ed., 2007) is 450 pages of excellent ideas and lessons. This is the leadership "Bible." The essays in Frances Hesselbein & Ron Johnston, *On Mission and Leadership* (Drucker Foundation, Jossey-Bass, 2002) are a terrific resource (chapters by Warren Bennis, Anita Roddick, Daniel Goleman, Patrick Lencioni, Bill Pollard, Dee Hock, David Lawrence, and others). You can't do much better than study *Built to Last* (1994) and *Good to Great* (2001). In the latter book, Jim Collins describes "Level Five Leadership"—what it takes to move a company from good to great. Surprising conclusions.

The USC business profs are also great. Anything on leadership by Warren Bennis is well-written, insightful and convincing. Forget the pop writers: buy Bennis, *Leaders: Strategies for Taking Charge* (with co-author Burt Nanus;

HarperBusiness, 1997) and *On Becoming a Leader* (Perseus, 1989). Also from USC, James O'Toole's *Leading Change: The Argument for Values-Based Leadership* (Ballantine Books, 1995) is readable and brilliant.

Four other books worth adding to your own leadership library are Max DePree, *Leadership Is an Art* (Doubleday, 1989) (slim little volume of wise insights from former Herman Miller CEO; best of his little books); Susan and Thomas Kuczmarski, *Values-Based Leadership: Rebuilding Employee Commitment, Performance, and Productivity* (Prentice Hall, 1995); Richard R. Ellsworth, *Leading with Purpose: The New Corporate Realities* (Stanford, 2002); and Marvin T. Brown, *Corporate Integrity: Rethinking Organizational Ethics and Leadership* (Cambridge, 2005). Ellsworth and Brown will require some attention and effort, but these are two brilliant and challenging contributions to our thinking about business leadership, ethics, and values.

NOTES

[1] Andrew Savitz, *The Triple Bottom Line* (Jossey-Bass, 2006), pp. 82-84.

[2] David Packard, *The HP Way: How Bill Hewlett and I Built Our Company* (HarperCollins, 1995).

[3] Jim Collins, *Good to Great* (HarperCollins, 2001), pp. 41 ff.

[4] James Kouzes and Barry Posner, *The Leadership Challenge* (Jossey-Bass, 4th edition, 2007).

[5] Jim Collins, *Good to Great* (HarperCollins, 2001), p. 39.

[6] Two different angles on saying "No" are provided by Jana Kemp, *No! How One Simple Word Can Transform Your Life* (Amacom, 2005) and Bill McKibben, *Enough: Staying Human in an Engineered Age* (Henry Holt/Times Books, 2003).

[7] James O'Toole, *Leading Change: The Argument for Values-Based Leadership* (Ballantine, 1995).

[8] William P. Robinson, *Leading People from the Middle* (Executive Excellence Publishing, 2002).

[9] C. William Pollard, *The Soul of the Firm* (HarperBusiness, 1996).

Re-Developing Our Business World

Executive Summary

We hear a lot about business development and some about community re-development. Here is a concluding call for re-development of our business world itself. We have so many resources, so many mistakes to learn from, so many good examples to emulate, so much opportunity, and so much need. It's time for this generation of business leaders to stand up, step up, rise up to lead a charge toward business that is both ethical and excellent at a level never seen before.

D espite all the scandals, problems, and terrible things that have too often happened in business, I remain staunchly pro-business, pro-entrepreneurship, pro-development . . . provided such development is in the effective and ethical service of a mission to create something good, useful, and beautiful, or to help fix something broken or help someone hurting. A truly vast territory is opened up by such a business perspective, and we can never exhaust the possibilities. We will never all agree on all matters of how to carry out such business development. We will have disagreements and dogfights on various matters. But we can't let a perfectionist impulse paralyze us from acting when so many individuals and communities are dying for lack of meaningful good work and business.

The essential foundation for good business development, in my view, is a *re-development of the business world itself.* Some places in our business world have become run-down, vice-infested "slums." Too much predatory, value-challenged harm to the residents. Too much ugliness and blight. There are exceptions, of course—good business "neighborhoods" where we can see how it could be. But Southwest Airlines is a true exception in the airline neighborhood. In'n'Out Burgers is a rare exception in the fast food neighborhood. Costco is an exception in the big box discount retail neighborhood. Whole

179

Foods (and Paradise Foods) are exceptions in the grocery neighborhood. Of course, there are lots more great stories we could tell. And the company examples I give are not immune from mistakes and problems themselves. But we are not being anti-business when we look at the overall landscape and say that some basic re-thinking and "re-development" is called for in many places.

> *The essential foundation for good business development is a <u>re-development</u> of the business world itself—where there now exist too many run-down neighborhoods, where too many people are getting mugged and sick these days.*

Adam Smith published *The Wealth of Nations* in 1776—the most influential statement of the theory and values of free-market capitalism ever written. Smith's contemporary fans cry out "Let the market decide"—the "invisible hand" of the market will make the best choices in the end. Any quacks, crooks, and con-artists taking advantage of free markets will be found out and the market will not support them any longer. (Too bad that invisible hand couldn't save the guy in the last town who bought that contaminated potion). Those who are charging exorbitant prices will lose business to new competitors who will come on the scene, seeing an opportunity to make money at a more reasonable and just level. (Too bad if a monopoly has eliminated all conceivable competitive challenges to that business over there).

The role of government in keeping the free market as level and free as possible is not something I am writing about. But I want to say something about the role of ethics. A robust, shared ethics and values is an assumption that Adam Smith had that has often been lost on his fans. Smith also wrote *The Theory of the Moral Sentiments*. His fuller argument about economics and markets is that free markets only work if the population has a sound moral/ethical foundation. Sorry, but "the love of money" does not provide such a foundation.[1]

In short, then, what we need, and what I am calling for, is a flourishing of authentically "Smithian" free enterprise, an explosion of business entrepreneurship and creative development bringing jobs, products, and wealth to the participants. But to be authentically Smithian, and genuinely good for our world, this needs to include an *ethical re-development* in the business world itself—the existing businesses as well as the new ones that spring up. Businesses must re-develop themselves into ethically healthy organizations. As I have tried to make clear in this book, this project is not about more "damage control" ethics—the popular but misguided, narrow, reactive prodigal offspring of the grand tradition of ethics and values in world history.

Any ethics that is authentic and worthwhile here is the classic kind, the kind that is about excellence. It is a "mission control" ethics. It's all about mission-driven, vision-pursuing organizations with value-embedded cultures and principle-guided practices. When we get on with this re-development process, we soon discover that is not some zany, soft, philosophical idealism—it is a coherent, common-sense, tough-minded, practical way of building profitable, sustainable business of which we can be proud.

NOTES

[1] James R. Otteson's *Adam Smith's Marketplace of Life* (Cambridge, 2002) is a superb study of how Smith's economic and ethical thought fit together.

Appendix A

Gill's Ten Traits of Ethically Healthy Organizations

Executive Summary

The consistent message of It's About Excellence *is that organizations need first to figure out what their mission and vision are going to be, and then, second, to figure out what appropriate core values should be embedded in their organizational culture. You can't borrow some other organization's core values. Still, there are some commonalities in great organizational cultures, and this chapter reviews ten powerful values/themes that often characterize great, ethically healthy companies.*

Reflecting on and discussing these traits/values at a staff retreat—or one-by-one over ten staff meetings—could help you take your career and your company leadership to the next level.

In chapter five of this book, we looked at the process of building strong, value-embedded corporate cultures. The basic argument was (1) get the mission straight, then (2) figure out what core values and traits need to be embedded in the organization to achieve that mission. The particular values (or corporate traits) that are essential to your success follow from the nature of your mission. There can be no standard account or one-size-fits-all template.

Nevertheless, I have come to believe that there are some cross-organizational, even cross-cultural, perhaps transhistorical, commonalities in the traits of ethically healthy organizations. Of course, at an even deeper level, that of mission and vision, I hypothesized earlier that great company missions/visions often tap into one or both of two basic themes: (1) "build/create/innovate something useful or beautiful," and (2) "help somebody in need, fix something broken." And in Appendix B which follows, I will propose ten basic principles of ethical decision and action.

At all three levels (mission/vision, culture/values, and practices/principles), I am not arguing that everyone *must* agree with my hypotheses. But I do find that when I ask people to "try this on for size" in their thinking, I almost always get substantial agreement. So maybe there is some kind of underlying "truth" in these matters, but it is not my purpose to try to sell you on any philosophical or anthropological conclusion of that sort. My purpose is simple—to give you a point of reference to stimulate your own thinking on these matters.

A few years ago I was with the late, great writer and teacher Neil Postman at a conference, and over dinner I asked him how he dealt with questions in his own mind about some of his opinions and hypotheses. He told me that he had always wanted to write "Or vice versa" on the last page of his books, and that he actually did it in one book (I forget which one). I'm not quite ready to put an "or vice versa" at the end of my list here, but I do insist that it is just my best attempt to summarize a complex subject.

Anyway, coming out of my studies of various corporate cultures and core values over the years, here is a list of "Gill's Ten Traits of Ethically Healthy Organizations." In each case I have given some explanation of what I mean by each key term and some business examples of it being played out. I put my name on the list for two reasons. First, as I confessed above, this is my personal take on the subject, not a "universal truth" every business needs to accept. Second, an edited version of my list (presented as "Eight Traits") was published in May of 2002 in a magazine I was working on at the time and is still floating around cyberspace. What you see in this appendix was back then, and is still now, the best, most complete take on the subject, in my opinion and experience.[1]

These ten traits are not randomly presented. Each one builds on the preceding one, and sets the stage for what follows. I think the eighth trait is really the pinnacle, where you have a culture of people and ideas drawn together in exciting ways, all in pursuit of a meaningful, gratifying common mission and purpose. Anyway, see what you think.

Gill's Ten Traits of Ethically Healthy Organizations

1. **Loyalty.** *Tenaciously preserve core mission and vision; hang in there with the team; no traitors.*

2. **Openness & Humility.** *Teachability from top to bottom of organization; no arrogant know-it-alls.*

3. **Accountability & Responsibility.** *All individuals and teams stand up; no blaming, no excuses.*

4. **Freedom.** *Creative risk-taking encouraged; no micro-managing control freaks.*

5. **Ethics & Excellence.** *Insatiable hunger for both "doing the right thing" and "doing things right."*

6. **Mistake Tolerance.** *Learn and try again; avoid punitive, fearful, repressive reactions.*

7. **Honesty, Integrity, & Transparency.** *Consistency of thought, talk, and walk; no hidden agendas or evasions.*

8. **Collaboration & Integration.** *Bringing people together . . . bringing ideas together.*

9. **Courage & Persistence.** *Guts in the face of difficulty.*

10. **Joyfulness & Fun.** *Stay positive even in hard times.*

---

1. Loyalty: Tenaciously preserve core mission & vision; hang in there with the team; no traitors.

Loyalty is the capacity and the inclination to remain faithful and steadfast, the disposition to stay committed, to hang in there, to not "bail out" or disappear even when things are tough. It is not simplistic, unquestioning conservatism—thoughtlessly or fearfully clinging to traditional ways. Loyalty needs to be given to the right things—two things actually—to our core mission/vision and to our team.

Jim Collins and Jerry Porras have presented a compelling case for the first aspect: loyalty to the mission. They call it "preserving the core."[2] Great, enduringly successful companies don't wonder what their purpose is and change fundamental direction from year to year. They are ferocious in staying anchored to their "core ideology." Stimulating creativity, innovation, and risk-taking without first and then simultaneously strengthening this core, they argue, is a recipe for disaster. Nikos Mourkogiannis's *Purpose: The Starting Point of Great Companies* (Palgrave Macmillan, 2006) and Richard R. Ellsworth's *Leading with Purpose* (Stanford, 2002) powerfully underscore this same message: It all begins with loyalty to the right mission, vision, and purpose.

But loyalty is also about personal relationships on the team.[3] It used to drive me crazy when my dean (back in the late 1980s) would threaten to quit my administration whenever things got tough for him. I see now that after the second episode I should have helped him pack and hit the road. His disloyalty—a deeply embedded character trait—was extremely destructive all the years he worked at that institution (despite his other stellar abilities). We can learn something from the priority the Army and Marines give to this value of loyalty. If you are expecting to be in combat, loyalty to mission and team are critical. Without it, we are just not going to be competitive. The SAS software firm (with a brilliant record of success and a 97 percent employee annual retention rate) and Southwest Airlines (profitable thirty-four years in a row, the only major airline that knows how) are two shining examples of corporate cultures that stress the kind of loyalty I am talking about.

None of this means that we keep people on forever who are not performing or that we are blockheaded about re-tooling aspects of our mission and vision. This is one of the traits, the first one, but not the whole list. But we will be paralyzed and undone if we don't have some tenacity to our core mission and some loyalty to our team.

2. Openness & Humility: Teachability from top to bottom of the organization; no arrogant know-it-alls.

Openness is the companion virtue to loyalty. Openness (in individual character or organizational culture) is not the same thing as emptiness; it doesn't mean abandoning everything. G. K. Chesterton used to say it was important to have an open mind—but not open at both ends. But a radical openness, anchored by loyalty to one's core mission and values, is a critical component in a healthy culture. Think of the opposite traits: arrogance, closed-mindedness, narrowness, and rigidity. These vices stifle creativity and freedom. They kill off learning and growth and blind us to our own weakness. Strength comes out of receptivity and a willingness to learn from others. This is why "loyalty" (the first great trait) must be to the right things: the mission and the team. A fierce, unbending loyalty to *everything* else, "the way we always did it," is paralyzing and destructive.

Collins and Porras argue in *Built to Last* that great companies both "preserve the core"—and "stimulate progress" by reaching for "big, hairy, audacious goals" and by cultivating a "try lots of things, keep what works" approach. They say it is a yin/yang relationship, a both/and dialectic. Having a deep anchor allows for wide ranging experimentation. It is common sense. Even if we are doing well, adding the best ideas from someone else can make us even better. Openness and a humble teachability are not signs of weakness but of strength.

Openness needs to be practiced in at least three directions. First, openness is directed toward *people*; it is inclusive rather than exclusive.[4] Second, openness is directed toward *ideas*—"intellectual openness"—new thoughts, innovative, fresh concepts and ways of doing things. Third, it is directed toward *criticism*. It is easy to be open to ideas that reinforce our opinions, harder to hear criticism. But such openness to criticism is a source of strength, helping us discover problems and cut our losses while they are relatively small, rather than getting really nailed farther down the road.

The 3M company is justly famous for its openness to new ideas. And certainly you have to hand it to Toyota and other Japanese automakers for beating Detroit to a pulp—mainly by their openness to innovation and the ideas of others, while Detroit closed up and suffered the competitive consequences. Finally, think about who you want to work for. Isn't it obvious that we flourish when we get to work for bosses who are open to our ideas and even our critique and suggestions for improvements?

3. Accountability & Responsibility: All individuals and teams stand up; no blaming, no excuses.

The third characteristic is related to the previous one in that openness suggests there will be a "need to learn" and even a "need for improvement or correction." And wherever there is a need or a weakness, there is an opportunity for denial, blame, and excuses. A healthy culture is one where we accept personal responsibility and where we hold ourselves and each other accountable for our actions (including our weaknesses). A culture of irresponsibility breeds dissension and distrust among colleagues and customers and long-term disaster and loss for the company.

Responsibility literally means "answerability" or "accountability." The responsible party is the one deserving praise or blame for what happens. A responsible person (or company) willingly accepts accountability, agrees to care for something, and can be counted upon to do what they say they will. A culture of responsibility and accountability must be based, in turn, on four things: knowledge, freedom, forgiveness, and relationship. First, if we want people and organizations to accept responsibility, they must be given access to the *knowledge* required for wise decisions. That was implied in the previous characteristic about teachability. Second, holding people responsible without their having *freedom* to choose and to act is a sham and a farce—like a tyrant who hangs some poor souls, blaming them for the bad weather. If we ask others to accept responsibility, we must give them freedom and opportunity (the next trait on this list). Third, responsibility and accountability won't work without forgiveness, and a culture that learns from mistakes rather than punishing them. That comes up later on this list. Fourth, responsibility entails a "response" to someone. We can be accountable to others because our lives and interests are interdependent. We will have to live and work with those who share the consequences of our failure. This relational trait comes up eighth on this list.

The Body Shop is a great business success that has made responsibility and accountability core values. Responsibility for the environment and for animal welfare as well as for the health and satisfaction of Body Shop customers is well known and widely applauded. It is not easy for most of us to swallow our pride and say "That was my fault" or "I'm going to need some help on this." A culture of accountability and responsibility has to start at the top. Nobody is fooled by CEOs pretending to be all and know all. A powerful cynicism spreads through such CEOs' companies. So from the top down, let's not just be humble and open but also accountable and responsible.

4. Freedom: Creative risk-taking encouraged; no micro-managing control freaks.

The fourth trait is about managers and organizations giving up control. It is about a culture of freedom for risk-taking, giving others space—limited only by loyalty to mission and team, openness, and accountability. Freedom, in this context, has to do with giving up, or at least sharing, control. Joe Caruso's *The Power of Losing Control* (Penguin/Gotham Books, 2003) understands how important this is in organizations. The vice that is the counterpart to this virtue is micro-management, "control-freakism." Are you going to try to micro-manage that teachability piece or that accountability piece we just reviewed—or can you let things ferment without your hands-on direction? It's about how we manage people and their issues and growth. We could be a learning culture and an accountability culture and still fail by oppressively trying to control everything. That is the message here. Control freaks kill trust in cultures. If you can't trust and let go, either you need to leave or the objects of your control will shut down (or flee at the first opportunity).

Of course, we can't be healthy with an excessive, reckless risk-taking—any more than with a stifling, fearful control. It's all about a culture of freedom—within appropriate limits, i.e., the mission and vision. However we use our freedom, it must align with the mission. Everything is not up for grabs; we stay anchored in loyalty to the core mission and to our team. But then, we give people space and freedom.

The 3M company is an example of openness and freedom that exhibits this trait as well as any company (see the descriptions in *Built to Last*). The old

Hewlett-Packard with its flexible hours and other policies was also a culture of freedom in the sense we are using it here. Business leaders will create healthier organizations if they will keep this value in their top ten list and actively live by it—disciplining themselves to not intervene immediately to straighten everyone and everything out. Give your people some space.

5. Ethics & Excellence: Insatiable hunger for both "doing the right thing" and "doing things right."

The fifth value shares the passion and activism felt in the first one, "loyalty." Loyalty was about passion and tenacity vis-à-vis the core mission, vision, and team. The next three values feel more passive, or we could say "preparatory"—openness, responsibility, and freedom. But those three are creating the capacity to better see what is really excellent and ethical (the fifth character trait). Without openness, teachability, and freedom, I don't think we can really see excellence and ethics clearly. The classical term "justice" (Greek, *dikaiosyne*), much like the term "virtue" (Greek, *arête*), suggests both doing the right thing and doing it right, both the ethics side and the excellence side. This close combination has been a constant theme through this book, and I don't like to separate them into two different concepts on the list. This perspective sees excellence and quality as a moral/ethical imperative—and it sees ethical integrity as being (not just leading to) true individual and organizational excellence.

What we are talking about is an organizational culture that has a real passion to get things right—in financial terms, technical/engineering terms, legal terms . . . and ethical terms, of course. It is about excellence in all those directions. Mediocrity is easy; excellence is hard work, and there are many temptations for short-cuts. But a search for excellence (as the bestselling business book of the 1980s was titled) always inspires both inside and outside an organization.[5] Harris & Associates captures this double message in its core values by making "integrity" their first value and "quality" their second—other terms for ethics and excellence. Starbucks is another company making both ethics and excellence core values in the culture. It starts with a leadership that is not satisfied with second-best or ordinary results. This is where we can let our perfectionist streak run wild. We aim as high as possible and go for it.

6. Mistake Tolerance: Learn and try again; avoid punitive, fearful, repressive reactions.

An organization that aims high is not always going to achieve its ambitious goals. A sure way to kill off such ambitious attempts at greatness is to punish failure. Punishing honest mistakes stifles creativity. Learning from mistakes encourages healthy experimentation and converts negatives into positives. There is a place for mercy and for generosity in business. As we noted earlier on this list, if we want people to step up and be accountable and responsible, we must not overreact and crush them. If we want them to aim high, they may come short, and we must not crush them at that moment.

The basic principle of justice and fairness is proportionality: to each his/her due. Accountability and responsibility mean that people stand up and take what they deserve. But the passion for justice, ethics, and excellence must be qualified. If we take a larger view of the context in which business goals are pursued, an honest—but failed—effort at achieving something great should not be viewed in the same way as an effort that failed for lack of preparation or care. Some business leaders have told me that a mistake might be tolerated once, but repeating the *same* mistake twice is another story. Perhaps it is not a mistake but true negligence the second time around.

Certainly companies with an emphasis on research and new product development (e.g., pharmaceuticals, technology, entertainment) have to embrace this cultural trait. When bad things happen, part of the learning is to put safeguards and backup systems in place the next time to minimize the impact if something starts to go awry. Such companies must have learn to tolerate mistakes made in good faith efforts—and turn those mistakes into learning experiences. The business payoff is a workforce without fear of trying things that are new or difficult, a workforce that learns from its mistakes rather than living in denial or blame or the likelihood of repeating them.

7. Honesty, Integrity, & Transparency. Consistency of thought, talk, and walk; no hidden agendas or evasions.

All of the foregoing corporate cultural traits must be authentic and real if the organization is going to achieve its potential. An organizational leadership that only pretends, Machiavelli-like, to care about loyalty to the mission, teachability, accountability, freedom, excellence, and mistake-tolerance may sometimes succeed in the short term. But longer term, such dishonesty will come back to haunt the company. Business requires trust—and trust requires integrity, "trustworthiness." Integrity is about consistency, the "integration," of what is inside with what is outside, of what is thought, known, and believed with what is said and done.

Relationships thrive on clarity, transparency, honesty, and reliable follow-through. Integrity and trust can be destroyed in a moment; they take a long time to be rebuilt. Integrity simplifies life: If we live with integrity we are relieved from having always to be covering our tracks, maintaining a facade, or looking over our shoulder. Max DePree, William Pollard, Warren Bennis, and many of the other business leaders and authors we have heard from earlier in this book have stressed the critical importance of integrity in companies and their leadership.

From another angle, Don Tapscott and David Ticoll's *The Naked Corporation* argues that in our Internet age, it has become almost impossible to hide anything. Those e-mail memos that ridiculed someone will almost certainly come back to haunt their author. What we do, say, and think is more likely than ever to come out in the open. Therefore, the authors suggest, companies might as well embrace transparency, divulge their true reality, and live consistently with it. Integrity is the virtue that makes transparency pay off. Harris & Associates hits this basic value from two directions. Their first core value is integrity, second is quality, third is reliability. The first and third, integrity and reliability combine to make a powerful commitment to organizational consistency and trustworthiness.

8. Collaboration & Integration. Bringing people together . . . bringing ideas together.
Collaboration and integration in pursuit of excellence on a mission—that's what a company is all about. Teams thrive when there is an inspiring mission, a passion for excellence and ethics (doing the right thing and doing it right), with an atmosphere of mistake tolerance and a high degree of integrity. The eighth trait has two sides to it, a people side and an idea side. On the idea side it is about integrating ideas into more holistic and powerful perspectives, bridging across traditional disciplinary boundaries with new thinking, drawing together the best ideas and practices from various fields. Narrow, silo thinking is the vice to be avoided; holistic, integrative thinking is the virtue.

On the people side, companies are groups of people "co-laboring"—*collaborating*. If we could do it better alone, why form a company? If we are going to make the most of our opportunity, we need to put an emphasis on team play, not just on individual stardom. Turf wars are deadly. Integrating the best people into collaborative teams multiplies organizational strength.

"Collaborationist" used to refer to someone who cooperated with the invading enemy. Collaborators were traitors. In a strange way, this negative connotation points to something basic: Rather than regarding competitors (internally or externally) as enemies, it is often wise to find ways to work together. Life and business are not a zero-sum game. Two businesses creating similar products (or two employees competing with each other) may actually have greater success by working together. Of course, competition is also part of human nature (and often produces better results than its absence). And ego and other narrow interests often disrupt or destroy cooperation and community. Collaboration is not an easy option, but it is worth pursuing and making a value in our companies. Wisdom, creativity, and innovation are usually to be found in a diversity of voices collaborating around a common goal and task.

Jody Hoffer Gittel's *The Southwest Airlines Way: Using the Power of Relationships to Achieve High Performance* (McGraw-Hill, 2003) is a superb demonstration of how collaboration can bring business value as well as workplace happiness. At the Harris & Associates company, the fourth value, "respect," underlines the importance and value of each individual employee. The fifth of their six values, however, is "teamwork." The message is that no matter how great we are as individuals, we can be even better collaborating together. On the idea side, Jon R. Katzenbach and Douglas K. Smith's *The Wisdom of Teams* (HarperBusiness, 1993), and now James Surowiecki's *The Wisdom of Crowds* (Anchor, 2004), make the case that thinking together in teams produces better results than individualism.

9. Courage & Persistence: Guts in the face of difficulty.
The ninth trait is necessary because the business playing field is not always level and life is not always fair. Much of what we deal with in the marketplace, the global economy, or the environment is unfair. Who can predict natural disasters or epidemics or terrorism or war? Even without such large-scale forces, it is difficult to manage a workforce, adapt to change, and make wise decisions in a swirling global marketplace. Problems and even defeats will come, sometimes wholly undeserved. But healthy organizational cultures will be unintimidated and undeterred by these difficulties. Courage, persistence, and "guts" means that they "keep on keeping on" despite the struggles, setbacks, and pain.

Our terms "guts" and "determination" are about courage. Courage (bravery, fortitude) was one of the "cardinal virtues" in antiquity. The ancients thought of it as the "readiness to fall in battle." Courage is the capacity to do the right thing even when you don't want to and it costs something. Aristotle described courage as a "mean" between two undesirable extremes: cowardice (too little "courage") and recklessness (too much "courage"). Courage does what is right—but in a wise and appropriate way, not in a blind, rash reaction. Such a steady, indefatigable persistence was demonstrated by Casntor Fitzgerald after losing much of their business and workforce in the 9/11 attack on their building. Resilience is now one of their stated core values. Levi Strauss lists courage among its four core values—highly appropriate in a global textile business. Jack and Suzy Welch have written that "Business is about managing risk, not running from it"[6]

10. Joyfulness & Fun: Stay positive even in hard times.

The final characteristic suggests that in a healthy culture we don't stop with a grit-your-teeth, grim determination, but we try hard to find some joy and laughter. It may only the tenth on the list, but I think it needs to be there. Max DePree writes that "Joy is an essential ingredient of leadership. Leaders are obligated to provide it."[7] Work is often carried out in the sweat of our brow. One of the synonyms of work is "toil." It feels like that some times. It is important to try to inject humor into the process and help our organizations find joy at work.

Dennis Bakke's management reflection on his years at AES, the energy company, is called *Joy at Work*. AES had fun as one of its core values. Bakke argues that "The key to joy at work is the personal freedom to take actions and make decisions using individual skills and talents."[8] Fun results from a workplace where individuals are given the challenge and opportunity to be innovative, to use their creativity to make something good. Give the workers some control. Challenge them to use their freedom—and they will do so with great results for the company and finding joy for themselves.

Whole Foods and Southwest Airlines are two other companies that have explicitly made fun one of their core values. If you fly Southwest very often, you know how different the atmosphere is among the employees from the experience on most other airlines. It goes back to founder Herb Keleher's personal insistence on its importance. Harris & Associates also list fun as a core value. "More than just a job" is their slogan next to "fun."

Afterthought & Confession

Here is another part of the inside story of my list. I don't just teach business ethics, although that has been my main concern for several years. In another domain and for another, narrower, audience I have studied and taught Christian ethics—trying to re-articulate the ethical teaching of Jesus for our era. As I was studying the Sermon on the Mount, Jesus' most famous statement, back in the 1980s, I started thinking about the opening passage called the "Beatitudes" (from the repeated language "blessed....") and how these seemed to describe the basic characteristics that Jesus wanted his followers to seek for their community and organizational life together in order to be the "salt of the earth" and the "light of the world." For at least the first couple hundred years, it seems that these characteristics were pretty much what the movement was known for (too bad that is far from the case today, but that's another story)—and it gradually permeated the Roman Empire and led to a sort of internal revolution by the 4th century. In other words, these core values or traits did seem to help create and maintain a movement that people wanted to be part of and which achieved its mission in many ways.

> *The longer I studied these eight beatitude characteristics the more I was struck by how similar that message was to what I was getting from business leaders and writers about healthy business (not religious) cultures. For example: "Blessed are the poor in spirit" (openness, teachability), "Blessed are the pure in heart" (integrity), "Blessed are the peacemakers" (collaboration). While the parallels are undoubtedly not persuasive to everyone—and don't need to be—my "Ten Traits" track (loosely or tightly, depending on your perspective) with that ancient list of Beatitudes (with "loyalty" representing the initial commitment of the disciples). For what it's worth . . .*

NOTES

[1] I did write a series of my "Benchmark Ethics" columns in *Ethix Magazine* on most of these traits, between June 1999 and February 2001. When I took my "Ten Traits" to our *Ethix* art director she insisted that it must be eight, not nine or ten, because we had already published lists of "Nine Reasons" and "Ten Principles." Under publication deadline pressure, I wimped out. See *Ethix*, Issue 23 (May-June 2002), p. 11.

[2] Jim Collins and Jerry Porras, *Built to Last: Successful Habits of Visionary Companies* (HarperBusiness, 1997).

[3] See Dennis C. McCarthy, *The Loyalty Link: How Loyal Employees Create Loyal Customers* (John Wiley & Sons, 1997) for an excellent study of how customer loyalty flows from internal loyalty of employees and management ("the link").

[4] Francis Fukuyama's *Trust: The Social Virtues and the Creation of Prosperity* (Free Press, 1995) makes a massive historical case that cultural openness and the capacity to trust others is critical to economic success.

[5] Tom Peters & Robert Waterman, *In Search of Excellence: Lessons from America's Best-Run Companies* (Harper & Row, 1982).

[6] Jack and Suzy Welch, *Winning: The Answers* (Collins, 2006), p. 27.

[7] Max DePree, *Leadership is an Art* (Doubleday, 1989), p. 133.

[8] Dennis Bakke, *Joy at Work* (PVG, 2005), p. 65.

Gill's Ten Principles of Highly Ethical Leaders and Organizations

Executive Summary

Just as with core values and traits of organizational cultures, ethical principles and guidelines must be grounded in a particular mission and vision to have the desired impact. Nevertheless, perhaps because we share a common humanity in some important ways, there may be some common themes in the best ethical schemas. Here is a list of Ten Principles that, in one way or another, find their way onto many codes of ethics for individuals and organizations. This list can be used to stimulate reflection not just on a company code of ethics but on one's own set of core ethical principles. If not these principles, what do you bring to the ethics table?

In Chapter Six, we looked at "principle-guided practices." My argument was that the ethical principles or guidelines of a company code of ethics need to be developed by the practitioners in an organic way. What are the business practices and activities on which we should be spending our time in pursuit of our organizational mission? That's the first question. Then: What are the guidelines that tell us *how* to do these things we do, how to do them *right*, how to avoid messing up either the company or anyone impacted by our activities? This code of ethics is and must be specific and customized to each particular company and situation.

Nevertheless, on a more general level, I have come to think that there are certain basic ethical principles for the ethical leadership of people and organizations. Back in the early 1980s, I started developing the list below and I have given literally hundreds of speeches and taught dozens of classes on these principles over the past quarter century. Part of my inspiration, I should say, was Stephen R. Covey's *Seven Habits of Highly Effective People*. I didn't much like the terminology of "effective people" (by itself). Ethics types often react, "Yes, but effective to what end?" We don't want tyrants and thieves to be effective. The concept of "effectiveness" begs for some guidance regarding its mission and objectives. So I countered by articulating the "Principles of Highly *Ethical* People." But there are ten, not seven.

Unfortunately, versions of my list are circulating through cyberspace, sometimes with some glitches and variations that I think weaken the overall argument. I can't undo the downside, but I'd like add to the upside by including the list here with some explanation and illustration of what I have been driving at. As in the case of the "Ten Traits" of Appendix A, I brand it as "Gill's Ten Principles" partly to acknowledge that this is only my take on the principles, not some universal Truth binding on all humanity, and partly to re-stake a public claim to this (almost) lifetime project of mine.[1]

One way I have used this list is as a sort of values and principles template against which to help people clarify their own top ten ethical convictions and principles (the form I use is at the end of the Appendix). One important result of this sort of exercise is that it helps you know what you have to bring to the table when ethics is discussed.

I do follow my own advice (in Chapter Six) and state these principles first in a positive way (i.e., as ethical mandates); then as negatively stated ("Never . . . ") boundary conditions. "Always" and "never" language makes some people nervous, but remember, these are *principles* to inspire us and give us guidance. When they come into conflict or are difficult to apply we must not be paralyzed by perfectionism, guilt, or weariness. This is a map, remember. We don't live for the map itself. The map is to help us live.

Gill's Ten Principles of Highly Ethical Leaders and Organizations

1. Treat all people as unique, valuable individuals.
Never treat anyone as worthless, dispensable, or "just a number."

2. Support the freedom and growth of others.
Never view anyone through stereotypes and images, or as fixed and unchangeable.

3. Communicate to others by name with respect.
Never ignore people—or use demeaning, trivializing, or derogatory names/labels.

4. Model and encourage a balanced life of good work and rest.
Never adopt policies or make demands on others that undermine balanced lives.

5. Honor and respect the families and friends of others.
Never undervalue the significance of families and friends of employees.

6. Protect the life, safety, and health of others.
Never harm or jeopardize the physical well-being of anyone.

7. Keep commitments and agreements in a trustworthy, reliable manner.
Never betray your relational commitments or undermine those made by others.

8. Promote fairness in matters of money and property.
Never tolerate unfair wages, prices, or financial practices.

9. Communicate truthfully and constructively.
Never mischaracterize people, products, services, or facts.

10. Cultivate a positive and generous attitude.
Never give in to negativity, anger, greed, or envy.

1. Treat all people as unique, valuable individuals: Never treat anyone as worthless, dispensable, or "just a number."

The first principle really is foundational to ethical management. It is not just a soft, sentimental affirmation to make the weak feel better. It is the truth. The fact is that every person is unique (unique fingerprint, DNA, temperament, history, abilities, etc.). We are only recognizing the reality of life by this principle. The second aspect is a bigger stretch, i.e., that everyone is *valuable* somehow, somewhere. This is the management challenge: finding a place for each person's abilities to flourish—or helping them move on to some other employment setting. But certainly everyone performs better when treated this way, and general morale improves when this is a value in the culture.

Here are some of the ways this principle has been articulated: First, by the philosopher Immanuel Kant, "Act in such a way that you treat humanity, whether in your person or in the person of another, always at the same time as an end and never simply as a means."[2] Here is David Packard's statement: ". . . Our strong belief that individuals be treated with consideration and

respect . . . Every person in our company is important, and every job is important."[3] Finally, a study of several successful businesses by Stanford professors
Charles O'Reilly and Jeffrey Pfeffer concluded, "These places are also better
at attracting and retaining people as a byproduct of how they operate. That is
because great people want to work at places where they can actually use their
talents, where they are treated with dignity, trust, and respect . . ."[4]

HP, UPS, AES, Men's Wearhouse, and Harris & Associates are just some
of the companies that make this a key principle in their organization. It is a
different way of thinking, speaking, and acting toward people. Remember: It
doesn't mean that everyone is equal or the same in ability or appropriateness
to your business—or that they have a right to screw up and then criticize you
for calling them on the carpet. But it does radically change the way we manage people. It is principle #1 in ethical organizations.

2. Support the freedom and growth of others: Never view anyone through stereotypes and images, or as fixed and unchangeable.

The fact is that everyone actually *is* capable of learning and growth (hard
to believe sometimes, but it is true). People are bored without challenge and
change. Further, it is dehumanizing and insulting to be stereotyped and limited
("just a secretary," "engineers can't really lead people," "managers will never
understand the science," "blonde, so . . ." "black, so . . ." "female . . ." etc.).
The exceptions make the case: stories of hidden talents that came out when
given a chance, stories of superb leadership when given the responsibility.
Individual growth and unleashed creativity lead to higher team productivity in
the organization. Depression and resentment come when boxed in by stereotypes.

Bill Pollard, former CEO of ServiceMaster described a core concern of his
company as ". . . that basic ethical question of the marketplace: What is happening to the person in the process? Is she developing and growing as a whole
person?"[5] David Packard also wrote that "It has always been important to Bill
and me to create an environment in which people have a chance to be their
best, to realize their potential . . ."[6]

Think about how you feel when boxed in, when stereotyped. By contrast,
how do you feel when given opportunity and responsibility to solve a problem? When you get to choose to try something new? When you accomplish a
creative task? When you know your team valued your creativity and help?
Like the first principle, this one may not come naturally to every leader, but it
has a lot of good authority behind it—both the philosophy and science and the
concrete business experience of many successful leaders. I used to always ask

my direct reports during their annual one-on-one reviews: "Tell me one way you would like to grow this coming year? Is there one new skill you'd like to add to your bag of tricks? A class you would like to take?" I never saw anything but upside payoffs for this approach. On the other hand, I have had long lines of people griping to me over the years about bosses who took them for granted, boxed them into some stereotype, etc.

3. Communicate to others by name with respect: Never ignore people—or use demeaning, trivializing, or derogatory names/labels.

The first point here is that it is dehumanizing and discouraging to be ignored. It is discouraging not to be known by name by our supervisor or colleagues. Second, it is degrading to be addressed or labeled with an unwelcome, negative, or trivial name or label. Human beings are language-using beings. Names matter. Communication matters. Frequent, respectful, meaningful communication leads to higher morale and increased productivity. Somebody knows my name. "I'm amazed that he/she remembered my name," someone will say (gratefully) about a boss.

Max DePree, the much admired CEO of Herman Miller, wrote "Communication is an ethical question. Good communication means a respect for individuals. . . We owe each other truth and courtesy. . . There may be no single thing more important in our efforts to achieve meaningful work and fulfilling relationships than to learn and practice the art of communication."[7] The Harris & Associates code of ethics says: "Communicate (voice, written, e-mail, or otherwise) in a respectful and professional manner to fellow workers, clients, partners, contractors, competitors, and all others."

How do we practice this principle? First, we learn the names and labels people choose for themselves. Learn how to pronounce their name the way they say it (a person's name has huge symbolic importance—it represents who they are, and your use or misuse of their name is your first symbolic recognition of who they are; it is a profound wound and disrespect not to do this). Related to this: If you refer to "girls," you had better say "boys" as well; better by far is to say "men" and "women." But never "men" and "girls." If Black people want to be referred to as African-Americans—then they should be referred to that way. If someone of Chinese descent prefers "Chinese-American" over "Asian-American," that decides it. The point is to show respect by letting people name themselves (do not invent nicknames and impose them on people; you may think of it as cute and affectionate, but it is much more likely that it is boneheaded and offensive—even if your intimidated employee says otherwise).

Second implication: Take the initiative to speak/communicate to people. Relationships depend on such communication. Silence and being ignored are often deadly. Failure to respond is a bad message by itself. Learn how to manage a long list of communications efficiently so this task doesn't bury you. Take a few moments to wander by your people and say hello. Be an active, respectful communicator.

4. Model and encourage a balanced life of good work and rest: Never adopt policies or make demands on others that undermine balanced lives.

This principle has a work side and a rest side. All people need the opportunity to work—and to relax. Both work and rest are about human health; both are basic human needs. Good work not only provides for our financial and material needs, it gives us an opportunity to be creative and express our humanity and character. Good rest gives us a chance not just to recuperate physically and emotionally in order to be good workers again—it has a kind of intrinsic value. It's about enjoying our "being" not just our "doing."

The principle is to model both good work and good rest. Being a workaholic is little, if any, better than being work-aversive. Managers practice this principle by working for (on behalf of) their people—but also taking a little time to be with those people (coffee, conversation, etc.). It takes both aspects to have a complete relationship (true for friends and family also: Work *for* them, but also devote some quality time to just hanging out *with* them). People generally respond with gratitude, loyalty, and even greater effort when we do something for them—and also stop to be with them.

Leaders must not just set a good example here but do whatever else can empower and encourage their people to live balanced lives. Anne Mulcahy, the Chair & CEO of Xerox has written, "Work/life benefits allow companies meaningful ways for responding to their employees' needs; they can be a powerful tool for transforming a workforce and driving a business' success." David Gilmour decided to go against the flow when he created Paradise Foods. Everyone, Gilmour included, works very hard to make this the best market in Marin County (California), but the store is never open past 8:00 p.m., and it is always closed on Sundays. "Our message to our customers is 'Life is more than shopping,' and to our employees, 'Life is more than working,'" Gilmour says. Despite all the naysayers who point to the competition which is always open 24/7, Paradise Foods has year-in, year-out exceeded all its ambitious growth projections. Balanced lives of work and rest do not mean business failure. Quite the contrary.

**5. Honor and respect the families and friends of others: Never underval-
ue the significance of families and friends of employees.**

Few, if any, people are without relationships to "significant others" who
mean much to them: parents, partners, children, house-mates, friends. The
fifth principle of highly ethical leaders and organizations is to treat those significant others with respect. How you treat those "others" affects how people
feel about you and the company. Wayne Alderson, based on his experience as
President of the Pittron steel company and then as a consultant and advisor to
many other businesses, has written, "One of the foremost ways for an organization to show respect for its employees is to recognize and respect each
employee's family. An employee is nearly always connected to others—a
spouse, parents, children, roommates."[8]

How do we practice this management principle? Part of it is the little, day-
to-day things of showing interest in the lives and relationships of our people.
Take a look at the family and friend photos in the cubicle. Ask about someone
you heard was ill—or graduating from school. Part of it is a policy matter—
promoting sensitive and supportive family leave and emergency leave policies.
Welcoming friends and family to tour the workplace at appropriate times, or to
participate in some company social events, can also support this principle of
ethical management.

**6. Protect the life, safety, and health of others: Never harm or jeopardize
the physical well-being of anyone.**

The sixth principle is sort of obvious, but it needs to be stated clearly and
remembered at all times. We have seen in earlier chapters that "harm" is at the
core of what makes something unethical. Harm can come in many ways, but
the sixth principle focuses on the most basic aspect: life, health, and safety.
Illness, injury, or even the fear or significant threat of such, undermine
employee performance as well as any likelihood of continuing customer, partner relationships (i.e., if your products or activities make them sick or endan-
ger their lives, they will go elsewhere).

Perhaps this principle is especially relevant in dangerous businesses such
as construction, energy, air travel, pharmaceuticals, and food handling. Here is
some of the language used by Harris & Associates for their construction and
project management firm: "Protect life, health, and safety. . . Rectify or report
immediately any unsafe or threatening situations. . . Accept responsibility for
any unsafe conditions we may have caused or contributed to and take corrective action. . . Pursue the highest standards in safety, whether on Harris property, in transit, or at a project site, . . Never compromise safety at any stage from
project design, to execution, to final inspection." Paradise Foods, a grocery

store, is concerned with "Cleanliness everywhere in our store and among our staff, with special concern to maintain the highest standards in sanitary food storage and display are critical requirements."

The sixth principle is important in all arenas where life, health, and safety might be at risk. We can try to maintain healthy, non-hostile workplaces . . . provide (or assist with) basic health care for our people . . . ensure adequate product safety testing . . . ensure positive environmental impact of our business activities and products . . . assist conflict resolution—not exacerbation . . . tame public and private rhetoric (no insults, etc.), and work to improve attitudes (anger management, etc.).

7. Keep commitments and agreements in a trustworthy, reliable manner: Never betray your relational commitments or undermine those made by others.
Humans are not just individual physical beings whose bodies need protection but relational, social beings whose commitments and agreements also need protection. Reliable, trustworthy covenants and commitments are essential in every sector of life: business, family, friendship, community, and politics. The first, direct way we practice the seventh principle is to deliver on both the letter and spirit of promises, commitments, contracts, and handshakes we have made. It is to show loyalty and fidelity to people counting on us, inside or outside our business. Second, the principle calls us to never undermine or attack other people's important covenants and relationships, inside or outside the workplace.

One obvious interpersonal aspect of this application is to respect people's marriages and romantic relationships and not exploit possible opportunities in the work environment (including business trips and after hours activities) to attempt to lure colleagues away from their commitments into inappropriate relationships with us. Abusing our power and position by pressuring others in this way is profoundly unethical. Even worse, if such attention is not reciprocated and is clearly unwanted, it is not just flirting but harassment, which is both illegal and ethically wrong. Betraying your own marriage or similar commitment is just as ugly.

This principle also applies to business commitments and relationships. Here is some of the language used in the Harris & Associates Code to preserve this principle: "Fulfill commitments, contracts, agreements, and promises. . . . Follow through completely and reliably on agreements made with clients, business partners, and fellow employees." "Refer interested individuals to the Harris web site and to our Human Resources department. Do not engage in 'raiding' of employees of other firms."

8. Promote fairness in matters of money and property: Never tolerate unfair wages, prices, or financial practices.

Everyone, every business, and every community has need of a basic material infrastructure for life (shelter, food, clothing, financial security, "stuff"). Fairness (justice) in how these material goods are distributed is at the core of the eighth principle. A fair distribution of money and property is essential to good work, sustainable and successful business, and a peaceful world. This principle requires us to promote fairness in compensation, wages and benefits, in pricing services and products that we sell, in tax rates and policies, and in matters of inheritance. Intellectual property is also a concern here. Fairness in opportunity and in access to nature and education, is part of it. The principle applies to workers or customers who might be tempted to steal or misuse company property, and it applies to employers who might be tempted to extort unfair payments from desperate or gullible customers—or to refuse to pay fair wages to employees desperate for any level of work and wage—or to evade paying their fair share of taxes.

The Harris & Associates Code develops the basic principle, "Maintain fairness in business and financial matters," with several elaborations of what they mean: Avoid both the appearance and the reality of any kind of financial or business impropriety. . . . Deliver the full value service that has been purchased from Harris. . . . Compensate employees, sub-consultants, and business partners fairly for services rendered. . . . Ensure that invoicing and billing practices are accurate and fully justified, whether dealing with clients, business partners, or personal expense reimbursements. . . Avoid real or potential conflicts of interest that could arise from giving or receiving gifts, dealing with relatives or close friends, or from any other source. . . . Avoid improper tampering with the employees, operations, inside information, or intellectual property of other companies."

Over centuries of human history, this topic has been debated at length. Barbarians and thugs have argued that what is fair is "whatever I can take from everyone else." Civilized people have always concluded that that argument is not good enough. Economic justice and fairness are not decided by your power, but by other criteria such as what you deserve, how hard you work, how much you produce, the quality of products and services, the proportionality of one situation or person to another. Job danger and risk matter, as do stress, experience, responsibility, and availability. If my gain comes with your gain, that is different than my gain at your loss. Every one of these criteria bring up debatable issues. Very little is simple in this domain. The bottom line principle, though, is that highly (or even moderately) ethical people seek fairness—not just personal wealth maximization.

There are CEOs who are committed to some kind of fairness in their own compensation. Gary Kelly of Southwest Airlines, John Mackey of Whole Foods, and Jim Sinegal of Costco, are just three major CEOs who are committed to fairness in compensation (for themselves, for their employees). You can read every day in the business pages about the long list of others who practice the "greed is good" philosophy. Suffice to say here that this great, historic principle is in grave danger today. When we are ruled by people of power rather than people of justice, the clock of revolt and insurgency begins to tick.

9. Communicate truthfully and constructively: Never mischaracterize people, products, services, or facts.

Lying and falsehood break down the trust that is essential to good business and leadership. Lies lead to ever more complex, time- and energy- consuming cover-ups. Truth is simpler. Lies and mischaracterizations can harm people's health, relationships, finances, and reputation. Lies also corrupt and degrade the liar. This principle is about telling the truth *to* colleagues, customers, partners, investors, other stakeholders——and telling the truth *about* people, products, finances, and services.

Max DePree has written, "Access to pertinent information is essential to getting a job done. The right to know is basic. Moreover, it is better to err on the side of too much information than risk leaving someone in the dark. Information is power, but it is pointless power if hoarded . . . We owe each other truth and courtesy . . . To liberate people, communication must be based on logic, compassion, and sound reasoning."[9] Telling the truth gets complex in the information age. Who "needs to know" this or that . . . and when is the appropriate time? Can too much information ("infoglut") obfuscate rather than clarify and empower? Truth can be as cruel as the lie, which is why the principle says not just to communicate truthfully but constructively.

The American Marketing Association Code of Ethics emphasizes that "Marketers shall uphold and advance the integrity, honor, and dignity of the marketing profession by . . . being honest in serving consumers, clients, employees, suppliers, distributors, and the public. . . . Participants in the marketing exchange process should be able to expect that . . . communications about offered products and services are not deceptive." The Harris & Associates Code devotes two basic principles and a number of elaborations to this topic which are worth quoting at length to illustrate how to approach this principle: "Never compromise on truthfulness and accuracy. Maintain clarity, consistency, and accuracy in all communications with clients, contractors, business partners, employees, governmental agencies, and the public. Never submit deceptive, incomplete, or inaccurate proposals, financial reports, or inspections. Do not over-promise on schedules, project outcomes, or personnel; disclose any contingencies and concerns. Correct mistakes, mis-statements, and misleading communications immediately. Respect privacy and protect confidential and proprietary information. Protect the privacy of individuals and their records, whether Harris employees or not. Protect the confidentiality of the proprietary information, business plans, and communications of Harris and its clients and business partners. Do not accept or misappropriate any confidential information or proprietary data from a competitor company; respect always the rights of the rightful owners of information."

We live in an era transformed radically by information and communications technologies. This practice area needs the guidance of our ninth principle.

10. Cultivate a positive and generous attitude: Never give in to negativity, anger, greed, or envy.

The final principle is parallel to the final "trait" of ethically healthy organizational cultures; it is here not just as a trait we seek to embed in our culture, but as a principle of practice, decision, and action. We should choose and act in a way that preserves a positive and generous attitude. Attitude is the root of speech and action. A bad (or good) attitude is almost impossible to conceal or disguise. Even if it is mostly concealed, a bad attitude corrupts the person who harbors it. Business ethicist Robert Solomon has written, " 'Greed is good' is a contradiction . . . Greed (avarice) is an excess. It is like gluttony, an embarrassment . . . unbridled vulgarity . . . Greed is not vision. It is lack of vision . . . Better to listen to what the Talmud says: 'The rich man is one who is satisfied with what he has.' Contentment might not seem to be a virtue, especially in a world where ambitiousness is thought to be one, but there is real wisdom in knowing when enough is enough, not being greedy, and allowing oneself to simply be satisfied."[10]

Of course, a bad performance is not saved by having a good, positive, generous attitude alone. And we are not suggesting a superficial "rah-rah" froth over everything. There may be a time to show some aggravation and disappointment. But as a general principle, leaders should not be governed by anger, jealousy, envy, negativity, and greed. Leaders need to personally demonstrate a good, resilient attitude and then infect others and try to create the conditions in which others can also be positive. Southwest Airlines, AES, and Whole Foods are three companies that explicitly focus on this good attitude principle.

Gill's Ethical Principles Personal Inventory

What ethical values and principles do you bring to the table? What does your own "moral compass" tell you as a leader?

How would you rank (from "1" (highest) to "10" (lowest)) the following ten basic ethical management principles in your own value system?

Is there another principle (not on this list) that would be on your own "top ten" list? Write it at the bottom.

#___ **Treat all people as unique, valuable individuals.**
    Never treat anyone as worthless, dispensable, or "just a number."

#___ **Support the freedom and growth of others.**
    Never view anyone through stereotypes and images, or as fixed and unchangeable.

#___ **Communicate to others by name with respect.**
    Never ignore people—or use demeaning, trivializing, or derogatory names/labels.

#___ **Model and encourage a balanced life of good work and rest.**
    Never adopt policies or make demands on others that undermine balanced lives.

#___ **Honor and respect the families and friends of others.**
    Never undervalue the significance of families and friends of employees.

#___ **Protect the life, safety, and health of others.**
    Never harm or jeopardize the physical well-being of anyone.

#___ **Keep commitments and agreements in a trustworthy, reliable manner.**
    Never betray your relational commitments or undermine those made by others.

#___ **Promote fairness in matters of money and property.**
    Never tolerate unfair wages, prices, or financial practices.

#___ **Communicate truthfully and constructively.**
    Never mischaracterize people, products, services, or facts.

#___ **Cultivate a positive and generous attitude.**
    Do not give in to negativity, anger, greed, or envy.

#___

#___

#___

#___

Afterthought & Confession

As in the case of the previous Appendix A, there is another "secret history" to this list of Ten Principles. What lies in the background in this case is the most famous list of ethical principles in history: the Ten Commandments. Back in the early 1980s I was giving a talk on ethics and the Ten Commandments to a graduate student group at the University of Nevada at Las Vegas. Until that occasion I had always thought that the first part of the commandments (no other gods, no images/idols, etc.) was only about religion and theology—and only the second part (no murder, no theft etc.), was about people and ethics. But it suddenly dawned on me that evening that all ten of these guidelines expressed a perspective that was equally relevant to relationships with God and relationships with human beings.

For example, in the first commandment, God insists that no one else be given his place ("no other gods before me"), in the second that he not be replaced by any fixed images, in the third that his name be used respectfully, in the fourth that people work for him six days but take a day off ("Sabbath") just to be with him, etc. Atheists, such as Karl Marx or Ludwig Feuerbach, would argue that the ancient adherents of the Decalogue actually wanted such treatment for themselves, but, oppressed and unable to achieve their liberation, they falsely projected these ideals and desires onto a god they invented. So fundamentally, in their essence, the Ten Commandments express not God's wishes but human wishes for how to be treated.

The alternative way of explaining this relationship is to say, with the Jewish-Christian-Muslim tradition, that there is a God who created man and woman "in his image and likeness"—hence the similarity between what we want for ourselves and what God appears to command for himself. The theological explanation for why men and women want to be treated as unique and valuable, not as replaceable, valueless parts, is because they have been made in the image of their Creator God, who wants to be loved that way and who has a basic right to be treated that way.

Personally, I have always preferred the theological explanation to the social scientific one, but that is not my subject here. And however one decides the matter does not change the basic message: That these, by whatever avenue, are ten key guidelines on how people wish to be treated. Still stronger, people believe they have a right to be treated in these ways, which makes them ten principles of justice, not just ten principles of love.

It has occurred to me, of course, that if all social scientists and cultural anthropologists of the Marxist and post-Marxist orientation, plus all Jews, Christians, and Muslims, could make common cause on these ten basic principles of ethical business—if this were possible—what a great day that would be.

NOTES

[1] Al Erisman and I published a slightly modified version of this list in our *Ethix Magazine,* Issue 21 (Jan-Feb 2002), p. 11.

[2] The "categorical imperative" in *Grounding for the Metaphysic of Morals* (1785).

[3] David Packard, *The HP Way: How Bill Hewlett and I Built Our Company* (HaperCollins, 1995), p. 127.

[4] Charles O'Reilly and Jeffrey Pfeffer, *Hidden Value: How Great Companies Achieve Extraordinary Results with Ordinary People* (Harvard Business School Press, 2000), p. 3.

[5] C. William Pollard, *The Soul of the Firm* (HarperBusiness, 1996), p. 26.

[6] David Packard, *The HP Way* (HaperCollins, 1995), p. 127.

[7] Max DePree, *Leadership is an Art* (Doubleday, 1989), pp. 91-96.

[8] Wayne Alderson, *Theory R Management* (Nelson, 1994), p. 100.

[9] *Leadership is an Art* (Doubleday, 1989), pp. 91-95.

[10] Robert Solomon, *A Better Way to Think About Business* (Oxford University Press, 1999), pp. 27-29, 81.

Appendix C

Case Commentaries

The following ethics cases were presented in Chapter Three on "Ethical ER: Trouble-Shooting and Crisis Management." Along with these cases, Chapter Three provides a case analysis method which can help us analyze and resolve such cases. I will not follow the case analysis rubric slavishly, line-upon-line, but in general outline that is the approach here.

Sample Case One: Under the Influence?

Your boss has been great to work for these past three years. But on a recent occasion you smelled alcohol on his breath when he arrived back at the office after a long lunch at an off site location. He has been such a great boss; he is scheduled to retire in two years; his personal life has brought him terrible pain recently.

Do we have an ethics problem here? How should it be handled?

Commentary:

Red flags are waving, but let's be real careful. We don't want to hurt this good guy who is going through some personal hell right now—but neither can we stand by and let him hurt others, the company, or himself. Harm is a key ethical value here, along with loyalty and care. But some factual discovery is critical: Was he driving back from lunch—or walking or taking a cab? Does the business have a stated policy prohibiting drinking or being under the influence on the job (or are you all employees at a brewery? Just asking!). Also—does he smell of alcohol because he finished lunch with one drink…or just burped…or someone spilled a drink on him…or because he really drank too much and is inebriated? If he is really drunk, if he was driving, if he is belligerent, if this has happened several times . . . you probably need to report him to a supervisor or whoever is in charge. We can't risk harm to innocent victims of his driving. We can't let this behavior create a precedent for others in the workplace. Nevertheless, if the transgression is less severe, my inclination would be to call a taxi and send him home for the day (or drive him home myself) and then have a heart-to-heart chat with him later, maybe helping him get some counseling support.

Sample Case Two: Google in China

Google has agreed with the Chinese government that it will censor its web site to comply with Chinese policy. In a widely debated example, a search of "Tiananmen Square" outside China gives photos and info about China's violent suppression of a free speech demonstration—but in China such a Google search deletes these negative images and facts. CEO Eric Schmidt defends the decision as necessary to reach the lucrative market of 111 million Internet users and argues that it is arrogant to walk into a new country and tell them how to operate. (*SF Chronicle*, 13 April 06)

How do you figure out what's right and wrong in this global business case?

Commentary:

It doesn't seem illegal, doesn't seem to break company ethical standards—though some observers will charge Google with "doing evil" in contradiction to their motto. In the end, this case requires a judgment call. It is not clear that there is one right way to go. It bothers most of our personal moral compasses to think of being party to a government deceiving its people. People are harmed by such disinformation (if they believe it). But think about it this way: If you were in China, would you rather have 99 percent of Google access—or no access until it is 100 percent? If you were computer-literate and politically savvy in China, would you be taken in by their Tiananmen censorship? Chances are you wouldn't believe a word they say under any circumstances. (After all, are you naïve about press releases and news spin from your own politicians and government? I didn't think so). And is Google permitted to occupy 99 percent of the info space and believe that the remaining 1 percent will come before very long? (This is a lot more than just getting the proverbial nose of the camel in the tent). Two suggestions: Let's try to ask some Chinese scholars and travelers over here, and even some Chinese citizens on the ground in China, what they would like Google to do in this case. Isn't it a bit patronizing for us to decide for them? Let's find out what they want Google to do. If the dominant voice of the Chinese people is "boycott"—then I'm for that. Final thought: Can Google just have NO entry for Tiananmen Square, rather than host a misleading flower show at that site? That way Google is making a quiet but clear statement: No partnership in deception.

Sample Case Three: Executive Compensation at Sun

Sun Microsystem's Board Chairman Scott McNealy's compensation rose from $4.2 million in 2005 to $16.5 million in 2006. CEO Jonathan Schwartz's compensation rose from $3 million in 2005 to $22.8 million in 2006. Meanwhile, in the past five years Sun has experienced annual layoffs, declining revenue, and a stock price decline of 93 percent.

Do we have an ethics problem here, or is this just a market reality? If it is ethically problematic, who should take responsibility? What should be done?

Commentary:

This case is a brief example of the executive compensation ethics debates that swirl around us. These kinds of compensation don't seem to be illegal or violate company or professional codes of ethics. But these practices do trouble many consciences and personal values (it seems to many people grossly unfair and out of scale to pay anyone like this—especially when revenue and stock price are plummeting). When publicized, these practices do create an uproar (a red flag, remember). And investors, if not also employees and customers, may be harmed by the diversion of so much money to two leaders in this manner and under these circumstances.

It is easy for those outside the executive suite to call this legalized "theft"—but easy for the recipients to call it "market value" for talented executives like McNealy and Schwartz. The range of effective responses to these practices (should one decide they are unethical) seems very limited (protest, write letters, foment unrest, appeal to Congress, quit working for the company, boycott company products). The problem here is twofold: (1) Are these compensation practices unethical? (2) What can we do about the problem? In my opinion, a great deal more research and discussion is needed to come to some agreement on the ethics of compensation (not just for executives, but at all levels—including questions about employee retirement, health care, etc.). And a great deal of work remains to be done to figure out how best to respond to the problem (whether to constrain unethical practices—or to better explain the justice of practices in the interest of peace).

For the moment, I'm just going to agitate and press for that bigger research and discussion.

Sample Case Four: Legal but Unethical?

You are a sales representative for a new synthetic fiber that has excellent properties in every respect but one. To this point no one has been able to treat or process it so it will be flame-resistant or flame-retardant. It has therefore been outlawed in the USA as a fiber for apparel. Sales have dropped drastically since the fiber is now legally permitted only in certain industrial products. Hundreds of jobs are at stake if this company fails to find a way to market its product soon.

Your customer surprises you by asking you to quote prices and delivery schedules for a large order of your fiber. When you remind her that the fiber is not legally useable in apparel, she says, "The law only prohibits selling such apparel in the USA. I'm going to manufacture it here but sell it in South America where there are no legal restrictions on this material."

Will you quote her a price? [Discuss the case without reading the next paragraphs; then move on]

_____

You find out that many children in the proposed market have inadequate clothing. The alternative may be between sleeping in cold, inadequate clothing—and sleeping in your warm, inexpensive but non-flame-resistant clothing.

Does this change your mind? [Discuss how this discovery might affect the case without reading the next paragraph; then move on]

_____

Then you find out that most of the prospective buyers of your product use open fire ovens and fireplaces for cooking and heating in their living quarters—a more dangerous environment for accidental fires and burns than the typical American home.

Does this affect your decision?

Commentary:

This case has, with various modifications, been on my desk since the mid-1970s. There are actual historical cases with many of these details. It seems anachronistic to have a case about manufacturing clothes in the USA when most of our textile and clothing manufacture is now offshored—although American Apparel seems to be a thriving Los Angeles-based clothing manufacturer these days.

The basic lessons of this case are about how our values can stay constant (always concerned to protect the health and safety of children, concerned not to let any racial or national prejudice allow us to treat others as less valuable, always concerned to save the jobs at our company) ... while our changing awareness of the facts pushes us to one conclusion or another. First, we won't sell ... but then we realize that this clothing is better than freezing to death ... but then we decide again not to sell because the risk is unacceptably high.

Here are some other things to think about: You may be the sales rep, but the stakes are too high here for you to play Lone Ranger: buy a little time and go back to consult with your boss. Also: Are American safety standards justifiable? Are the fire-retarding chemicals in the material themselves carcinogenic? (Technological progress is not automatically good—just think of the drugs that enter the market to great fanfare, only to be withdrawn after side effects become apparent).

What do the community leaders and parents in our proposed market think and want? (Let's not be patronizing and decide for them).

Are there creative, imaginative win-win solutions? (e.g., use the material as the lining in between two panels of fire-resistant cloth? Sell it with warning labels? Manufacture and sell spark-arrestor screens for housing in the proposed market?

Sample Case Five: Engineering Standards: Who Decides?

You are an engineer, widely respected in the whole industry for your expertise on tunnel design and safety. Six months ago you accepted a lucrative job offer to move from headquarters in Chicago to a booming branch office in San Francisco and serve as lead engineer on a new tunnel being built in a controversial, earthquake-prone area.

Now, six months after moving your family and deep into the project, you have reached an impasse. You believe that the California engineering standards have not caught up with the latest discoveries on tunnel earthquake safety. Your San Francisco boss, who recruited you from headquarters for this move, has rejected all of your arguments and insists that, for project budget reasons, the tunnel must be built in conformity with existing regulations, not at the more expensive, newer engineering level you believe that will better provide earthquake safety.

You have concluded that you may be fired if you push too hard. The job market is tight in your specialty area. The kids are just now getting comfortable in their new schools

What are the central ethical values and principles at stake here? How will you sort through the facts, values, and options and find the best, most ethical response?

Commentary:

Do we have an ethical problem here? I think so. Maybe everything complies with the law, but some engineers tell me it is unethical for an engineer to surrender professional judgment on a critical safety issue. If this conflict were a front page story, I think it would create a huge controversy. So where do we go? How do we resolve the problem? Seems like the Chicago headquarters boss should get involved—if for no other reason than to help move you back there again (the Southern California boss should help you move back also; you seem to have been brought out under slightly false pretenses. Your approval was wanted but not your expertise).

But it is also possible that you can broaden the conversation. Get more engineering (and finance) experts involved. Get the taxpaying community involved and find out their sense of priorities (e.g., extra safety margin at higher tax cost?). There is some fact-finding necessary here. This is a huge thing—earthquakes, tunnels, public safety—and it has to be understood that public safety trumps project schedules and budgets. It is not just a power struggle of me against you. Get more people involved! The public almost certainly needs to be made aware of what is happening. When people are significantly affected by a decision, justice requires that they be given some say in their own fate.

Sample Case Six: Blow the Whistle?

Jane, a recent college graduate, has accepted a great job as a scientist at a leading high tech research and development company. She will be involved in exciting research right in her interest area. The job pays very well—her old classmates are a little envious of her great opportunity—but she is mainly grateful for the salary so she can make life a little better for her ailing, aged parents.

Jane has been given a security clearance and is deeply involved in a research project which is expected to save thousands of lives around the world if it is successful. The stakes are high and she is excited to be involved. Her boss has emphasized over and over to her how important this project is and how critical it is to maintain loyalty, integrity and mutual trust on the research team.

While walking past a van parked on the street just outside the company parking lot one morning, Jane unintentionally discovers that Joe, the key genius on the research team, is sexually involved with the boss's wife.

Jane asks you, her friend, what, if anything, she should do about it. And you say . . .

_____

Jane decides to hold off, at least for the time being (but was she right to do so?). She then is amazed one day when Joe tells her (and she later confirms from her own observation) that their boss has a serious cocaine habit (using even in his office some times), and that he appears to be spending government grant money on his drug habit.

She asks for your advice again . . .

Commentary:

Oh my goodness, this is ugly. What a disappointment for Jane after such high initial hopes. She is the "new kid on block," and we can presume that all the other members of her team are not sleazy and corrupt. I would not urge her to jump into the leadership of a reform or whistle-blowing project quite yet. The sexual thing (are you absolutely sure Jane?) is offensive and unethical to many people, but we really don't even know if it might be going on with the boss's knowledge and permission (he prefers coke to sex?). The law usually doesn't prohibit sex between consenting adults, but it does prohibit embezzlement and mind-altering drug use on the job, especially in government settings. So the problem goes from possibly minor to definitely major with the coke and bucks phase.

My suggestion to Jane: Move slowly, but don't give up on it yet. Try to confide in a trusted colleague on the team and ask if they are aware of any weird stuff going on (I would not make any rash accusations on any of these issues). If you get a lot of self-protecting denial and find yourself alone with this after making some slow, wise, deliberate steps to share the problem with colleagues, I would advise you to quit. (Sorry, Jane, but if you sit on this and do nothing, you are implicated). Send an anonymous (or signed, I'm not sure how endangered you might be) letter to some higher-ups and to one or two muck-raking journalists at "60 Minutes," "Frontline," etc. Look for another job?

Sample Case Seven: Big Pig Waste Management

Will is the financial vice president of a community hospital. He is under heavy pressure from the president and board of directors to reduce the operating deficit. His job may be on the line if he fails.

The hospital has a long-standing policy of providing basic care to all in need. A huge list of uncollected and perhaps uncollectible bills for such services is part of the financial problem. But no one wants to abandon this Good Samaritan policy.

Will could balance the books by giving the contract for disposal of medical wastes to Big Pig Waste Management. But Big Pig is widely suspected of dumping medical wastes in unsafe ways and illegal places.

What are the ethical values and principles at stake here? What is the best way to work toward an optimum ethical outcome?

Commentary:

We have a real conflict of values here, it appears: Medical care for the poor vs. protection of the environment and the people who live in it. There is no real way to resolve that conflict per se—except if a specific patient or population was actually dying on the spot (then we say, "The heck with the garbage, save these lives"). But it is not quite that extreme (yet). There may really be a problem with the law, professional ethics, company ethics—the whole six-fold test. My main suggestion is to be very creative and think win-win. Share the problem more broadly. Leverage Big Pig into better practices and transparency. Appeal to their higher, better self. Embarrass them publicly, if it takes that to get them in line. Or work with the Urban Job Development Association to create a new business ("Good Samaritan Eco-Friendly Trash Co."?). Go public in the community. Have discussions, newspaper articles about the two concerns (health care for the poor, and environmental responsibility). You can really do something great here, Will: Go for it!

Sample Case Eight: Who Is the Boss?

Laura has been promoted to a supervisory position at her company and is now responsible for managing a department with a dozen other employees. Several of these workers are significantly older than her and have worked at the company many years longer than she has. But she recently finished her MBA and was very effective in leading some recent projects.

Unfortunately, three of the veterans (generally viewed as high performers) under her supervision are having a bad attitude about her promotion. They are regularly, it seems, going behind her back to her boss (an old friend and golf partner of theirs) with complaints and questions. They are late or inattentive at staff meetings she calls.

Laura has tried hard to be supportive of them and has gone out of her way to praise their work. She has asked them repeatedly to come to her with whatever issues they have. They just ignore her and complain to other workers about reporting to someone her age.

What are the ethical—and managerial—issues here? What is your recommendation?

Commentary:

Laura, I'm so sorry about this situation. You have done just the right things so far in speaking directly to these three malcontents. It is an ethical problem because people—and the company itself—can be harmed and no one would wish this treatment for themselves. If it was reported on the news, most public sentiment would be on your side.

So the first thing is to go to your boss and put it pretty strongly to him (stay calm, but be firm) that he must cut these guys off the moment they want to talk about any of your departmental business concerns—in fact, he should put some distance between himself and them and tell them you are his choice to lead; and they must get in line with a good attitude or get out, no matter what. I wouldn't hesitate to lay it on the line with the three guys again, one-on-one, and threaten them with a job demotion or transfer if you can. But tell them you don't want to think that way. You want them to accept reality, get over their old attitudes, and join with you in making the department a success. If they don't change (within a very short time frame), I would bust at least one of them (fire or transfer out). I might go over my boss's head if he won't support me. This is an impossible situation for a leader, and it must be resolved quickly. Looking for another job is an option, but why should you have to do it? You're good, Laura!

Acknowledgments

It just wouldn't be right (or ethical) if I didn't acknowledge some of the important influences on my thinking about business ethics. Obviously some of it is absorbed by a kind of osmosis difficult to identify and credit precisely, and some of it comes from the school of hard knocks and experience in the trenches. But certainly I can identify some people who play large here. It is hard to keep the list brief but here goes. My father, Walter Gill (1913-2004), had a long career as an accountant at the Crown Zellarbach Corporation, and an even longer career as an example of ethical integrity before his son's eyes. And since our own kids moved off to college, almost twenty years ago, my wife Lucia has worked in the executive offices of Citibank--meaning that, no matter what I thought of banking industry ethics, I always had at least one shining example of goodness to be impressed with.

My ethics formation has lots of sources but it is mainly anchored in the brilliant insights of my late intellectual mentor, the Bordeaux sociologist Jacques Ellul (1912-1994) who taught me, among other things, that values are embedded not just in individuals but in technologies, institutions, and cultures and that the most important realities are not in the latest headline stories but rather in the trends, forces, and main currents beneath the surface.

I owe a great deal to the ethical writings of Aristotle, their more recent philosophical expression by Alasdair MacIntyre, and their business ethics application by Professor Robert Solomon, whose premature death in 2007 was a terrible loss for business ethics and the other domains he touched. Jim Collins (*Built to Last, Good to Great*) is unquestionably my favorite business writer and analyst though I have learned from many others whose names occur throughout my text and footnotes.

I have been a professor of ethics since the early 1970s, often in theological schools such as my present post at Gordon-Conwell in the Boston area. This book owes most, however, to my years teaching business ethics to MBA students (and a few undergrads) at St. Mary's College (Moraga, California), North Park University (Chicago), Seattle Pacific University, San Jose State University, and the University of San Francisco. I also want to mention with gratitude several business educator/consultant friends whose encouragement, conversation, and collegiality have been incredibly valuable for my business ethics work in general, and often for this book in particular: Greg Zegarowski, Marvin Brown, Jim O'Toole, Lisa Newton, Randy Englund, Karen Frisbie, Reggie Mastin, Juan Montermoso, Linda Herkenhoff, Jim

Hawley, Ron Coverson, Kendall Mau, Phillippe Daniel, Clark Sept, David Batstone, Patricia Fisher, Dave Evans, Jana Kemp, and Kenman Wong.

Several of my MBA business ethics students (almost all of them working executives and managers at companies such as Kaiser-Permanente, Ericson, Oracle, Boeing, and a wide range of small and medium size companies) gave this book a careful review when it was a manuscript in process. I appreciate very much the comments and suggestions they gave me, especially those from Kristoffer Anderson, Rey Arante, Donald Card, Colin Crawford, Anne Erler, Janet Foster, Nuttakorn Leerattanapanich, Mary Livingston-Weston, Pablo Matute, Adam Odessky, Greg Regan, Justin Ribeiro, Mark Schilder, Eric Schumacher, and Aaron Thomas.

My ideas about organizational and business ethics have been shared, criticized, encouraged and refined not just in MBA class settings but in many professional lectures and presentations for organizations such as the Commonwealth Club, the Silicon Valley Marketing Association, the Tri-Valley Human Resources Association, the Contra Costa Council, the American Association of Healthcare Administrative Management, the Silicon Valley Public Relations Society, the Beta Gamma Sigma Business Honor Society, the Association for Practical and Professional Ethics, the National Association for Science Technology and Society, and others. I've also benefited from my colleagues and audiences at lectures I have given at the University of Washington and University of Wisconsin Graduate Schools of Business, the Arizona State University department of sociology, the Penn State University center for Science, Technology, and Society, the University of Poitiers (France) department of political science, and elsewhere.

Working on the ground with businesses is also a key part of the background to my understanding of ethics. I didn't just work out my ideas by reading books, teaching college students, hanging out with academic ethicists, and visiting web sites! In particular my business ethics consulting and training at Harris & Associates, Paradise Foods, Nikon Precision, East Bay Municipal Utility District, Swedish Covenant Hospital, and UNext.com were gratifying and instructive opportunities to put my ideas to the test in real world settings.

I have been very fortunate that even in the darkest hours of Enron-like gloom, I have always known---and sometimes worked closely with---business leaders whose ethics and excellence inspired me. These inspiring friends include Carl Harris, Guy Erickson, Vern Phillips, and Marie Shockley (Harris & Associates), David Gilmour (Paradise Foods), Mark Kvamme (Sequoyah Capital), Geoff Wild (Nikon Precision), David Stewart (State Farm), Doug Sterne (Pandora), Dean Levitt (Coopers & Lybrand), John Erisman (Hewlett Packard), Gary Ginter (Chicago Research & Trading), Duke Dayal (Citibank), Rand Morimoto (Convergent Computing), Kim

Farnham-Flom (Safeway), Carol Spencer (Russian Hill Bookstore), Larry Langdon (Hewlett Packard), and Peter Jackson (Intraware).

I owe a special debt to Al Erisman (and wife Nancy), with whom I co-founded and co-directed the Institute for Business, Technology, and Ethics from 1998-2003. Al was Director of Technology R & D at Boeing in the early 90s when we started a conversation about our very different takes on the same core topics and challenges in business and technology. This led to some exciting course and conference co-teaching (or should I say "counter-teaching"? some thought we were conjuring Ned Ludd vs. Victor Frankenstein but that is far too extreme) and then to the IBTE and our bimonthly magazine, *Ethix*. We shared a lot of common passion and struggled with some significant differences but even (or perhaps especially) when we dis-agreed, these were profound learning experiences for me. And I would always say that I never met a guy who integrated his personal philosophy and values with his business thinking as much or as well as Al.

I am dedicating this book to my son, Jonathan Gill. One of the greatest joys of any parent's life is when you wake up one day and realize that you are the learner---and the teacher you are looking up to or asking advice from is your son or daughter. I have that joy with both my daughter Jodie and my son Jonathan. I am frankly in awe of what Jonathan has done over the past decade and more in building Gill's Fitness literally from the ground up in an intensely competitive environment. I'm not just an inordinately proud dad; clients, employees, and San Diego newspaper writers sing his praises just as loudly. This is no flash in the pan success but a mission-driven, value-embedded, ethically-principled instance of business excellence. May God give the marketplace more entrepreneurs like this. And thank you Lord, for giving me this one as my son.

David W. Gill
August 2011

About the Author:

David W. Gill (www.ethixbiz.com)

David W. Gill is an ethics educator, writer, and consultant. He was educated at the University of California, Berkeley (B.A.), San Francisco State University (M.A.), and the University of Southern California (Ph.D.). He is currently Mockler-Phillips Professor of Workplace Theology and Business Ethics and Director of the Mockler Center for Faith and Ethics in the Workplace at Gordon-Conwell Theological Seminary in South Hamilton, Massachusetts. He served as Professor of Business Ethics From 2004 to 2010 in the Graduate School of Business and Economics at St. Mary's College (Moraga CA). He has also served as Adjunct Professor of Business Ethics on the MBA faculties of the University of San Francisco and Seattle Pacific University, and as visiting or adjunct professor of ethics at Regent College (Vancouver BC), and Juniata College (Huntingdon PA). From 1992 to 2001 he was Carl I. Lindberg Professor of Applied Ethics on the philosophy and business faculties of North Park University (Chicago IL). From 1978 to 1990 he served as professor of ethics on the interdenominational theology faculty of New College Berkeley.

Gill has lectured on ethics at the University of Poitiers (France), FEPADE (El Salvador), the University of Wisconsin School of Business, the University of Washington School of Business, Arizona State University, Penn State University, UC Davis, Wheaton College (IL), Pepperdine University, Sonoma State University and in many other college and university settings. He is author or editor of six other books on ethics, religion, and higher education. He has published more than two hundred chapters, articles, and reviews in various books, journals, magazines, and reference works, including the *Journal of Business and Professional Ethics, the Encyclopedia of Science, Technology and Ethics, the Bulletin of Science, Technology, and Society, Bridges, Ethix Bulletin, Radix Magazine,* and *Cahiers Jacques Ellul.*

Gill has served as business and organizational ethics consultant/trainer for Harris & Associates, Paradise Foods, the East Bay Municipal Utility District, Nikon Precision, Intelligent Information Systems, Swedish Covenant Hospital, UNext.com, the Marin Leadership Foundation, and other companies. He has been plenary lecturer or conference speaker for many professional groups such as the Commonwealth Club of California, the Contra Costa Council, the Silicon Valley Public Relations Society, the Tri-Valley Human Resources Commission, the Association for Practical and Professional Ethics, the Silicon Valley Marketing Association, and the Association of Health Care Administrators.